Also by Rosie Daley

In the Kitchen with Rosie: Oprah's Favorite Recipes

Also by Dr Andrew Weil

Eating Well for Optimum Health:
The Essential Guide to Food, Diet, and Nutrition

Eight Weeks to Optimum Health:
A Proven Program for Taking Full Advantage of Your Body's
Natural Healing Power

Spontaneous Healing:
How to Discover and Enhance Your Body's Natural Ability
to Maintain and Heal Itself

Natural Health, Natural Medicine:
A Comprehensive Manual for Wellness and Self-Care

Health and Healing

From Chocolate to Morphine:
Everything You Need to Know About Mind-Altering Drugs
(with Winifred Rosen)

The Marriage of the Sun and Moon:
A Quest for Unity in Consciousness

The Natural Mind:
A New Way of Looking at Drugs and the
Higher Consciousness

The Healthy Kitchen

**Photographs by Sang An, Amy Haskell,
and Eric Studer**

THE
HEALTHY
KITCHEN

Innovative Recipes for a
Better Body, Life, and Spirit

Dr Andrew Weil AND

Rosie Daley

EBURY PRESS
LONDON

First published in 2002

1 3 5 7 9 10 8 6 4 2

First published in the United Kingdom in 2002 by Ebury Press
Random House, 20 Vauxhall Bridge Road, London, SW1V 2SA

Random House Australia (Pty) Limited
20 Alfred Street, Milson's Point, Sydney, New South Wales, 2061, Australia

Random House New Zealand Limited
18 Poland Road, Glenfield, Auckland 10, New Zealand

Random House (Pty) Limited
Endulini, 5a Jubilee Road, Parktown 2193, South Africa

Random House Group Limited Reg. No. 954009

A catalogue record for this book is available from the British Library

ISBN 0 09 188422 5

Printed and bound in France by Imprimerie Pollina - L85876

Photographic credits:
Sang An: 4, 20, 36, 58, 78, 91, 102, 114, 130, 143, 151, 175, 198, 233, 238, 282, 289;
Amy Haskell: xiv, 71, 99, 117, 180, 245, 251, 278, 304; Bethany Jensen: 203;
Eric Studer: 19, 56, 57, 69, 100, 105, 164, 166, 167, 172, 174, 209, 219, 255, 270, 271, 272, 273, 274. All other images are made up of the photographs listed above.

To my friend Barry Bluestein,
who helped me write my first book and encouraged me
to do a second. He is, alas, no longer with us, but his spirit
and his passion for cooking and eating healthy
are here on every page.

—R.D.

To Jenny and Diana

—A.W.

Contents

Acknowledgements

I would first like to thank all the chefs who have inspired me to be a better cook: Miceal Strout, Jeff Hampton, Deborah from Charlie's, Gordon Smith, Cal-a-Vie Spa, and so many more (you know who you are).

Thank you and congratulations to all the professional chefs who have flourished in the public eye and continue to motivate people to cook.

A special thank you to all my friends who came to many recipe-tasting parties, gave me advice, and supplied me with comments about my cooking.

Thanks to my writing team: Rachel Isabell Gomez, for being my main writer and spending enormous amounts of energy and time in rewriting and changing recipes to better suit the public; Judith Jones, my editor, who gave me more than I could ask for – incomparable talent and professionalism, not to mention her love of cooking and unwavering faith in me that lifted my spirits and successfully guided me through two books.

Thanks to Lily Rose Neville, Beverly Lockheart, Marley St. John, Court Stark, Eva David, Natalie and Nicole Thomas, Danny Anderson, the Clinton O'Brien family, Ron Holder, Jill Wilson, Beverly Connors, Nan Self, and Kirt Smidley.

Thanks to the crew at Panikin Coffee for all their hospitality that saw me through my morning and afternoon work sessions.

Thank you always to all my previous employers, who gave me the chance to work with and learn from them. Thank you to Oprah Winfrey for the opportunity to share my love of cooking with such a wide audience and for giving me a reason to create my recipes in the first place.

Thank you to the group at Culinary Concepts Testing in Arizona who tested my recipes.

I am forever grateful to all the people who supported my previous book and for their desire to learn more about cooking.

Thank you to my co-author, Dr. Andrew Weil, for sharing his vast knowledge and understanding of nutrition and the immeasurable benefits that eating well offers all of us.

—R.D.

Thanks to Paul Bogaards at Alfred A. Knopf for making this idea a reality. It has been a pleasure to work with him as well as with my editors Jon Segal and Judith Jones, and, as always, my agent, Richard Pine.

Dr. Jim Nicolai helped me develop and test recipes and did a great deal of work to assist in the completion of the manuscript. It was fun to cook and eat with him. Lynn Willeford also provided recipe ideas.

Thanks to my office staff, especially Michele Hardin and Debra DuBois.

Judith Berger and Suzan Gross and the rest of the staff of Culinary Concepts in Tucson, Arizona, provided invaluable help in testing recipes and calculating their nutritional values.

Finally, thanks to my co-author, Rosie Daley, for showing me new ways of working in the kitchen and for bringing her boundless energy and enthusiasm to this project.

—A.W.

Rosie's Introduction

I have tried to give you throughout this book useful tips about shopping, cooking, planning meals, and making your food look attractive. But, above all, I hope the recipes, which are not only sensible but taste fantastic, will inspire you to cook. This is not a diet cookery book. Eating well is not about dieting, but a life choice. Adopting a healthy lifestyle through food should never leave us feeling deprived. I think most of us agree that eating is one of life's greatest pleasures and every recipe in this book will demonstrate how fulfilling good eating is.

The recipes vary in their level of complexity. Some are simple to prepare. Some take a bit more time and energy to put together. My hope is that you will take on the more advanced recipes when you are ready to. I've shared with you all the techniques that will help you to become more confident in your kitchen. You will notice your skill level growing with each new dish that you make. You will also probably develop a favourite activity in terms of food preparation. I love to make garnishes and to shop for food. You may love to cut vegetables 'julienne' style or poach fish or make spectacular salads or barbecue. The beauty of cooking is that everyone already knows how to do it – it is really a matter of just doing it. And, like anything else, the more you do it, the better you get.

Cooking takes some effort, no question, but kitchen stress and time pressures usually arise when certain needed items are not readily available to complete a dish. The first step in making your kitchen truly functional is to plan your shopping. Think about what you want to make, what you have at home, what ingredients can be used for other meals, and what you need to stock up on. Arrange it so that you don't have to shop more than once or twice a week. I buy perishable items only every few days, but I keep lots of frozen or dried foods on hand for whenever I need them. See my tips on Stocking the Storecupboard.

The one place I always shop is at my local farmers' market. I enjoy the entire process of gathering fresh foods for my meals. A great way to get in touch with the seasons is by becoming aware of what fresh foods are available at specific times of the year. This will also be helpful in your menu planning.

Timing is an essential component to making a great meal. First, review the recipe you want to make, see what can be done ahead of time, and then do it!

Don't be afraid to work with new ingredients, such as cooking with different grains, using tofu, or trying out a variety of peppers, herbs, and spices. Cooking should be varied because that's part of the fun, the creativity, and the learning. Involve your family by planning a meal in a leisurely way on the weekend and use your kids' energy – let them stuff vine leaves, roll up slices of aubergine, knead dough, or cut out biscuits.

Perhaps the most significant benefit cooking at home provides, besides quality sustenance, is sitting down in the company of loved ones and sharing a meal that you've made. Everyone's lives are indeed much busier today. But even if you relax at the table with family and friends to enjoy a home-cooked meal just once a week, it will help to relieve the stresses of everyday life and keep you in touch with the people who make life wonderful.

ANDY'S INTRODUCTION

'Good health begins in the kitchen.' I agree with that statement, because I believe that good nutrition is one of the most important influences on health. Most of us eat three times a day. Many of us eat more frequently. Each time we do, we have an opportunity to nourish the body, delight the senses, and calm the mind. It is a shame to waste those opportunities by eating food that is neither healthful nor delicious.

It is a fact of contemporary life that people spend less and less time in the kitchen, relying more on prepared food, fast food, and processed food. The statistics on the declining percentage of American families that have even one daily meal together are depressing. Some of this results from the undeniable pressure and fast pace of life in the twenty-first century. Where can we find the time to cook, to make meals from scratch? But some of it also comes from habit, from fear, from lack of knowledge.

Eating habits often develop in early life. For that reason, I encourage parents to involve children in food preparation. Kids love to help in the kitchen, and by having a hand in the creation of meals, they are more likely to want to try new foods, to develop a love of cooking, and to discover the joy of making and eating good food. I have read that most Italian men, by the time they are twenty, have mastered a basic repertory of kitchen skills and can turn out a good tomato sauce, for example. That is a result of their upbringing, of parents encouraging them to take part in cooking at early ages and is quite unlike the situation in most other Western countries.

I have heard health gurus over the years decry the dangers of various nutrients, foods, and diets – from fat in general and saturated fat in particular to carbohydrates in general and sugar in particular, from milk and meat and fish to soya beans and peanuts, from macrobiotic diets to Beverly Hills diets. All of this makes more people feel that food is the enemy and the dining table a minefield. It makes them throw up their hands and think they will never understand the science of nutrition or the relationship between diet and health. It makes them afraid and confused, and it drives them out of the kitchen and into the arms of fast-food merchants and makers of processed food.

At the same time we are seeing a tremendous upsurge in popularity of cookery books and of cooking shows on television. I suspect that many people turn to them more for entertainment than for practical information, because most of the books and shows feature celebrity chefs, who are producing food that the average cook could never reproduce in a home kitchen.

I am hardly a celebrity chef. I am a home cook and a physician who advocates natural medicine. As I said, I believe that eating well is one important determinant of health. By 'eating well', I mean giving your body the fuel it needs, using food to increase your resistance and natural healing power – and not sacrificing the pleasure of eating appetising, tasty, and satisfying food. In my time I have been served many dreadful dishes that were supposed to be 'health food'; I am unwilling to eat food that is boring, artless, and devoid of pleasure even if it's somebody else's idea of healthful.

My purpose in producing this book with Rosie is to show you that good food can be good for you and can also be easy and fun to prepare. Rosie and I do not see eye-to-eye on every culinary issue. (I think you will find that our disagreements make for interesting reading.) But we very much agree that a dish can be only as good as its worst ingredient, that it is worth getting the best and freshest ingredients, that recipes should yield good results without being overly complicated or taxing. Both of us enjoy good food. Both of us enjoy making good food. We want to share that enjoyment with you.

*Rosie and Andy picking vegetables and
fruits from his garden in Arizona*

NUTRITION AND HEALTH

The science of nutrition is full of controversy and disagreement. Given the amount of contradictory information from researchers and the media regarding dietary influences on health, it is not surprising that most people are confused. Not long ago we were told that eggs were good for us. Then we learned that eggs were bad. Now, once again, we hear that they are good. For years in the mid–twentieth century, doctors told us to shun butter and eat margarine made from vegetable oils. Now they tell us that margarine may be even worse for the heart than butter. Just as we were learning about the cancer-protective effects of soya beans, some experts began warning us that eating soya could increase cancer risks.

It doesn't help that our health professionals are so poorly educated about nutrition. Medical doctors get next to no training in this most important subject and so are unable to help us navigate through the confusion or interpret all the research findings. And because doctors' eating habits are often less than ideal, they are no better role models for healthful eating than anyone else. And sadly, the food served in most hospitals is awful.

Rosie and I both believe that our homes should be the best places to eat. We spend a great deal of time in the home kitchen: think how often people gather there, leaving the sitting room unused. This book would not exist if we did not believe that you can make the home kitchen the source of great food – food that provides optimum nutrition and is also delicious. We will show you how to do that, by giving you recipes, tips on meal planning and shopping, and practical hints for simplifying food preparation. In *The Healthy Kitchen* you will learn how to make dishes that are much more appetising than those served in 'health food restaurants', where people have not yet grasped that eating wonderful food and eating healthy food can be one and the same.

A number of dietary trends in Western society are cause for concern. We all know that too many of us are overweight – just sit in an airport and watch who passes by. Even more alarming is the epidemic of obesity in children; evidently, their weight problems begin very early. Recently, medical journals have reported another alarming trend – the appearance of type-2 diabetes, usually called adult-onset diabetes, in very young children, as young as seven years old. This is a completely new phenomenon. Along with other observations, it suggests that we are eating too much food and too much of the wrong foods (as well as not getting enough physical activity). The reason is that most people do not know how to select foods that will maintain optimum health as well as satisfy and delight the senses. Again, that is just what Rosie and I will help you do in this book.

The primary message given to us by nutritionists and dietitians is to eat a balanced diet – advice so vague as to be meaningless. Some people think it means to eat some of everything, including foods that are distinctly not good for our health. The concept of a balanced diet may be a good one, but to make sense of it, you need practical information about the components of diet and the roles they play in the body.

What we prepare and eat at home and what we eat elsewhere must supply fuel for the body's metabolic engine – that is, enough sources of energy to provide for all the body's needs. It must also supply materials for growth and for the maintenance and repair of the body's structure. And it must supply all other elements needed to keep us in optimum health.

Nutritionists divide dietary needs into two broad categories – micronutrients and macronutrients. Micronutrients are the 'little foods' needed in very small quantities to fine-tune our metabolism. They include vitamins, minerals, fibre, and a variety of beneficial compounds from plants called 'protective phytochemicals'. Eating plenty of fruits and vegetables ensures a proper intake of micronutrients. Macronutrients – carbohydrates, fats, and proteins – are the 'big foods' that supply energy needs (calories) as well as materials for growth and repair of tissue. How you choose them can affect how you live, feel, and age.

Macronutrients

Carbohydrates and fats are primarily sources of caloric energy, although the body also uses some special fats as building blocks (for cell membranes, for instance) and starting materials for synthesising hormones. The body can use proteins as fuel, but it depends on them mainly as raw materials for maintaining and growing body structures. A balanced diet must provide the right number of calories to replace those expended in the course of day-to-day living, and it should provide the right mix of carbohydrates, fats, and proteins to meet the body's needs. This is why daily menu planning is so important – more on that later. In addition, because there are better and worse carbohydrates, good and bad fats, and proteins that are more and less desirable, it should provide the best of the available macronutrients. Let me explain the differences.

Let's start with calories. You can look up in standard tables your average daily caloric need based on sex, body size, and level of activity. Most adults have to consume between 2,000 and 3,000 calories a day. Women, and smaller and less active people, need fewer calories, while men, and bigger and more active people, need more. If you consistently eat more calories than you expend, the chances are you will gain weight, and if you consistently eat fewer calories than you need, the chances are you will lose it. I have to say 'chances are' because some people are genetically programmed so that their metabolic rate changes in ways that keep weight constant despite variations in caloric intake. For most of us, unfortunately, the iron-clad rule is that calories in equal calories out, or else weight goes up or down. Most overweight and obese people are simply consuming more calories than they are burning up in their activities of daily living.

'Burning up' is an accurate term. Metabolism is the controlled burning of fuel by living organisms – that is, the chemical combination of foods with oxygen to release the energy they contain. The energy locked up in foods originates in sunlight that is captured by green plants in the process of photosynthesis. The first product of photosynthesis is glucose, a form of sugar and one of the simplest carbohydrates, the basic metabolic fuel of both plants and animals. In animals, glucose circulates in the blood as a ready source of energy that cells can take in and metabolise; one name for it is blood sugar. In addition, both plants and animals can use glucose as a starting material to build other, more complex macronutrients.

In thinking about the relative contributions of different kinds of foods to total caloric intake, it is important to know that fats are almost twice as calorie-dense as either carbohydrates or proteins; fats provide nine calories per gram versus five for the other two macronutrients. Therefore, a simple way to decrease caloric intake is to reduce fat consumption. To do that you need to know what fat is and where it occurs in foods. It is also important to know what carbohydrates and proteins are and where you encounter them.

Carbohydrates

The main sources of carbohydrates in the Western diet in decreasing order of magnitude are yeast bread; soft drinks; cakes, biscuits, quick breads, and doughnuts; sugar, syrups, and jams; potatoes; ready-to-eat cereal; milk; pasta; rice and other cooked grains; flour; juices and fruit drinks; frozen desserts; and crisps and popcorn. Other, less popular carbohydrate-containing foods are beans, sweet potatoes, and pumpkin. In general all these foods are relatively inexpensive, filling, and satisfying. Many people crave them. Recently, a number of diet experts have been forcefully telling us to avoid them on the grounds that they are the chief cause of obesity – more of a problem for our waistlines than fat. There is some truth in this statement, but I think it gets badly distorted in many popular diet books. It is unwise to shun carbohydrates.

There are two classes of nutritive carbohydrates, sugars and starches. Sugars include very basic ones like glucose and more complicated ones like sucrose or table sugar. They taste sweet to us, and we seek out that taste. In nature, sugars accumulate in ripe fruit, in some seeds (like sweetcorn), and some vegetables (like peppers, which are actually fruits because they contain seeds). They also occur in sap and nectar, which can be concentrated into products like syrup and honey. Starches, more complicated molecules than sugars, are used by plants for storing energy in roots (sweet potatoes), tubers (white potatoes), and seeds (grains). Animals also make a form of starch, glycogen, that is stored in the liver and muscles as a short-term energy reserve.

Nutritionists have told us for years to think of carbohydrates as either simple (sugars) or complex (starches) and to minimise consumption of the former in favour of the latter. That turns out not to be very useful advice. The important way that carbohydrate foods differ from each other is in how fast they convert to glucose and raise the level of it in the blood. Speed of conversion of a carbohydrate food to blood sugar is rated with a quantity called the glycaemic index (GI) on a scale from 0 to 100. Glucose has a GI of 100; it need not be digested and goes directly into the bloodstream. Table sugar has a lower GI (65) because it is a compound of glucose and fructose, also known as fruit sugar. The body does not digest fructose very well; it has a very low GI of 23.

Meals full of high-glycaemic-index foods like potatoes, bread, and sweet drinks cause rapid rises in blood sugar. They require the pancreas to secrete insulin, the hormone that allows glucose to enter cells. Insulin also affects fat metabolism, weight, and cardiovascular function. Many people who eat diets rich in high-glycaemic-index carbohydrates will gain weight, and develop unhealthy levels of fat and cholesterol in their blood. They may also develop high blood pressure and increased risk of diabetes. Too much of these kinds of foods in our diet probably accounts for a great deal of the obesity we see, including the epidemic of it in our children.

Glycaemic index depends on the chemical nature of a carbohydrate food as well as on its physical structure and method of preparation. If whole grains are eaten whole or cracked into large pieces, they convert slowly. The starch they contain gradually becomes glucose and does not provoke a rapid outpouring of insulin. But if grains are stripped of their fibrous coatings (bran) and pulverised into flour, the fine starch particles are easy targets for digestive enzymes that rapidly convert them to glucose, raising blood sugar and forcing the pancreas to work harder.

I like bread, but I much prefer dense, coarse, whole-grain 'peasant' breads to those made with finely milled flour, whether white or brown. If I eat porridge, I much prefer it made from the more coarse, 'old-fashioned' rolled oats to the usual mushy variety. These preferences guide me towards lower-glycaemic-index carbohydrates that are better for me.

Pasta has a lower GI than bread because the starch is in a denser form that resists quick digestion. If pasta is cooked al dente in the Italian manner, it is denser still, with an even lower GI. Beans are also low on the scale, because the fibre they contain slows down digestion of the starch.

In my opinion, diets based on elimination of carbohydrates are not very sensible. Carbohydrates are easily digested sources of energy for the body, and they should provide the largest share of calories you eat. It is important, however, to choose carbohydrate foods wisely and not overdo those at the top of the GI chart. Carbohydrates are certainly not bad in and of themselves, but the way we eat them may be. If you look at the most common sources of them in the diet, you will note that highly processed and refined foods dominate the list; beans, one of the best sources, with a low GI, are not even on it.

Just think of all the fluffy breads, pastries, savoury biscuits, crisps, mushy starches, and soft drinks that people consume today. In this book we try to emphasise better carbohydrate choices: whole grains, beans, pumpkin and other squashes, and fruit. And when we give recipes for waffles or rice pudding, which have higher GI ratings, we recommend topping them with fruit, such as berries or peaches, which have low GIs. The combination brings the glycaemic index of the dish down to the moderate zone.

Fats

Fats, also demonised in recent years and blamed by some for all of our dietary woes, are an even more efficient form of storing energy than carbohydrates. Plants pack it into seeds (in nuts, for example), and animals store it under the skin, both to insulate themselves and to provide a source of energy when food is scarce. Of course, many of us never lack for food, and we keep accumulating fat rather than burning it up.

Here are the main sources of fat in the American diet in descending order of magnitude: beef; margarine; salad dressings and mayonnaise; cheese; milk; cakes, biscuits, quick breads, and doughnuts; poultry; oils; yeast bread; crisps and popcorn; sausages; eggs; nuts and seeds; butter; ice cream. This is an interesting and, to me, distressing list. The first two items on it represent two sources of bad fat that offer two different kinds of dangers to health. The fat in beef, like that in other animal flesh, poultry, and milk, is saturated fat. Saturated fat is solid at room temperature. The body can easily burn it as fuel, but, in many people, excessive consumption of it drives up levels of cholesterol and blood fats and increases the risk of cardiovascular disease. If the major source of fat in the diet is saturated fat, risks of heart attacks and arterial problems increase in most people. The easiest way to reduce these risks through diet is to cut down on red meat and dairy products made from whole milk and to remove the skin (and accompanying fat) from poultry. Only a few vegetable fats are saturated – palm and coconut oils especially – and you are only likely to encounter them in some manufactured foods, so read the labels (see page xxxvi).

Most vegetable oils are unsaturated to one degree or another. The more unsaturated ones are called polyunsaturated and remain liquid and pourable even at cold temperatures. The less unsaturated ones are called monounsaturated and turn translucent and thick in the refrigerator but not completely hard like saturated fat. Margarine is made from liquid vegetable oils that are artificially saturated (with hydrogen) to make them semisolid. This process changes the fat molecules in ways that make them very unhealthful. Margarine and other partially hydrogenated oils damage arteries and raise the risk for heart attack. I believe they also promote cancer, inflammation, damage to the immune system, and premature ageing. Some of this harmfulness is due to their content of trans fats, which are unnatural fat molecules created in the hydrogenation process.

Look again at the list of fat sources in the American diet. At the top of the list you'll find mostly foods containing saturated animal fat or processed vegetable oils, both undesirable, as I have said. Some of the best fats are those found in nuts like walnuts, almonds, and cashews, and in seeds like sesame and pumpkin. Nuts and seeds are near the very bottom of the list of what people eat.

In recent years, Americans have repeatedly been told to 'get the fat out', and they have been eating more and more low-fat and non-fat foods. In my opinion, telling people to avoid fat is as misguided as telling people to avoid carbohydrates. As fat-free foods have proliferated in our society, people have grown steadily fatter, probably because they have been eating more calories, especially from low-quality carbohydrate foods. When food has too little fat, it very often just doesn't taste good. That isn't the kind of food you – or we – want to put on our tables. Fat conveys flavours to our taste buds and contributes to the pleasurable 'mouth feel' of good food. The problem is not to get the fat out but to avoid bad fat and get the good fat in.

From the standpoint of health, the best fats are the monounsaturated ones found in nuts, seeds, olives, and avocados. Most of the recipes in this book that call for oil specify olive oil, and many use nuts and seeds. Olive oil is a mainstay of the Mediterranean diet, one of the best ways of eating in the world (more on that later, too). Fortunately, it is now easy to find good quality (extra virgin) olive oil in ordinary supermarkets. If you don't want too strong a flavour of olive oil in a dish, you can try one of the 'light' brands or use a good, neutral-flavoured oil. My current favourite is grapeseed oil.

Never heat oils to the smoking point, and never breathe the smoke of burning oil; it is highly toxic and carcinogenic. (One of the reasons I favour grapeseed oil is that it has a high smoking point – that is, it can be heated to higher temperatures before it begins to smoke.) Also beware of rancid oils – those that have oxidised as a result of exposure to air, light, and heat. They not only have an unpleasant smell (like that of oil paint) that will make food taste bad, but they, too, are toxic and carcinogenic. Buy oils in smaller rather than larger containers, protect them from light and heat, use them up quickly, and throw them out if they smell odd. These same recommendations apply to foods that contain oils, like nuts, seeds, savoury biscuits, crisps, and baked goods.

One special group of good fats deserves particular attention. Omega-3 fats are a group of polyunsaturated fats that are absolutely essential for optimum health. The body needs them on a regular basis to synthesise hormones and build cell membranes, including those of nerve cells in the brain. Dietary sources of omega-3s are few, and, probably, most people are deficient in them. That deficiency may underlie our susceptibility to heart disease, inflammatory diseases (including forms of arthritis and auto-immunity), some forms of cancer, and a variety of nervous and mental disorders. Research on the preventive and therapeutic potential of omega-3 fats is currently a very active area of medical investigation.

The main food source of these good fats is fish, especially oily fish from cold waters: salmon, mackerel, herring, sardines, and (to a lesser extent) albacore tuna. Non-fish sources are few: walnuts, linseeds, hemp seeds, and the oils extracted from them. There are smaller amounts in soya beans and sea vegetables (such as nori and arame). A new source is fortified eggs produced by chickens fed dietary supplements rich in omega-3s. I cannot overemphasise the importance of including these foods in your diet and preparing them regularly. *The Healthy Kitchen* offers many recipes that will help you accomplish that.

If you keep your saturated fat intake to a minimum and avoid partially hydrogenated and other processed vegetable oils, concentrate on using olive oil and other monounsaturated fats, and make sure to eat enough omega-3 sources, you do not have to follow an ascetic, ultra-low-fat diet to enjoy optimum health. In fact, you can allow enough fat in your diet to make food delicious and yet also be assured that you are reducing disease and promoting general health.

Protein

The last category of macronutrients is protein. A lack of it results in severe wasting, especially in children, because the body needs protein to grow, maintain, and repair itself. Many people worry about whether they are getting enough protein and think that meals have to be built around dense portions of animal protein, like a steak or a roast – in other words, that a meal without meat would be nothing but side dishes and accompaniments. One of the things Rosie and I hope to accomplish in this book is to change your thinking on this, and to suggest ways you can build meals on far healthier protein sources that are delicious – meals that can be prepared easily and that you'll be proud to serve.

Here are the main sources of protein in the American diet today, again in decreasing order of magnitude: beef; poultry; milk; yeast bread; cheese; fish and shellfish (excluding canned tuna); eggs; pork; ham; pasta; cakes, biscuits, quick breads, and doughnuts. Who would have thought that bread would be so high on the list? Wheat and other grains contain protein along with their starch, and some bread contains milk, but most of it provides a great deal of high-glycaemic-index carbohydrate. And most people eat bread with fat, often a bad fat like margarine. Beans, an excellent protein source with low-glycaemic-index carbohydrate and no fat, do not appear on the list, because they contribute a maximum of only 1 per cent of the protein in the American diet.

There are several problems with relying on meat, poultry, milk, and cheese as primary protein sources. Meat and unskinned poultry contain a great deal of saturated fat and cholesterol, both of which increase risks of cardiovascular disease. Commercial meat and poultry also contain residues of drugs and hormones used to promote the growth of animals, and the raising of animals for food is very damaging to the environment (see page 149). Milk and cheese are also significant sources of saturated fat, and milk, especially, is associated with a number of common health problems (see page 34). For all these reasons, I recommend moving away from dependence on animal foods for your protein and looking more to fish and vegetable sources.

If you eat salmon, sardines, herring, and albacore tuna regularly, you can get omega-3 fats along with your protein. But take care when eating fish, too (see page 176); you want to select wisely the varieties you eat and learn to cook them in healthful ways. Rosie and I have included a number of fish dishes that we think are easy and delicious as well as good for you. We also give recipes for vegetarian dishes that are high in protein because they use beans, soya foods, and whole grains.

More and more enlightened dietitians recommend that people move towards 'plant-based' diets to reduce disease risks and improve well-being. That does not mean forgoing all animal foods and sticking to salad when you eat out. It does mean unlearning the habit of organising meals around centre-pieces of meat and poultry and becoming acquainted with the great variety of satisfying protein-rich dishes that can be made from vegetarian ingredients. Populations that eat plant-based diets live longer and enjoy better health than populations whose protein sources match those on the list above. We hope this book can inspire you to move in that direction.

By the way, far from not getting enough protein, most people get too much, often taking in their whole day's needs with a typical breakfast of eggs, bacon, toast, and milk. Protein deficiency is very rare in our society except among very poor people, the elderly, and some people on bizarre diets. If you eat more protein than your body needs to make and maintain tissue, the excess goes into the metabolic furnace to provide caloric energy. Protein is not as good a fuel as carbohydrate or fat, however. It is neither an efficient nor a clean-burning fuel, requiring more work on the part of the digestive system, especially the liver, and more work for the kidneys to eliminate the residues of its combustion. Those residues can irritate the immune system. Protein needs are increased in growing children, nursing mothers, and those recovering from illness and injury, but even for them the typical Western diet probably provides too much.

So how should the optimum diet break down in terms of macronutrients? I recommend the following percentages of total calories: 50 to 60 per cent from carbohydrates, 30 per cent from fat, and 10 to 20 per cent from protein. At the end of this chapter I will give more detailed recommendations.

Micronutrients

I want to start by reminding you that it is not necessary to worry about the details of these important elements, needed by the body in much smaller amounts for optimum functioning. All you have to do is be sure to eat a variety of fruits and vegetables, of good quality and in sufficient quantities (ideally five portions a day). This is all you need to supply all of your micronutrient needs and is easy to achieve.

Vitamins are essential nutrients obtained from food that are necessary for health and growth. Vitamins C and E occur mainly in plants, the B-complex occurs mainly in animal tissue, and others are in both plant and animal foods. The body can make vitamin D with exposure to sunlight, and bacteria in the gut make small amounts of B vitamins and vitamin K. Of course, you can make sure you are getting all your vitamins by taking a supplement, and there are good reasons for doing so (see page 145). Nonetheless it is useful to know that you can get all the vitamins you need by eating a varied diet that includes some animal foods (such as cheese and fish) and that is rich in fresh fruits and vegetables. People who avoid animal foods entirely are at risk for developing deficiency of vitamin B-12, which can cause severe illness in children and pernicious anaemia in adults; these people must take this vitamin in supplement form.

A number of minerals are also essential micronutrients and, again, their sources are mostly fruits and vegetables. Two that deserve special comment are iron and calcium. If you cut down on red meat, as Rosie and I suggest, you eliminate a major dietary source of easily assimilable iron. You can make up for this by eating more dried beans, dried fruit (prunes, raisins, figs), molasses, cocoa, and dark, leafy greens, as well as by doing some cooking in cast-iron pots. Be aware that iron is an oxidant that can promote undesirable changes in the body; it can raise the risk of heart disease, for example. Therefore, you should never take supplemental iron unless a blood test shows you to be iron-deficient.

Calcium, on the other hand, probably should be supplemented, especially in women at risk for bone loss and osteoporosis, such as those with family histories of these conditions. The problem may not be that the diet does not provide enough of this mineral but that other factors prevent its absorption and use or promote its loss. For example, inadequate vitamin D in the diet hampers the body's ability to use calcium, and high intakes of carbonated soft drinks, salt, caffeine, and alcohol all promote loss. Diets top-heavy in animal protein also lead to calcium loss. Dairy products are good sources of this mineral, as are spring greens, kale, broccoli, sea vegetables, sesame seeds, and some fortified foods like orange juice, soya milk, and tofu.

Fibre, another micronutrient, is necessary for proper intestinal function and may reduce risks of cardiovascular disease and some cancers. It is simply the indigestible part of food, otherwise known as roughage, that makes up much of the bulk of stool. There are various types of fibre, and all of them are 'resistant carbohydrates' – that is, carbohydrates too complex to be broken down by the human digestive system. Vegetarians take in a lot of fibre; people who eat mainly meat, potatoes, and white bread do not. Cooked beans are a good source, as are whole grains, nuts, and many vegetables and fruits. Berries are particularly rich in fibre, which occurs in the tiny seeds they contain. I do not recommend taking fibre supplements, because they can cause wind and bloating and interfere with absorption of minerals. If you eat more fruits, vegetables, whole grains, seeds, and nuts, you will get all the fibre your body needs.

The final category of micronutrients, and to me the most interesting, is the protective phytochemicals. These are a large and very diverse group of compounds found in fruits, vegetables, and mushrooms that strengthen our natural defenses against agents of disease, reducing risks of cancer and other serious illnesses. Scientists keep discovering new ones, and research on them is very promising.

One class of protective phytochemicals acts as antioxidants, blocking chemical reactions in the body that can damage tissues and promote cancer and premature ageing. For example, the red and purple pigments in berries, cherries, red grapes, and red cabbage are powerful antioxidants with many beneficial effects. So are the carotenoid pigments that give colour to carrots, pumpkins and other squash, sweet potatoes, tomatoes, orange-fleshed melons, and other yellow and orange fruits and vegetables. They also occur, but are not visible, in dark, leafy greens. This family of compounds is strongly cancer-protective. Another natural antioxidant, called EGCG, accounts for most of the health-promoting effects of green tea.

Again, you don't need to know the details of the chemistry or pharmacology or even the names of all the protective phytochemicals now known to medical science. Just remember to eat your fruits and vegetables.

Before ending this overview of nutrition and health, and moving on to how you can make use of this information in your everyday cooking, I would like to summarise for you the information about the optimum diet I recommend. This is the way of eating that I believe will help you attain maximum health and longevity. It should also give you all the enjoyment you want when you sit down to eat.

The optimum diet should:

- Supply all of your needs for calories, macronutrients, and micronutrients
- Support general health throughout life and maximise longevity
- Provide the pleasure you expect from eating.

General Characteristics of the Optimum Diet

- *Variety.* Cover all nutritional bases and minimise the intake of any harmful elements in foods.
- *Freshness.* The higher the percentage of fresh foods in the diet the better.
- *Unprocessed foods.* The lower the percentage of processed foods in the diet the better.
- *Abundance in fruits and vegetables.* The more fruits and vegetables you eat, the more protective phytochemicals you take in.

Calories

Depending on sex, body size, and activity level, most adults need to consume between 2,000 and 3,000 calories a day. Women, and smaller and less active people, need fewer calories; men, and bigger and more active people, need more. If you are eating the appropriate number of calories and not varying your activity, your weight should not fluctuate greatly.

The recommended distribution of calories is: 50 to 60 per cent from carbohydrates, 30 per cent from fat, and 10 to 20 per cent from protein.

Carbohydrates

Adult women should eat about 225 to 270 grams of carbohydrates a day, while men should eat about 288 to 345 grams. The majority of this should be in the form of whole, unprocessed foods with a low (i.e., below 60) glycaemic index, and everyone should try to eat some low-GI carbohydrate with each meal (whole grains, beans, vegetables, and non-tropical fruits). If you eat high-GI carbohydrates, try to include them in meals that also contain some low-GI foods.

Try to reduce your consumption of foods made with wheat flour and sugar and increase your consumption of beans.

Fat

On a 2,000-calorie-a-day diet, 600 calories can come from fat – that is, about 67 grams. Ideally, this should be in a ratio of 1:2:1 of saturated to monounsaturated to polyunsaturated fat, meaning that no more than 100 calories should come from saturated fat. You should reduce saturated fat by eating less butter, cream, cheese, and other full-fat dairy products, unskinned chicken, fatty meats, and products made with palm and coconut oil. Use olive oil as a principal oil in cooking. Limit your consumption of polyunsaturated vegetable oils (safflower, sunflower, corn, sesame) and avoid margarine, vegetable shortening, and all products made with partially hydrogenated oils. Also avoid fried foods in restaurants, especially fast-food restaurants.

Be sure to eat sources of omega-3 fats: oily fish, fortified eggs, soya foods, walnuts, linseeds, and hemp seeds.

Protein

Your daily intake should be between 50 and 100 grams on a 2,000-calorie-a-day diet. Eat less protein if you have liver or kidney problems, allergies, or auto-immune disease. Eat more vegetable protein, especially from beans, in general, and soya beans, in particular, and less animal protein, except for fish and reduced-fat dairy products. Avoid protein supplements.

Vitamins and Minerals

Eating a diet high in fresh foods with plenty of fruits and vegetables will provide most of the micronutrients you need. In addition, I recommend supplementing the diet with the following:

- vitamin C, 100 mg twice a day
- vitamin E, 400 to 800 IU of a natural form (d-alpha tocopherol together with other tocopherols)
- selenium, 200 mcg of a yeast-bound form
- mixed carotenoids, 25,000 IU
- a B-complex vitamin providing at least 400 mcg of folic acid
- calcium, 1,200 to 1,500 mg, preferably as calcium citrate.

Fibre

The optimum diet should provide 40 grams of fibre a day. You can achieve this by increasing your consumption of fruits (especially berries), vegetables (especially beans), and whole grains. Ready-made cereals can be good fibre sources, but read labels to make sure they give you at least 4, and preferably 5, grams of bran per 30 g (1 oz) serving.

Protective Phytochemicals

To get the maximum natural protection against cancer, degenerative diseases, and environmental toxicity, eat a variety of fruits, vegetables, and mushrooms, and drink tea, especially green tea.

Water

Try to drink six to eight glasses of pure water a day or drinks that are mostly water (tea, very diluted fruit juice, sparkling water with lemon). Use bottled water or get a home water purifier if your tap water tastes of chlorine or other contaminants or you live in an area where the water is suspected of being contaminated (see page 31). I recommend that you drink tea regularly for its antioxidant effects, especially green tea. Decaffeinated forms are available.

If you drink alcohol, red wine is probably the best choice because of the antioxidant effect of the red pigments (see page 39). I do not recommend using any form of alcohol excessively or on a daily basis.

Now, how can you put all of this information into practice? The recipes that Rosie and I have devised for this book are mostly consistent with the recommendations for the optimum diet, except for some desserts, which should be reserved for special occasions. You also have to think about shopping, menu planning, time management in the kitchen, and the storage and use of leftovers. Throughout *The Healthy Kitchen* you will find sidebars that address some of these matters. In her recipes, Rosie frequently offers tips from her kitchen to help you simplify food preparation and make the most efficient use of time in your kitchen. Before I end this chapter, I'd like to give you some general advice on putting meals together that take account of the facts of human nutrition.

A first consideration is whether the day's meals approximate the number of calories you need and the right amounts of macronutrients and micronutrients. For example, if you are going to have a main course of chicken or fish for dinner, you may not want to serve a protein-rich breakfast. If you are going to have a dish with a high-fat content, try to cut back on fat in the other dishes you eat. If you are serving a high-glycaemic-index carbohydrate food like waffles, make sure to serve berries with them to lower the GI of the meal.

Where will you get your omega-3 fatty acids today? From fish? Walnuts?

Fortified eggs? Linseeds? Ask yourself how you can get the recommended number of servings of fruits and vegetables in a day. Here is one possibility: have a banana and a glass of orange juice with breakfast, a big mixed salad and some vegetable juice at lunch, a serving of broccoli with dinner, and some berries and a slice of melon for dessert. That will more than take care of your needs for micronutrients.

In planning menus, think about the preparation time involved, so that you do not find yourself in a last-minute frenzy. What can you prepare in advance? If you are making an elaborate main dish, you might want to serve simple sides to accompany it. Do you expect to have leftovers? If so, think about how you can use them in later meals. By getting in the habit of planning in this way, you can make your healthy kitchen an efficient one also.

Rosie and I want you to have fun in the kitchen, not to knock yourself out. We hope this book will help you discover the pleasure of making, serving, and eating food that is both good and good for you. —**A.W.**

Stocking the Storecupboard

In general, most all of my recipes call for ingredients that are readily available, but occasionally you'll come across something that has to be bought in a speciality store, such as an Asian, Middle Eastern, or health food shop. In those instances I have alerted you and indicated where the item is to be found. But there are certain ingredients that I use frequently which you will want to have on hand on your cupboard shelf or in your refrigerator so you'll know they are there when you want to make a recipe from this book.

So let's stock the storecupboard before we begin.

Oils

Toasted sesame oil and olive oil are essential for sautéing and adding flavour and texture to a dish. Grapeseed and walnut oil are optional but good to have for salad dressings and for sautéing, particularly grapeseed because of its high smoke threshold. Note that we always call for toasted sesame oil, which is the Asian variety; it is readily available these days in supermarkets. Store oils in a cool, dark place and don't buy more than you can use up in a month or so.

Oriental Products

Soy sauce: We always call for a natural soy sauce, such as tamari (see Andy's comments on page 58). Available at supermarkets. Get a good supply; it keeps indefinitely.

Mirin: A sweet, low-alcohol rice wine that adds an aromatic flavour to many dishes. Possibly available at a supermarkets, but you may have to get it at a Japanese or Oriental food shop. Keeps well, unrefrigerated.

Rice vinegar: Milder than Western-style vinegars, although you could substitute cider vinegar. Available at most supermarkets.

Coconut milk: Available in cans and packets in most supermarkets – low-fat variety preferred. Store in a lidded jar and refrigerate after opening; keeps for up to ten days.

Wasabi: This is a fiery root-herb that resembles horseradish, although it is not related to it. It is used frequently in Japanese dishes. Available in

Japanese and Oriental food shops in either powder or paste form. Use sparingly. Refrigerate well-sealed after opening.

Miso paste: Made from soya beans. Available in Japanese and Oriental food shops. Organic, brown-rice miso or light yellow preferred. Refrigerate after opening. Keeps a long time.

Pasta

I have recipes using buckwheat and cellophane noodles (also called transparent or bean thread noodles) as well as Italian-style pasta. Look for the former in supermarkets or Oriental food shops.

Rice and Grains

You'll need brown, basmati, jasmine, and (optional) wild rice. Also, quinoa, bulgur wheat, cornmeal, couscous, oat bran, and millet. All these are best bought at a health food shop where you can get organic products; buy them in bulk if you have a big household and are going to use them a lot. Store them in tightly sealed jars on the cupboard shelf, except during very hot, humid weather when you might want to refrigerate the grains.

Flour

I use both plain white flour and wholemeal flour as well as wholemeal pastry or cake flour. Pastry or cake flour is a high-starch, fine-textured flour that makes delicate pastries and cakes.

Nuts and Seeds

Walnuts, almonds, pine nuts, sesame seeds, and sunflower seeds are frequently used. Try to get organic nuts and seeds in health food shops and keep them tightly sealed, in the refrigerator or freezer.

Herbs and Aromatics

Some herbs are so much better when used fresh that it is worth growing your own. (See Rosie's Tips on Growing Herbs, page 100, and Andy's About Herbs, page 98.) But some keep their character and aroma very well when dried, and I would recommend that you have the following dried herbs on hand: thyme, sage, oregano, mint, rosemary, and tarragon. Dried basil loses a lot of its character, but when combined with seasonings as in the Cajun mixture below, it is acceptable. Keep your fresh herbs in tightly sealed jars in a cool, dark place, preferably the refrigerator. Dried herbs do not have to be refrigerated. Replace them when they lose their bloom (your nose is your best guide); if they've lost their aroma, throw them out.

Seasonings and Spices

Again, if you cook a lot, you may want to buy the spices you use most frequently in bulk at a health food shop. Store in tightly sealed containers in the refrigerator.

Italian seasoning herbs: I call for this quite a lot. If you don't have it on hand, you can make up a batch by crushing and mixing together 1 teaspoon sage, 1 tablespoon thyme, and 1 tablespoon oregano.

Mexican seasoning: You can buy this in a jar or make your own by combining 1 tablespoon garlic powder, 1 tablespoon ground cumin, and 1/2 teaspoon each black pepper, paprika, onion flakes, and crushed thyme.

Cajun spice blend: Available in jars or make your own by mixing 1 tablespoon paprika, 1/2 tablespoon cayenne pepper, 1 tablespoon salt, 1/2 tablespoon oregano, and 1/2 tablespoon basil.

Curry powder: Indian cooks would mix their own but since it is made up of about twenty spices, I recommend that you buy a good prepared brand.

Turmeric: One of the principal spices that go into curry, it is what produces the deep yellow-orange colour; it can be a little bitter if you use too much.

Saffron: Very expensive, but a little goes a long way and gives a dish a deep yellow colour and a subtle flavour.

Cumin: A spice that gives a distinct flavour to Mexican foods, which I use to give a kick to all kinds of dishes.

Chillies: You can buy them powdered, as cayenne or chilli powder; as dried flakes; as chilli oil; or as chilli paste (the latter should be kept in the refrigerator after opening). If you don't have exactly what is called for you can use the above interchangeably, but it is hard to give exact measurement equivalents, so you will have to let your tastebuds guide you. Add a little, taste, and then use more if you like it hot.

Paprika: A Hungarian sweet chilli powder that gives subtle flavour and brilliant colour.

Fennel: A spice with a liquorice flavour (but not as sugary sweet as liquorice suggests). It is better to buy it whole and grind or crush it as needed. (I call for it sprinkled on tofu and on some vegetables.)

Cinnamon, ginger, cloves, nutmeg, and allspice: These aren't just limited to sweets and baked goods in our recipes, so you'll want to have them on hand to add interesting flavour to some sauces, soups, and stews. Unless used in baking, the ginger we call for is fresh root ginger and it should always be available in the vegetable drawer of your refrigerator. (Allspice is aptly named because it tastes like cinnamon, cloves, and nutmeg combined.)

Nutmeg should be bought whole so you can grate it fresh (the small holes of any grater will do) because once powdered it loses its flavour rapidly. Freshly grated nutmeg perfumes not only sweets but many a savoury dish of ours.

Sweeteners

When you want to sweeten desserts or drinks, sugar isn't the only way to go. I use honey, maple syrup, crystallized ginger, and natural fruit preserves.

Onions and Garlic

Fresh is always best. We use these aromatics a lot, so be sure to have them in your vegetable bin (no need to refrigerate). Avoid powdered onion and garlic in any form and never buy the peeled and sometimes chopped garlic you find in jars at supermarkets these days. It's easy to peel a clove of garlic: just smash it with the flat side of a big knife and the skin will split so that it can be pulled off. If you don't like the smell of garlic on your hands, rub some salt on them to remove it.

Fruits

Always try to have lemons, oranges, and limes when in season in your refrigerator. Both of us use them a lot in our recipes. It is also useful to have dried fruits on hand, such as mangoes, apricots, figs, currants, and sultanas, which keep well in tightly sealed plastic bags.

—R.D.

READING FOOD PRODUCT LABELS

The most important piece of advice I can give you about shopping for food is to read product labels. We are fortunate to live in a country where a great deal of information about food products must be disclosed on labels. It is foolish not to take advantage of that in deciding what to buy.

You can start by reading the list of ingredients on a package. These will be in descending order, from those present in the greatest weight to those present in the least. I recommend that you reject any product whose list of ingredients is too long, the print too fine, or the space on the label barely adequate to contain it. If you do not recognise a lot of the ingredients, that should also be cause for rejection. And think about how you would make something equivalent at home; if the ingredients on the label differ markedly from what you would use in your own kitchen, do not buy the product. Finally, look for the presence of unhealthy ingredients, such as partially hydrogenated oils and artificial colours. (Below, I'll list some other additives to watch out for.)

Next, check the nutritional information, if given, starting with calories per serving. Make sure that the serving size is realistic. A bag of crisps might say it contains eight or more servings, but you might eat half of it all at once. Note the total amount of fat and how much of it is saturated. Also note cholesterol and sodium content. Check the total carbohydrates and the amount of sugar, plus fibre, if any. Also look for the presence of vitamins and key minerals like iron and calcium.

Here are the basic rules to follow when you are trying to be good label detectives:

- Try to buy foods that contain the same ingredients you would use at home.
- Avoid products that have many unfamiliar ingredients or just too many ingredients.
- Avoid products containing partially hydrogenated oils, artificial colours, artificial sweeteners, nitrites or nitrates, sulfites, potassium bromate, and brominated vegetable oil. In my opinion, all of these pose health risks.

- Minimise consumption of products containing MSG (monosodium glutamate), aluminium, and the preservatives BHA, BHT, and TBHQ. In my opinion, these may pose health risks.
- In checking nutritional information on food labels, make sure the serving size is what you would actually eat, and adjust the arithmetic if it is not.

—A.W.

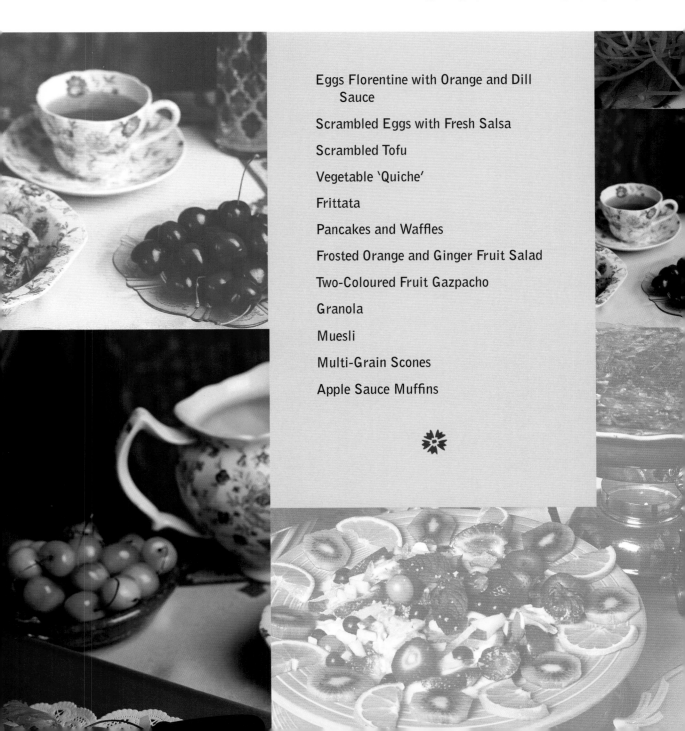

Breakfast

Eggs Florentine with Orange and Dill Sauce

Scrambled Eggs with Fresh Salsa

Scrambled Tofu

Vegetable 'Quiche'

Frittata

Pancakes and Waffles

Frosted Orange and Ginger Fruit Salad

Two-Coloured Fruit Gazpacho

Granola

Muesli

Multi-Grain Scones

Apple Sauce Muffins

BREAKFAST

I always eat breakfast, and recommend that you do too. We all need food in the morning to resupply ourselves with sources of glucose, which is not stored in the body and is needed to fuel the brain. Studies show that those who eat breakfast are more productive at school and work than those who skip it. But there is disagreement over what should be eaten for the first meal of the day.

I myself like leftovers. I've never cared for most of the common American breakfast foods and feel just terrible if I eat some of them (pancakes, Danish pastries, and fried potatoes, for example). I do fine on a traditional Japanese breakfast of steamed rice, grilled fish, miso soup, pickled vegetables, seaweed, and green tea. I also like fruit, nuts, some fresh cheese, and olives. You will have to experiment to find out what you like and what works best for you.

In any case, eating breakfast makes it easier to meet your daily nutritional requirements. Research shows that people who eat breakfast get more vitamins A, C, and E, folic acid, calcium, iron, and fibre than those who skip it. They also do better with weight control, because they are less prone to overeat at other meals or load up on high-calorie snacks later in the day.

Perhaps the most common excuse for skipping breakfast is lack of time; but considering the nutritional importance of the first meal of the day, you should try to find ways of eating something in the morning that is quick and easy to prepare. (And I don't mean a cup of coffee and a doughnut.) Breakfast should provide one-quarter to one-third of your day's protein, some good (i.e., low-glycaemic-index) carbohydrate, and some fat. Here are some ideas:

- A bowl of whole-grain cereal with calcium-fortified soya milk and some fruit. The most nutritious fruits are kiwi, orange-fleshed melon, papaya, mango, blueberries, strawberries, and bananas. Add a tablespoon of freshly ground linseeds as a source of essential fatty acids.
- A soya shake: blend 1/2 cake of silken tofu, 120 ml (1/2 cup) apple juice, 255 g (1 cup) frozen, organic strawberries, and 1 banana.
- Keep some hard-boiled eggs on hand, or scramble up a few eggs to eat with whole-grain toast. Include a glass of calcium-fortified orange juice or a container of plain yogurt to which you can add some berries or other fruit.

Finally, if all you take in the morning is coffee, try switching to green tea for the protection it provides against cancer and heart disease. —A.W.

Eggs Florentine with Orange and Dill Sauce

The orange-dill sauce drizzled over the poached eggs has a faint fruit flavour due to the orange juice, a spiciness from the balsamic vinegar, and a hint of the exotic, penetrating flavour of turmeric – a spice relative of ginger. This dish makes a vibrant breakfast – colourful, easy, and healthy.

SERVES 6

PER SERVING:

CALORIES 236.2

FAT 12.5 G
  SATURATED FAT
  5.5 G
(46.5% OF CALO-
  RIES FROM FAT)

PROTEIN 11.6 G

CARBOHYDRATE
  20.7 G

CHOLESTEROL
  266 MG

FIBRE 2.6 G

450 g (1 lb) washed spinach, stalks removed

ORANGE AND DILL SAUCE

1 egg yolk
60 ml (1/4 cup) freshly squeezed orange juice
1 teaspoon balsamic vinegar
2 teaspoons lemon juice
1/2 teaspoon turmeric
1/2 teaspoon salt

45 g (11/2 oz) butter, at room temperature
2 teaspoons chopped fresh dill

1 teaspoon white vinegar
6 eggs
3 English muffins, split in half
2 beefsteak tomatoes, sliced

GARNISH

Fresh cracked black pepper (optional)

Fill a medium pan with water and bring it to the boil. Drop in the washed spinach and cook for 3 minutes, stirring several times. Drain the spinach in a colander. Put a bowl or plate directly on top of the spinach, inside the colander, and press down to squeeze all excess water from the leaves. Cover and set aside.

Fill the bottom of a double boiler halfway with water and place over medium heat. Set the top pan over the water and drop in the egg yolk. Add the orange juice and stir until blended. Stir in the balsamic vinegar and the lemon juice, then the turmeric, salt, and butter. Add 1 teaspoon of the dill and whisk until all the ingredients are thoroughly blended and the sauce has a thick creamy consistency (approximately 2 minutes).

Remove the top part of the double boiler and set aside. Pour

Eggs Florentine with Orange and Dill Sauce

the white vinegar into the water in the bottom pan and heat it just to the boiling point. Gently crack the eggs one by one, into the simmering water, and poach for 3 minutes. Remove the eggs with a slotted spoon and let the water drip from the spoon so they aren't watery. Transfer the eggs to a warm platter and cover.

Toast the English muffins under the grill (or in a toaster). Remove them from the grill and put them on plates. Place a tomato slice on each muffin half and spoon one-sixth of the cooked spinach on top. Arrange 1 poached egg on top of that and drizzle a spoonful or so of the orange-dill sauce over everything. Sprinkle some of the remaining 1 teaspoon of chopped dill and black pepper (optional) over the sauce as a garnish. Serve immediately.

Tips from Rosie's Kitchen

This recipe uses a double boiler. If you do not have one, you can improvise by setting a medium stainless-steel bowl inside a large saucepan, so that the top of the bowl fits snugly onto the top of the pan. If you use this setup, be careful not to burn yourself – the steam from the bottom pan gets very hot!

ANDY SUGGESTS

I would happily substitute olive oil for the butter in the Orange and Dill Sauce.

ARE EGGS GOOD FOR YOU?

It's hard to keep up with medical opinion about eggs. First they were good, then they were bad, now they're good again. Egg yolks contain a dazzling array of essential vitamins and minerals, particularly vitamins A, D, E, and K and iron, while the whites are a great source of high-quality protein. The egg's once-tarnished reputation had to do with its yolk, a source of saturated fat and cholesterol. As fat and cholesterol became Public Health Enemies Numbers One and Two, health-conscious consumers scratched eggs off their shopping lists. The egg industry then launched advertising campaigns to tell us exactly how many eggs a week are safe to eat without increasing the risk of heart disease. The really interesting news, however, is that certain eggs can actually improve cardiovascular health because they provide omega-3 fatty acids.

My favourite source of omega-3s is fish, particularly salmon and sardines. Linseeds, hemp seeds, and walnuts are other sources. Eggs may now join these foods, provided that hens get omega-3s in their diets, which in turn will be incorporated in the yolks of their eggs. Most of the eggs in supermarkets come from factory-farmed chickens, which do not get to eat the required sources, such as soya beans and greens. In order to obtain the benefits you want from eggs, choose those from free-range, organically fed hens.

Recently, farmers have begun to produce 'designer' eggs, containing more omega-3 fatty acids than regular ones. They do this by fortifying chicken feed with a meal made from algae or linseed. These new eggs taste better than regular eggs – and they're better for you. They also cost more, but I think they're worth the extra money.

Even if you eat only the best eggs, you should still not eat them with abandon. Dietary cholesterol may not be as great a culprit as many people think – its negative effect on serum cholesterol is dwarfed by the effect of saturated fat in most people's diets – but whole eggs turn up in so many prepared dishes and processed foods that we can easily end up eating too many of them, especially in combination with sugar, milk, cream, butter, and cheese, classic recipes for atherosclerosis and heart disease. You can often substitute egg whites for whole eggs in recipes or even leave out eggs altogether. Experiment. If you like eggs, I think it's fine to eat one or two a day, as long as you cook them without a lot of fat and use them in dishes that are consistent with the guidelines for healthy eating. —**A.W.**

Scrambled Eggs with Fresh Salsa

There are two words for this dish: easy and nourishing. Everybody has time to make scrambled eggs! This meal is a good combination of protein from the eggs and carbohydrate from the bread. If you want to forgo the toast, wrap the scrambled eggs inside a warm flour tortilla (wrap) to make an egg burrito. No matter how you serve the scrambled eggs, the fresh salsa is what really makes this traditional breakfast food better than usual.

Keep in mind that if you are concerned about cholesterol, you can make this dish using only egg whites and get just as much nutritional value from it.

SERVES 6

PER SERVING:

CALORIES 204.9

FAT 8.2 G
  SATURATED FAT
  2 G
(33.3% OF CALO-
  RIES FROM FAT)

PROTEIN 10.2 G

CARBOHYDRATE
  26.5 G

CHOLESTEROL
  216 MG

FIBRE 4.6 G

❋

SALSA

1 bunch fresh coriander
180 g (1 cup) chopped tomatoes
30 g (1/4 cup) diced red pepper
40 g (1/4 cup) diced red onion
1 small green chilli, seeded and
  finely chopped
2 tablespoons freshly squeezed
  lime juice

1 tablespoon olive oil
35 g (1/2 cup) sliced mushrooms
60 g (1/2 cup) sliced spring onions

60 g (1/2 cup) chopped red pepper
60 g (1/2 cup) chopped yellow or
  green pepper
6 eggs
1 teaspoon salt
60 ml (1/4 cup) skimmed milk

GARNISH

6 slices whole-grain bread
6 slices honeydew melon

Make the salsa: hold the coriander under running water to wash off the dirt. Pinch the leaves off the stalks, coarsely chop the leaves, and put them in a small bowl with the remaining salsa ingredients. Toss thoroughly until everything is blended together. Cover and refrigerate until ready to use.

Smear a nonstick medium sauté pan with 1/4 teaspoon of the oil and set it over medium heat. Sauté the mushrooms, onions, and peppers in the pan, tossing them occasionally, until limp, about 2 minutes. Remove from the heat.

Whisk the eggs, salt, and milk together in a small bowl. Coat the bottom of a separate pan with the remaining olive oil, set it over low heat, pour in the eggs, and partially cook them for 3 minutes, stirring with a wooden spoon until they are no longer runny. Transfer the partially cooked eggs to the pan with the vegetables and cook everything together for 1 minute, stirring with a wooden spoon or spatula. Remove from the heat and cover to keep warm.

Cut each bread slice diagonally, put them on a baking sheet, and toast them under the grill for less than 30 seconds on each side. Serve the eggs with the toast, a slice of honeydew melon, and a small ramekin of salsa.

Scrambled Tofu

Don't worry, you egg eaters, you aren't deprived of flavour here. So have some variety in your breakfasts, alternating between eggs and tofu (see more about tofu from Andy on page 192). This dish is light, well seasoned, and, like eggs, full of protein for get-up-and-go energy. Turmeric is what lends the colour and mild flavour to this dish.

SERVES 6

PER SERVING:

CALORIES 98.3

FAT 7.5 G
 SATURATED FAT
 1 G
(65.9 % OF CALO-
 RIES FROM FAT)
PROTEIN 5.5 G

CARBOHYDRATE
 3.5 G

CHOLESTEROL
 0 MG

FIBRE 1.3 G

❋

450 g (1 lb) firm tofu
3 cloves garlic, peeled and thinly
   sliced
3 tablespoons diced red pepper
2 tablespoons olive oil
1/2 teaspoon turmeric
1/2 teaspoon salt
1/4 teaspoon freshly ground
   black pepper

95 g (3/4 cup) sliced spring onions
   or chives, or 80 g (1/2 cup)
   finely chopped onion
2 teaspoons soy sauce

GARNISH

Fresh salsa (page 8)
Corn tortillas

Drain the tofu and crumble it, using clean hands. Sauté the garlic and diced pepper with the olive oil in a medium sauté pan on medium heat, for about 2 minutes. Stir in the crumbled tofu first, then add turmeric, salt, pepper, spring onions (or chives or onions), and soy sauce. Cook the tofu for 3 more minutes, stirring occasionally. Serve with salsa and warm corn tortillas.

Tips from Rosie's Kitchen

You can use the scrambled tofu to make a 'tofu-salad sandwich' with lettuce and tomato, as opposed to an egg-salad sandwich, or you can mix the scrambled tofu with a little bit of the Pesto (page 160) for more of a side-dish type food.

Vegetable 'Quiche'

This fresh vegetable 'quiche' is made with a light, crispy potato crust and a filling of vegetables and herbs and spices.

This 'quiche' makes a wonderful morning brunch or lunch or a simple dinner, served with a salad and a small, toasted baguette. If you should not be eating egg yolks, you can make it using only the egg whites.

120 ml (1/2 cup) purified water
30 g (1/4 cup) dry-pack sun-dried tomatoes
225 g (8 oz) asparagus or broccoli florets
1/2 medium onion, chopped
2 cloves garlic, sliced
2 tablespoons olive oil
1 carrot, cut into small cubes
5 mushrooms, sliced
1 tablespoon chopped fresh basil or 1 teaspoon dried
1 tablespoon chopped fresh parsley
1/8 teaspoon dried chilli flakes
1/8 teaspoon freshly grated nutmeg

1/2 teaspoon salt
1 teaspoon freshly ground black pepper
3 small red potatoes, washed and thinly sliced
50 g (1/2 cup) grated cheese, such as Gruyère
60 ml (1/4 cup) milk
120 ml (1/2 cup) low-fat soured cream or reduced-fat crème fraîche
6 eggs
1 medium tomato, sliced (seeds squeezed out)
3 tablespoons freshly grated Parmesan cheese

SERVES 8

PER SERVING:
CALORIES 205
FAT 12.6 G
  SATURATED FAT
  4.9 G
(53.8% OF CALO-
  RIES FROM FAT)
PROTEIN 10 G
CARBOHYDRATE
  14.3 G
CHOLESTEROL
  175 MG
FIBRE 2.3 G

Preheat oven to 190°C.

Boil the water, pour over the sun-dried tomatoes, and allow to soak for about 15 minutes until they become soft and plump. Strain off any remaining liquid, and coarsely chop the tomatoes.

Cut off about 2.5 cm (1 in) of the coarse ends of the asparagus stalks, and discard or save them for soup. Cut the remaining stalks into about 6 pieces or chop coarsely. If you are using broccoli, cut into florets. Blanch the asparagus by boiling it in a medium pan of water for 2 minutes or less. Asparagus should be bright green and firm to the bite. Drain, rinse the asparagus in cold water, and drain again in a colander.

Sauté the onions and the garlic in the olive oil over low heat until the onions are translucent, approximately 10 minutes. Add the carrots, mushrooms, basil, parsley, chilli flakes, nutmeg, salt, and pepper and continue to cook for 5 more minutes. Remove from the heat.

Lightly grease the bottom and sides of a 23 cm (9 in) pie tin. Line the bottom with the potato slices, overlapping them slightly. Whisk together the cheese, milk, sun-dried tomatoes, soured cream (or crème fraîche), and the eggs in a large bowl. Mix in the sautéed vegetables and the blanched asparagus, coating everything with the milk and egg mixture, then pour into the potato-lined tin. Arrange the tomato slices on top and sprinkle with Parmesan cheese. Bake for 1 hour, covering after 45 minutes if top browns. Completely baked quiche should be very firm. Cool for 15 minutes before slicing and serving. Leftovers can be wrapped and kept in the refrigerator for up to 3 days.

Tips from Rosie's Kitchen

Try to grate fresh nutmeg and Parmesan cheese yourself because it makes a noticeable difference in the flavour.

Drop the potato slices into cold water to prevent them from discoloring.

To blanch fruits and vegetables, boil them for about 2 minutes and then plunge them into cold water – this stops the cooking and sets the colour. Blanching is also done to loosen the skins of fruits or vegetables such as plums or tomatoes.

SPICES AND SPICY FOOD

Skilful use of spices is a mark of a good cook. Once precious beyond measure for their ability to preserve food and mask off-tastes in days before refrigeration, the spices of the world are now available to anyone in the nearest supermarket. You just have to learn how to work with them.

A good starting point is to take one at a time. Get to know its aroma and flavour and think about which foods you would want to taste it in. Try allspice, the tiny dried fruit of a West Indian tree, so called because it is reminiscent of clove, nutmeg, and cinnamon. Recipes often tell you to add allspice to sweets like biscuits, but it is quite wonderful in savoury dishes like beans and soups. Cumin is a major spice in Latin America, the Middle East, and India, extremely versatile, and a good one to experiment with. In India it is usually used with coriander, the two together forming a backbone of the aromatic personality of curry. Chinese cooks often use ginger and garlic together in stir-fries. Try that combination – both are assertive flavours and complement each other.

After you gain familiarity with individual spices and have a sense of how and when you want to employ them, you can play with combinations. It is also important to develop a sense of how much spice to add, because too little will not command attention and too much can detract from the dish as a whole. A tomato sauce made too pungent with marjoram and oregano is a disaster, as is a stuffing with too much sage. Knowledge here comes with practise and a lot of tasting along the way. Remember: you can always add more.

When most people talk about spicy food, they mean hot and spicy, particularly from the presence of chilli, black pepper, mustard, ginger, and other hot spices. But food can be spicy without being pungent. In Ayurveda, the traditional system of lifestyle medicine from India, food is generally prepared without the hot spices but with liberal amounts of aromatic ones like cardamom, cumin, and coriander. Some people say that spicy food does not agree with them, failing to notice that the hot and spicy food they have encountered may have been poorly prepared, greasy, or otherwise likely to cause digestive distress. Most authorities agree that judicious and balanced use of spices stimulates appetite and digestion, and that many spices have specific beneficial effects. For example, ginger and turmeric are powerful anti-inflammatory agents, and garlic is a natural antibiotic.

Make sure the spices you use are fresh. Protect them from light and heat (I keep mine in the refrigerator), and throw them out if their colours and aromas fade. I can't imagine cooking without spices. They enable me to enhance, adjust, and balance the flavours of my dishes and are essential to me when I cook. —A.W.

Frittata

SERVES 6

PER SERVING:

CALORIES 166.4

FAT 13 G
  SATURATED FAT
  3.3 G

(67.8 % OF CALO-
  RIES FROM FAT)

PROTEIN 7.9 G

CARBOHYDRATE
  6 G

CHOLESTEROL
  183 MG

FIBRE 1.7 G

❀

Frittatas, or Italian omelets, are a bit easier to make than omelets, though the techniques are similar. I like frittatas because they are a substantial dish – dense with eggs, vegetables, and seasonings. You can eat a slice or two for breakfast, brunch, or lunch, or you can warm up a slice for a quick dinner on those evenings when you get home late from work. I like to serve the frittata with a mixed green salad.

5 eggs
2 tablespoons grated Parmesan
  cheese
1 clove garlic, finely chopped
40 g (1/4 cup) chopped onion
1 tablespoon olive oil
1 teaspoon Italian seasoning herbs
1/2 teaspoon freshly ground black
  pepper
1/2 teaspoon salt
20 g (1/4 cup) sliced mushrooms

60 g (1/2 cup) sliced courgettes
70 g (1/2 cup) asparagus, coarse
  ends removed, spears cut into
  5 cm (2 in) pieces
2 tablespoons grated Cheddar
  cheese

GARNISH

1 avocado, cut into wedges
1 tomato, cut into wedges

Preheat the grill to high.

Lightly beat eggs and Parmesan cheese in a bowl. Put the garlic, onions, and olive oil in an ovenproof sauté pan and cook over medium heat until the onions become limp. Add the spices. Add the mushrooms, courgettes, and asparagus and sauté until the onions are limp and translucent, about 2 1/2 to 3 minutes. Pour the egg batter over the vegetables, shaking the pan to keep the eggs from sticking to the bottom. Loosen the edges of the omelet with a spatula and tilt the pan so that the uncooked part runs around the pan. Just before the eggs are about to set, sprinkle the grated Cheddar cheese on top and remove from the heat. Put the pan under the grill until the top becomes brown, about 2 minutes. Slide the frittata onto a platter and cut into wedges. Garnish with avocado and tomato wedges. Serve immediately.

Tips from Rosie's Kitchen

For a denser version of this frittata, I replace the courgettes with artichoke hearts and the asparagus with diced potato.

Pancakes and Waffles

The aroma and taste of home-made American-style pancakes or waffles is irresistible! The batter in this recipe makes feathery light pancakes, or light and crispy golden waffles.

You'll definitely want to make these for a breakfast or brunch with friends or family, or on that free weekend morning.

SERVES 12

PER SERVING:

CALORIES 150.9

FAT 2.8 G

SATURATED FAT
0.7 G

(16.2% OF CALO-
RIES FROM FAT)

PROTEIN 5.2 G

CARBOHYDRATE
27.2 G

CHOLESTEROL 3 MG

FIBRE 2.6 G

❋

BLUEBERRY
PANCAKES

PER SERVING:

CALORIES 218.2

FAT 1.8 G

SATURATED FAT
0.9 G

(7.2% OF CALORIES
FROM FAT)

PROTEIN 5.8 G

CARBOHYDRATE
46.4 G

CHOLESTEROL 4 MG

FIBRE 4.3 G

4 eggs
80 ml (1/3 cup) fresh orange juice
1 teaspoon pure vanilla extract
300 ml (11/4 cups) milk
190 g (11/2 cups) unbleached plain flour
65 g (1/2 cup) wholemeal flour
1 teaspoon baking powder
1/4 teaspoon salt

FOR MEDALLION-SIZED BLUEBERRY PANCAKES

410 g (1 pint) blueberries, washed

FRESH FRUIT COMPOTE FOR PLAIN PANCAKES

340 g (1 pint) strawberries, washed, hulled, and sliced in half
410 g (1 pint) blueberries, washed
120 ml (1/2 cup) pure maple syrup

WAFFLE TOPPING
(Per Serving)

1/2 banana, sliced
30 g (1/4 cup) chopped walnuts
1 tablespoon pure maple syrup

Crack the eggs, letting the whites fall into a clean, dry mixing bowl and dropping the yolks into a separate bowl. Beat the whites with an electric mixer on high speed, or a balloon whisk, for about 2 minutes until the egg whites become fluffy and then firm. Be careful not to overmix, or they will flatten out.

Mix the egg yolks with a fork. Add the orange juice and vanilla and whisk everything together until it becomes foamy. Add the milk, barely stirring.

Place the dry ingredients together in a separate bowl and stir with a wooden spoon until everything is thoroughly blended. Slowly stir the dry ingredients into the egg yolk mixture and continue to mix until all the dry ingredients are wet and there are no clumps of flour. Slowly fold in the egg whites and stir only once or twice.

Prepare the fruit compote by mixing all the ingredients together until all the fruit is completely coated with syrup.

To make medallion-sized blueberry pancakes: coat the bottom of a flat griddle or large frying pan with 1/4 teaspoon butter or grapeseed oil and set it over medium heat for about 1 minute. Drop 2 tablespoons of batter onto the hot pan, placing them far enough apart so that the pancakes don't touch. Distribute 1 tablespoon (about 5) blueberries on top of each pancake, letting the berries sink into the batter. When bubbles begin to appear on the surface, in about 2 minutes, flip the pancakes over. Cook the blueberry side for 3 minutes. Transfer pancakes to a hot platter and stack them to keep them warm. Continue cooking the pancakes until all the batter is used up. (You do not need to add more butter to the pan.) Serve immediately. Makes 30 medallion-sized pancakes.

To make larger plain pancakes: coat the bottom of a flat griddle with 1/4 teaspoon butter and set it over medium heat for about 1 minute. Pour 3 tablespoons of batter onto the griddle and cook until bubbles start to form on top of each pancake. Turn them over and cook for about 2 minutes more. Transfer the pancakes to a hot platter and stack them to keep them warm. (No butter is needed after the first set of pancakes.)

When all the batter is used up, top each of 3 pancakes with 3 tablespoons of the fruit compote. Makes 12 regular-sized pancakes.

To make waffles: preheat the waffle iron until the signal comes on indicating it is ready. Pour enough of the batter evenly over the iron to fill it (usually about 120 ml/1/2 cup) and let the batter cook until the edges are golden brown. Turn out onto a warm plate and top with the banana, chopped walnuts, and maple syrup.

Tips from Rosie's Kitchen

The orange juice in the batter acts like a natural sweetener, alleviating the need for more syrup.

Separating the eggs is important, because the beaten whites make the pancakes puff up to perfection and the waffles light on the inside and slightly crunchy on the outside. Be sure to incorporate the egg whites slowly into the batter.

If you prefer, you can take some of the blueberries and spoon them into the smaller pancakes as they are cooking. You'll need about 2 tablespoons of blueberries to sprinkle on each pancake.

Frosted Orange Ginger Fruit Salad

For the same reasons this fruit salad makes a great breakfast, it also makes a great snack. It is light, naturally sweetened, and smothered in a smooth yogurt and ginger topping. Often, we find ourselves so busy that we quickly grab less-healthy foods to satisfy us. Make this ahead of time and keep it in the refrigerator, or take it to work in a covered container.

SERVES 12

PER SERVING:

CALORIES 84.6

FAT 0.9 G
    SATURATED FAT
    0.5 G
(12.3% OF CALO-
    RIES FROM FAT)

PROTEIN 1.3 G

CARBOHYDRATE
    13.8 G

CHOLESTEROL 9 MG

FIBER 2 G

350 g (2 cups) washed and sliced fresh strawberries

100 g (2 cups) grapes

115 g (1 cup) washed, cored, and diced apples

3 oranges, peeled, seeded, and cubed

60 ml (1/4 cup) freshly squeezed orange juice (from the 3 peeled, seeded, and cubed oranges)

240 ml (1 cup) plain low-fat yogurt (optional)

90 g (1/2 cup) chopped crystallized ginger

2 tablespoons honey

GARNISH

12 sprigs mint

Toss all the fruit together in a medium bowl. Whisk the orange juice, yogurt, ginger, and honey in a separate bowl. Pour the dressing over the fruit. Cover and refrigerate for at least 2 hours to marry the flavours.

Spoon the coated fruit into 12 small dessert dishes or parfait glasses. Garnish each with a sprig of mint.

Tips from Rosie's Kitchen

Crystallized ginger can be bought at most health-food shops in the bulk-food section. It gives the yogurt a subtle tangy yet sweet taste. If you choose not to use the yogurt, just mix the orange juice, crystallized ginger, and honey to make a glaze for the fruit.

Use a serrated knife when you peel, seed, and cube the oranges, because its edge will cut the flesh cleanly and precisely. Put an orange on a shallow dish or plate to catch the juice; then cut off the top and bottom so both ends are flat. Cut off the rounded parts of the orange, being careful not to slice too much into the flesh. You will have an orange with square corners. Pull the orange open and you'll be able to see the seeds. Pick them out and discard. Save all the juice.

Frosted Orange and Ginger Fruit Salad

Two-Coloured Fruit Gazpacho

What is more pleasurable to eat than a fruit soup? This isn't only great to eat; it is good to look at because of the colour. This gazpacho will cool you and your friends and family off on any warm afternoon.

SERVES 6

PER SERVING:

CALORIES 208.7

FAT 0.9 G
 SATURATED FAT
 0 G
 (3.7% OF CALORIES
 FROM FAT)

PROTEIN 2.4 G

CARBOHYDRATE
 52.1 G

CHOLESTEROL 0 MG

FIBRE 9.7 G

500 g (1 1/2 pints) fresh raspberries
20 ounces packaged unsweetened
 frozen raspberries, defrosted
3 tablespoons sugar
16 ounces lime-flavoured
 sparkling water
6 fresh mint leaves, shredded
5 kiwi fruits, peeled

2–3 tablespoons freshly squeezed
 lime juice
170 g (1 cup) finely diced
 honeydew melon
160 g (1 cup) finely diced orange-
 fleshed melon

Process the raspberries and sugar in a food processor until they are smooth. Strain the raspberry purée through a sieve to trap the seeds and transfer it to a big bowl. Add the sparkling water and mint and stir.

Process the kiwis and the lime juice in the food processor until smooth. Pour equal amounts of the raspberry purée into each of 6 small, chilled soup bowls. Pour equal amounts of the kiwi–lime juice purée in the middle of the raspberry purée in each of the 6 bowls. Sprinkle equal amounts of the diced melon into each soup bowl.

Two-Coloured Fruit Gazpacho

FRUIT

Nature clearly intends us to eat fruit. Juicy fruits have evolved into attractive and nutritious foods so that animals, including us, will eat them and disperse their seeds. Natural toxins occur commonly in roots, stems, and leaves to deter predators from eating the plants; they occur very rarely in fruits. Not only does fruit offer quick energy in the form of sugar, it is a cornucopia of health-protective elements: vitamins, minerals, fibre, antioxidant pigments, and other phytochemicals that reduce risks of disease. We all know we should eat fruit, even without nutritionists constantly telling us so.

The problem is often how to get good fruit. The quality of much of the fruit sold in supermarkets is not always great. Usually it is unripe, picked in a condition that is favourable to the shippers and distributors but not to those eating it. Worse, the varieties of fruits selected for mass production are often those that merely look good rather than taste good and that again offer more benefits to growers and distributors than consumers. The Red Delicious apple is a case in point. It looks the way people think an apple should, but more often than not it is mealy and insipid, distinctly inferior to varieties produced elsewhere, like the Fuji apple from Japan. I am not sorry to see the American apple industry in trouble as a result of trying to foist the Red Delicious variety on us for so many years – people are no longer buying.

Then there is the problem of residues of agrichemicals. I try to get organic fruit if I can. If I can't, I peel fruit when possible or wash it in a weak soap-and-water solution to remove what's on the surface. In my discussion of organic produce (see page 107), I mention that with some crops, such as strawberries, dangerous systemic pesticides are used that permeate the fruit and cannot be washed off.

Some diet gurus tell people to avoid fruit because of its sugar content. This is nonsense. The nutritional benefits of fruit far outweigh any problems related to the sugar in it. Do keep in mind, though, that fruit juices are concentrated sugar sources, both natural and, in many cases, added. It is not a good idea to let kids drink them to excess or to think of fruit juice as a substitute for water. Dried fruits also contain concentrated sugar. Enjoy them in moderation, but don't overdo.

I am very fond of berries, and am delighted to have read research findings that confirm their nutritional benefits. Not only are they low on the glycaemic index, they are full of micronutrients, especially fibre. (Raspberries are one of the best sources; the fibre is in the little seeds.) Berries are particularly rich in pigments called proanthocyanidins that are strong antioxidants and cancer fighters. Blueberries help fight urinary tract infections and have anti-ageing properties. But I don't think about all this when I sit down to eat a bowl of berries. I just think about how beautiful and delicious they are. And I am happy that I can keep bags of frozen organically grown berries on hand year-round. Thawed slightly, they make a fine dessert, with or without a scoop of fruit sorbet. —A.W.

Granola

Home-made granola makes a great snack alone, as a topping for yogurt or vanilla ice cream, or as a cereal with cold milk or rice milk, topped with bananas or peaches. You can mix anything you want with it, such as raisins, currants, or a different type of nut, to create your own home-made version of granola.

2 tablespoons grapeseed oil
75 g (1/2 cup) sesame seeds
170 g (1/2 cup) honey
1 tablespoon pure vanilla extract
160 g (2 cups) rolled oats
60 g (1/2 cup) slivered almonds

1 tablespoon grated orange zest
45 g (1/2 cup) desiccated coconut
1 tablespoon ground cinnamon

SERVES 6

PER SERVING:

CALORIES 403.3

FAT 20 G
  SATURATED FAT
  4.1 G

(42.8% OF CALO-
  RIES FROM FAT)

PROTEIN 8.7 G

CARBOHYDRATE
  51.4 G

CHOLESTEROL
  0 MG

FIBRE 4.5 G

Preheat oven to 180°C.

Put the oil, sesame seeds, honey, vanilla, oats, almonds, orange zest, and coconut in a large bowl. Stir everything together until thoroughly coated. Turn out onto a greased baking tray or tin and spread out the ingredients. Sprinkle the cinnamon on top and bake for 20 minutes, moving everything around a couple of times with a palette knife until all the oats are evenly browned. Let cool for 5–10 minutes. Store in a zip-lock plastic bag in the freezer until ready to eat.

Muesli

Instead of eating ordinary breakfast cereals, which can be laden with sugar – or, worse, skipping breakfast altogether – treat yourself. The combination of fruits in this natural cereal makes it sweet to perfection, and the walnuts provide a splash of protein. You will have to soak the oats and the fruit overnight, so plan ahead if you want to take this to work when you anticipate a busy morning. Or enjoy it any day of the week for breakfast.

SERVES 4

PER SERVING:

CALORIES 193.6

FAT 3.4 G
  SATURATED FAT
  0.8 G
(14.8% OF CALO-
  RIES FROM FAT)

PROTEIN 5.6 G

CARBOHYDRATE
  38.1 G

CHOLESTEROL
  2 MG

FIBRE 4.4 G

80 g (1 cup) rolled oats
4 sun-dried figs, pitted prunes, or apricots, chopped
4 pitted dates, chopped
2 tablespoons sun-dried raisins or dried cranberries
8 almonds, chopped
1/2 teaspoon ground cinnamon

1 pinch freshly grated nutmeg
240 ml (1 cup) apple juice
1/2 medium apple

GARNISH

1 banana, sliced
360 ml (11/2 cups) plain low-fat yogurt

Mix the oats, figs, dates, raisins or cranberries, almonds, cinnamon, and nutmeg together in a large bowl. Pour in the apple juice and soak overnight. After the oats and fruit have absorbed all the apple juice, grate the apple, with the skin, and stir it into the oat mixture until it is thoroughly distributed throughout. Divide evenly among 6 bowls. Garnish each serving with a few slices of banana, top with 60 ml (1/4 cup) yogurt, and serve.

Multi-Grain Scones

These scones are the perfect answer for the morning rush! Unlike a lot of low-fat foods, which can be so loaded with sugar that you feel hungry soon after eating them, these are quite filling – you can eat just half of one and still satisfy the need for morning sustenance. Plus, you get in a nice amount of bran for the day, an appropriate source of fibre.

1 egg
100 g (1/2 cup) caster sugar
5 tablespoons grapeseed oil
1/8 teaspoon grated lemon zest
40 g (1/2 cup) porridge oats
15 g (1/4 cup) bran
190 g (1 1/2 cups) unbleached
   plain flour
2 tablespoons millet
2 tablespoons poppy seeds

1/2 teaspoon salt
1 tablespoon baking powder
1/2 teaspoon ground cinnamon
120 ml (1/2 cup) milk

ZESTY LEMON TOPPING

3 tablespoons freshly squeezed
   lemon juice
30 g (1/4 cup) icing sugar, sifted

MAKES 6 SCONES

PER SERVING:

CALORIES 375.3

FAT 10.7 G
   SATURATED FAT
   1.5 G
(25.4% OF CALO-
   RIES FROM FAT)
PROTEIN 8.6 G
CARBOHYDRATE
   62 G
CHOLESTEROL
   23 MG
FIBRE 5.2 G

Preheat oven to 190°C.

Whisk the egg, sugar, and oil together in a bowl. Mix the lemon zest and all the dry ingredients together in a separate bowl and stir with a wooden spoon until all of them are evenly dispersed throughout. Slowly add the dry ingredients into the egg, sugar, and oil, and mix to create a thick dough. Add the milk and mix well.

Lightly grease a baking tray. Scoop up tablespoonfuls of the dough and drop them one by one in mounds onto the baking tray, leaving 5 cm (2 in) of space between. You should have 10 scones. Bake for 15–20 minutes, just until the crust is barely golden brown and the dough is dry. Remove from the oven and let cool for 10 minutes.

With a fork mix the Lemon Topping ingredients until the sugar is completely dissolved. Drizzle 1 tablespoon over each scone.

Tips from Rosie's Kitchen

If you want to make these scones completely dairy-free, substitute soya milk for regular milk. I also sometimes add 125 g (1 cup) of chopped walnuts for crunch and texture.

Apple Sauce Muffins

These are light and moist because of the apple sauce, and they have a surprising blast of chewy fruit and smooth preserves in the middle. I make them to eat with a cup of coffee or tea in the morning, or I'll cut one in half to satisfy a midday or late-afternoon sweet tooth.

MAKES 12 MUFFINS

PER SERVING:

CALORIES 152.8

FAT 1.3 G
  SATURATED FAT
  0.2 G

(8.1% OF CALORIES
  FROM FAT)

PROTEIN 4.1 G

CARBOHYDRATE
  36 G

CHOLESTEROL
  18 MG

FIBRE 3.8 G

190 g (1 1/2 cups) wholemeal flour
60 g (1 cup) oat bran
2 teaspoons baking powder
1/2 teaspoon bicarbonate of soda
1 teaspoon ground cinnamon
1 teaspoon ground allspice
1 egg
100 g (1/2 cup) soft brown sugar

100 g (1/2 cup) chopped dates
370 g (1 1/4 cups) Fresh Apple sauce (page **249**), or ready-made
80 g (1/4 cup) raspberry or any all-fruit jam

Preheat oven to 180°C.

Mix the flour, bran, baking powder, bicarbonate of soda, cinnamon, and allspice in a large bowl. Make a well in the centre and add the egg, brown sugar, and dates. Gradually stir in the apple sauce. Mix thoroughly.

Spoon half of the batter into 12 American-style muffin tins, then drop 1 teaspoon of jam on top of each one. Drop the rest of the batter on top of the jam. The jam will fall into the batter when it bakes. Bake for 25–30 minutes, until the tops are light brown.

EATING MINDFULLY

An exercise in mindfulness training, a Buddhist meditation practice, is to put a raisin in your mouth and see how long you can keep it there while paying attention to its taste and texture. Mindfulness is the technique of bringing all of our awareness to the here and now, to the sensations in our bodies and our breathing, for example, rather than letting much of it slip away in contemplation of the past and future or of other subjects that are not real. The assumption is that when we act with full awareness, our actions are more likely to achieve what we intend, and that when we feel with full awareness, we are more likely to feel fulfilled.

Many people perform the act of eating semiconsciously, swallowing food without really tasting it or focusing their attention on the next bite before they have enjoyed the present one. Others talk, read, or watch television while eating, directing their attention incompletely to their food. One consequence of unmindful eating is overeating. Who has not mindlessly shovelled in quantities of popcorn or crisps while watching a movie or staring at a television screen? Another consequence of unmindful eating is failure to get full sensory pleasure from food.

I notice that if food is really good, conversation at the table is reduced to a minimum, and people concentrate on the enjoyment of the moment. Then they are likely to eat less and enjoy it more.

We eat automatically out of habit. To break the habit requires motivation and practice. Try the raisin exercise to see how long you can go without chewing it up or swallowing it. When food is served to you, take a moment to fully appreciate its appearance and aroma before starting to eat. When you first taste it, try to give it your full attention. I think you will find, as I have, that eating mindfully heightens the pleasure of the experience. —**A.W.**

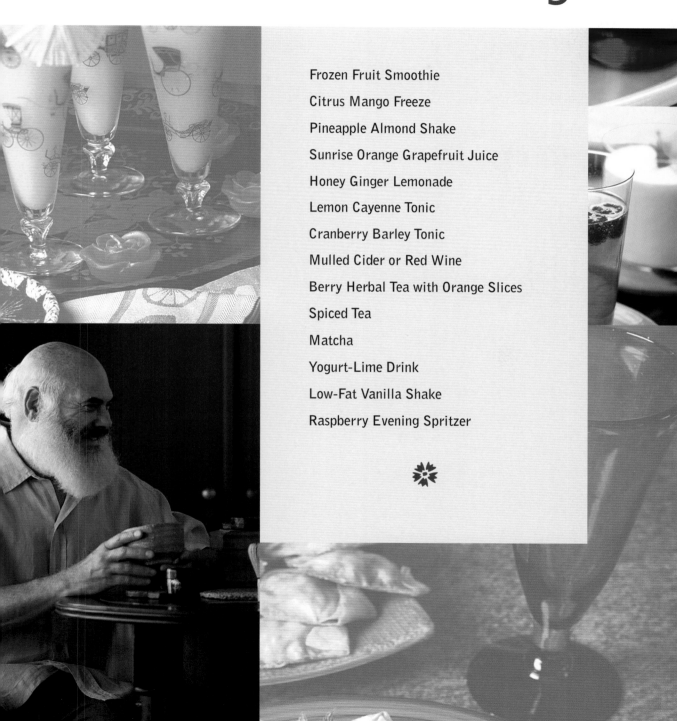

Beverages

Frozen Fruit Smoothie

Citrus Mango Freeze

Pineapple Almond Shake

Sunrise Orange Grapefruit Juice

Honey Ginger Lemonade

Lemon Cayenne Tonic

Cranberry Barley Tonic

Mulled Cider or Red Wine

Berry Herbal Tea with Orange Slices

Spiced Tea

Matcha

Yogurt-Lime Drink

Low-Fat Vanilla Shake

Raspberry Evening Spritzer

THE IMPORTANCE
OF WATER

We hear a lot about the importance of drinking water. Mostly we are told about the quantity of water we should drink, rarely about quality. To my mind water quality is all-important, not only for drinking but also for use in preparing food. If your tap water contains impurities that can hurt you – arsenic or lead, for example – food that you make with it will put those impurities into you, even if you use bottled water for drinking. I have rejected otherwise excellent bread because it tasted of chlorine to me, obviously from the chlorinated water used to make the dough.

I might use tap water to boil pasta or steam or boil vegetables. In these cases the water is mostly not consumed. But if I'm making soup or adding water to a recipe, I want it to be free of toxic impurities as well as unpleasant odours.

Bottled water is convenient, but over time it is expensive. And unless the manufacturer provides good information about its purity – in Europe they are more rigorous about this, and we should be in America too – you may be paying for a product that is not significantly better than tap water. I have long had a water-purifying system in my home and enjoy having an adequate supply of pure water for both drinking and cooking at reasonable cost. Because many different types of systems are available, I recommend that you do some homework before investing in one. A good first step is to have your water tested to determine what kind of impurities it contains.

I use a steam distiller to purify my water, because I believe distilled water is the cleanest you can get. Home distillers are efficient and convenient, but the initial cost is higher than that of other methods. If the main problem is off-odours or tastes, as from chlorine, you may be happy with a simple carbon filter. Another system I recommend is a carbon-block–KDF unit, which fits under the sink and runs the water through two cartridges (which must be changed periodically), one containing solid carbon, the other an alloy of copper and zinc. It removes most of the common impurities and is reasonably priced.

You can find more information on toxins in water and ways to remove them by consulting my book *Eight Weeks to Optimum Health*.

And remember to drink enough water – six to eight glasses a day. This can include tea, mineral water, or sparkling water with a hint of fruit juice. **—A.W.**

Frozen Fruit Smoothie

SERVES 3

PER SERVING:

CALORIES 75.7

FAT 0.3 G
  SATURATED FAT
  0.1 G
(3.1% OF CALORIES
  FROM FAT)

PROTEIN 0.6 G

CARBOHYDRATE
  19.1 G

CHOLESTEROL 0 MG

FIBRE 1.3 G

Frozen fruit smoothies are great for snacks, breakfast, or an after-dinner pleasure. You'll need to freeze the bananas for a couple of hours in a zip-lock bag or lidded plastic container. Frozen bananas act like fruity ice cubes, giving the smoothie a thick consistency that makes it so much fun to drink.

150 g (1 cup) peeled and sliced bananas, frozen

170 g (1 cup) peeled and sliced fresh peaches, or washed, hulled, and sliced ripe strawberries

360 ml (1 1/2 cups) unfiltered apple juice

GARNISH

1 sprig mint or a small handful fresh berries

Put all the ingredients in the blender. Cover and blend on low speed until smooth. Pour into 3 large wineglasses and serve immediately. Garnish with mint leaves or berries.

Tips from Rosie's Kitchen

You may need to pulse the fruit when blending to break it up. You can also turn off the blender and use a wooden spoon to shift the fruit around, and then blend again until smooth. To cut down a little on the acidity of the fruit, and to add some calcium and protein to the smoothie, you can add 2 tablespoons yogurt or your favourite soya/whey protein powder. Most blenders have only the capacity to make 3 servings of this smoothie at a time. If you want more just repeat the procedure.

To blanch almonds, remove their skins, drop them into a small saucepan of boiling water, and boil for 5 minutes. Drain the almonds and rinse with cold water to cool them. With your fingers, rub and squeeze the almonds to remove the brown skin, which will slide off easily. This is the part that children love. Sometimes the almonds pop out of their skins so readily that they skid across the floor.

Citrus Mango Freeze

I serve this with Chicken Tostadas (pages 217–18) because it has the same kind of festive feel to it, but you can make this any time you're in the mood for a cold blast of blended fruit.

3 ripe mangoes, sliced
180 ml (3/4 cup) freshly squeezed
    orange juice
60 ml (1/4 cup) freshly squeezed
    lime juice
60 ml (1/4 cup) freshly squeezed
    lemon juice

120 ml (1/2 cup) ice, crushed or
    cubes
120 ml (1/2 cup) soda water

GARNISH

6 fresh strawberries, hulled
1 lime, sliced

Put the mango slices and the juices in a blender. Add the ice and soda water and blend until smooth. Divide among 6 small martini glasses. Drop 1 strawberry in the middle of each and garnish the rims with a lime slice. Add fancy straws for fun.

SERVES 6

PER SERVING:

CALORIES 133.1

FAT 0.9 G
  SATURATED FAT
  0.1 G

(5.4% OF CALORIES
  FROM FAT)

PROTEIN 1.8 G

CARBOHYDRATE
  33.9 G

CHOLESTEROL 0 MG

FIBRE 5.9 G

Pineapple Almond Shake

The almonds in this invigorating shake make it a terrific source of protein, and blanching your own almonds is a great kitchen activity for kids.

35 g (1/4 cup) blanched almonds
155 g (1 cup) chopped pineapple
120 ml (1/2 cup) ice, crushed or
    cubes

1/2 teaspoon pure maple syrup
60 ml (1/4 cup) rice milk or soya
    milk
120 ml (1/2 cup) pineapple juice

Grind the almonds in a blender to a fine powder, as for making Andy's Nut milk (pages 34–5). Add all the ingredients and blend until smooth. Pour into 3 large drinking glasses. (If you want to make more, repeat the recipes. Most blenders will accommodate only enough for 3.)

SERVES 3

PER SERVING:

CALORIES 96.7

FAT 5.2 G
  SATURATED FAT
  0.5 G

(45.5% OF CALORIES
  FROM FAT)

PROTEIN 2.5 G

CARBOHYDRATE
  11.6 G

CHOLESTEROL 0 MG

FIBRE 1.3 G

GOT (TOO MUCH) MILK?

A great deal of propaganda from the dairy industry tells us that we never out-grow our need for milk and that milk is nature's perfect food. I'm sure it is for baby cows, but even they quickly outgrow their need for it. In nature, animals drink milk only in infancy. And throughout the world a great many people con-sider it distinctly unwise to drink milk. In fact, most people, other than those of Northern European origin, cannot digest lactose, the sugar in milk. As they grow out of childhood, they stop making the enzyme needed to break it down and experience major digestive upsets – bloating, cramps, and diarrhoea – if they drink milk.

Butterfat, the fat in cow's milk, is the most saturated fat in our diet. In many dairy products, such as cream, soured cream, butter, ice cream, and cheese, the percentage of butterfat is much higher than that of milk. Butterfat is a principal contributor to high cholesterol levels in the blood and to atheroscle-rosis, the artery-clogging disease that leads to heart attacks and strokes.

The protein in milk, casein, irritates the immune system in people with certain inherited predispositions (such as a propensity for allergy and autoim-munity). Casein also stimulates mucous production and so tends to aggravate chronic bronchitis, sinusitis, and ear infections. Introduced too early in life to susceptible people, cow's milk can trigger the onset of juvenile diabetes, asthma, eczema, and a variety of allergic conditions.

In addition, most commercial milk contains residues of antibiotics, drugs, and hormones, which are used to keep dairy cows producing abundantly. Milk also contains environmental toxins that cows concentrate in their fat. So clearly I have reservations about the dairy industry's contention that milk is a health food.

A number of milk substitutes – made from soya beans, rice, oats, pota-toes, and almonds – are on the market. Except for soya milk, these are not pro-tein sources, which must be kept in mind if they are given to children in place of cow's milk. Many of them are fortified with calcium, none contain lactose or casein, and all have fats that are much better than butterfat for our bodies. Some are sweetened and flavoured and work well on cereal or in beverages; others taste insipid or unpleasant. The best work well in recipes – soups or sauces, for instance – that call for milk or cream. To cut down on your intake of cow's milk, experiment with these products to find ones you like.

One option is nut milk, which you can make yourself. To prepare nut milk, grind raw nuts (cashews and blanched almonds are delicious) to a fine powder in a blender or food processor, then add water and blend at high speed for two minutes. The ratio of water to nuts determines the richness of the end result – the 'milk' – which can be made as heavy as cream for pouring over berries or as lean as skimmed milk. You can improve the texture of nut milk by straining it through a fine sieve, pressing as much liquid as possible from the residue, and discarding the residue. You can then use the nut milk in any recipe, such as a cream soup. It offers these advantages: no lactose, no casein, and mono-unsaturated fat instead of saturated. I use cashew milk instead of coconut milk in Thai curries. It is delicious and much better for you than the saturated fat of coconut. —A.W.

Sunrise Orange Grapefruit Juice

The cool, invigorating flavour of this fresh-squeezed citrus fruit juice will liven up your morning. Just a small amount will give you your daily supply of vitamin C without any added preservatives, sugars, or acids that you might find in store-bought juices. You'll be amazed at the intensity of the taste that just-squeezed juice offers. Pink grapefruits are my favourite because the pink they add to the orange juice puts the sunrise in each glass. I like the way they taste and they are higher in vitamin A than their other grapefruit relatives. The sweetness of the oranges and the mildly bittersweet taste of the grapefruit make a spirited drink.

4 oranges   2 grapefruits

Cut the oranges and grapefruits in half and squeeze, using a hand juicer. Mix both juices together in a small jug, serve in small juice glasses, and enjoy!

MAKES 6 SERVINGS

PER SERVING:

CALORIES 86.3

FAT 0.4 G
  SATURATED FAT
  0.1 G
(3.7% OF CALORIES
  FROM FAT)

PROTEIN 1.8 G

CARBOHYDRATE
  22.6 G

CHOLESTEROL 0 MG

FIBRE 4.1 G

Front: Berry Herbal Tea with Orange Slices; rear left: Citrus Mango Freeze; rear right: Frozen Fruit Smoothie

Honey Ginger Lemonade

Capture the essence of the summer sun and the natural goodness it brings in this invigorating beverage. I like to combine fresh honey my neighbour gives me with fresh-squeezed lemon juice and a twist of ginger to add a unique kick to this old-time summer refresher.

240 ml (1 cup) freshly squeezed lemon juice
170 g (1/2 cup) honey
40 g (1/4 cup) peeled root ginger slices

7 sprigs fresh mint
480 ml (2 cups) purified water
4 cups ice cubes

Put the juice, honey, ginger, and 1 chopped sprig of the mint in a large jug and stir, pressing the mint and ginger to release flavour. Add the water and stir until the honey dissolves, then add the ice. Pour into six tall glasses and garnish each glass with a sprig of mint and a fancy straw.

Tips from Rosie's Kitchen

Children three years old and younger can become seriously ill from honey, so please don't give them a glass of this lemonade. However, you can use local honey to help battle against seasonal allergies for older children and adults. Honey's thick coating with the vitamin C in lemons combine perfectly to soothe a sore throat and help treat a cold. To really combat a cold try Lemon Cayenne Tonic:

Lemon Cayenne Tonic

180 ml (3/4 cup) freshly squeezed lemon juice
85 g (1/4 cup) honey

240 ml (1 cup) purified water
1/2 teaspoon cayenne pepper

Mix everything together to create a syrupy, feel-good tonic. Drink hot or cold.

SERVES 6

PER SERVING:
CALORIES 104.8
FAT 0.1 G
  SATURATED FAT
  0 G
(0.8% OF CALORIES
  FROM FAT)
PROTEIN 0.5 G
CARBOHYDRATE
  28.7 G
CHOLESTEROL 0 MG
FIBRE 0.3 G

MAKES 6 SHOT-SIZE
SERVINGS

PER SERVING:
CALORIES 51
FAT 0 G
  SATURATED FAT
  0 G
(0.5% OF CALORIES
  FROM FAT)
PROTEIN 0.2 G
CARBOHYDRATE
  14.4 G
CHOLESTEROL 0 MG
FIBRE 0.2 G

Cranberry Barley Tonic

Barley was one of the first grains harvested and cultivated by man. Throughout time, it has been used in breads, cereals, soups, and even curative drinks. This is a very clean beverage that is excellent for those times when you feel you haven't eaten well and want to cleanse your system, or if you want to drink something purifying yet flavourful.

SERVES 8

PER SERVING:

CALORIES 77.7

FAT 0.3 G
  SATURATED FAT
  0.1 G

(3.7% OF CALORIES
  FROM FAT)

PROTEIN 1.5 G

CARBOHYDRATE
  17.8 G

CHOLESTEROL 0 MG

FIBRE 1.8 G

❊

100 g (1/2 cup) pearl barley
720 ml (3 cups) purified water

480 ml (2 cups) cranberry juice
2 tablespoons raspberries

Put the barley and the water in a large saucepan, cover, and simmer for 1 hour. Remove from the heat and let the water cool briefly. Strain the barley water through a fine sieve into a bowl. Mix the barley water with the cranberry juice and pour it into eight glasses. Garnish with 3 raspberries in each glass.

Tips from Rosie's Kitchen

Don't throw away the cooked barley! Use it in place of pasta in the Mixed-Bean Minestrone Stew (page 126), or to make a barley pilaf, which you can flavour with sun-dried tomatoes.

WINE

Many people throughout the world drink wine with their meals. I am not one of them, I'm afraid. I am not a great consumer of alcohol in any form, and if I am going to drink, I usually prefer premium Japanese sake, which I like cold. (Sake is made from rice and so is technically not wine.) I find it agrees with me more than other alcoholic beverages, never giving me a sour stomach, a headache, or a hangover, all symptoms I experience, not infrequently, from wine.

For some years I have followed the debate about the health benefits of alcohol in general and wine in particular. Here are some of my thoughts on the matter:

Alcohol is known to be toxic to liver and nerve cells. It is also addictive, and the addiction can be hard to break. Many people use alcohol to relax, especially at the end of the workday, and as a social lubricant because of its disinhibiting effects. Used moderately for these purposes, the benefits of alcohol may well outweigh its risks, especially since most of us need to relax. Recently, wine has received a lot of attention for possible beneficial effects on health – especially cardiovascular health, and especially red wine. If red wine, in fact, is heart healthy in ways that white wine and other forms of alcohol are not, the reason must be that there are unique elements in red wine, elements other than alcohol. Likely candidates are the red pigments, because these have significant antioxidant properties and can retard the oxidation of cholesterol in the blood that damages arteries. You can include these same antioxidant pigments in your diet by drinking red grape juice or eating red and purple fruits, especially berries. By doing so you would avoid risks of addiction to alcohol and any of its toxicity. Of course, you would not then get the pleasure that so many people experience from wine.

It is also possible, however, that alcohol itself has healthful as well as harmful properties and that all forms of it provide them, including white wine and spirits. Aside from its relaxing effects, alcohol appears to raise HDL cholesterol, the so-called good cholesterol that circulates in the blood and counteracts the influence of bad LDL cholesterol. Regular aerobic exercise also increases the HDL fraction; otherwise, it is hard to raise good cholesterol without resorting to pharmaceutical drugs.

Whether alcohol improves health directly by some biochemical mechanism or indirectly as a result of relaxing us, the key to using it wisely is moderation. A glass or two of wine with a good meal can be a good thing. Much more than that day in and day out may not be so good. Try saving wine for special occasions or for out-of-the-ordinary meals. Be conscious of the amount you consume at any one meal. If you drink wine regularly, try to give your body one or two alcohol-free days a week.

Finally, be aware that wine contains many additives that do not have to be listed on labels. In general, inferior wines have more of them than superior wines. I think that the unpleasant symptoms I develop from drinking wine are the result of sensitivities to additives, and I experience fewer of them from expensive wine. In recent years more organically produced wines have appeared in both America and Europe, some of very good quality. I prefer them and find that they are much less likely to cause unwanted effects.

My bottom line: used moderately and with awareness, wine can add to the pleasure of eating and improve both physical and emotional well-being. —A.W.

Mulled Cider or Red Wine

SERVES 6

PER SERVING:

CALORIES 188.8

FAT 3 G

SATURATED FAT
0.6 G

(12.4% OF
CALORIES FROM
FAT)

PROTEIN 1.2 G

CARBOHYDRATE
46.2 G

CHOLESTEROL
0 MG

FIBRE 7.2 G

This smooth and yummy beverage is perfect to serve in the autumn and straight through the holidays for a Christmas brunch or a cold winter evening by the fire. You can use either wine or apple cider or juice. It depends on what you feel is appropriate for the occasion and your guests.

840 ml (3¹/2 cups) apple cider or
   juice, or 1 bottle red wine
240 ml (1 cup) purified water
100 g (¹/2 cup) caster sugar

2 cinnamon sticks
¹/2 lemon, cut into slices
12 whole cloves

Put all the ingredients into a saucepan and bring to a low boil, then reduce the heat and simmer for 3 minutes. Strain and serve in cups or heat-resistant clear glasses.

Berry Herbal Tea with Orange Slices

I love the idea of fresh fruit in a drink! I use it a lot in the summer when I make tea for my friends and family, and it is always a big hit. You can serve this drink cold during the heat of the day, or warm during the cool of the evening.

720 ml (3 cups) purified water
4 Red Zinger tea bags
1/2 orange, sliced
240 ml (1 cup) apple or cranberry juice

75 g (1/2 cup) fresh strawberries, washed and hulled, or frozen strawberries, cut in half, or fresh raspberries, washed

Bring the water to the boil in a medium saucepan. Drop in the tea bags and orange slices. Pour in the apple or cranberry juice. Remove from heat. Cover and let the tea steep for 3 minutes. Remove the tea bags. Drop an orange slice into each of 6 heat-resistant glasses, distribute the berries evenly among them, and then pour the tea over. Serve hot or chilled.

SERVES 6

PER SERVING:

CALORIES 28.4

FAT 0.1 G
  SATURATED FAT
  0 G
(3.0% OF CALORIES
  FROM FAT)

PROTEIN 0.2 G

CARBOHYDRATE
  7 G

CHOLESTEROL 0 MG

FIBRE 0.5 G

Spiced Tea

SERVES 6

PER SERVING:

CALORIES 39

FAT 0.1 G
  SATURATED FAT
  0 G

(2% OF CALORIES
  FROM FAT)

PROTEIN 0.1 G

CARBOHYDRATE
  9.7 G

CHOLESTEROL 0 MG

FIBRE 0.1 G

Drinking hot tea is a pleasure guaranteed to take the chill from your bones in the dead of winter. The ambrosia of spices will warm your kitchen and welcome your guests in from the cold or complete an evening meal.

1.4 litres (6 cups) purified water
2 chamomile tea bags or 2 tablespoons bulk chamomile tea in a
  tea infuser

2 apple-spice tea bags
480 ml (2 cups) apple juice
Cinnamon sticks (optional)

Bring the water to the boil in a pan, then remove from the heat. Drop in the tea bags or the infuser and let the tea steep for 5 minutes. Pour in the apple juice and stir. Pour into large coffee mugs and serve. If you wish, add 1 cinnamon stick to each mug.

Tips from Rosie's Kitchen

A tea infuser is a stainless steel mesh basket that holds loose tea leaves and can be bought at any kitchen shop. If you don't have one, you can just strain the tea through a fine mesh strainer after it has steeped.

COFFEE AND TEA

Coffee is a strong stimulant that can be addictive and can cause or aggravate a number of medical problems. It can irritate both the upper and lower digestive tract, disturb urinary and prostate function, cause or worsen cardiac arrhythmias, and wreak havoc with moods, energy cycles, and sleep patterns. If you enjoy coffee, if it does not affect your physical or mental health, and if you can use it non-addictively – meaning without suffering withdrawal when you stop – go ahead and drink it. But I'm going to try to persuade you that tea is better for you.

Even though tea leaves contain more caffeine than coffee beans, not as much of it winds up in the finished brew. Most people find tea to be less jangling than coffee and less likely to cause any unwanted symptoms. And more people are becoming aware of its health benefits.

Both green and black teas are made from the same plant, *Camellia sinensis,* an attractive shrub. For green tea the leaves are briefly steamed, then dried. For black tea, the leaves are heaped up and 'sweated' before being dried, a natural fermentation process that changes their colour, chemistry, aroma, and flavour. Oolong tea, now produced mainly on Taiwan, is in between; shorter fermentation gives it qualities intermediate between green and black tea. Scented teas are mixed with dried flower petals (as in jasmine tea) or essential oils (as in Earl Grey). Herbal teas are made from plants other than *Camellia sinensis* and do not have the beneficial properties of that species.

A number of recent studies on tea – some quite extensive – show that both green and black tea offer significant protection against both heart disease and cancer. This is so because tea has strong antioxidant activity, mainly due to its content of polyphenols, one of which, EGCG, is among the most powerful antioxidants known. Green tea contains more of it than black tea, which is why I recommend it as a daily beverage. Green tea also contains L-theanine, an amino acid that produces a state of relaxed alertness and may account for the difference in the quality of stimulation from that of coffee.

Much of the green tea I see in America is more yellow or brown than green and often tastes like hay. The green tea I drink in Japan is really green and has a rich, aromatic taste with a slight bitterness. The highest quality, *gyokuro,* has a deep, rich flavour. Another form I like very much is *matcha,* powdered green tea that is whisked to a froth in a tea bowl and used in the Japanese tea ceremony. And I sometimes drink *genmaicha,* a mixture of green tea and toasted brown rice that gives the tea a nutty taste. All of these are now available in America at tea shops, from mail-order catalogues, and from online tea suppliers on the Internet. I often order iced tea as a beverage when I eat out, not just in summer but year-round. And I enjoy trying new varieties of tea. I'm currently experimenting with some delicious oolongs and a rare Chinese 'white tea' that brews into an almost colourless infusion with a very delicate taste but appears to have even more antioxidant activity than green tea.

Japanese research suggests that for the best effect on health, one should drink about four cups of green tea a day. If you don't want so much caffeine, you can find decaffeinated forms. At the moment, far more Americans are drinking coffee than are drinking tea, but more of us are learning how to select and make good tea, and more high-quality tea is obtainable here – a far cry from the tea bags most of us grew up with. If you are a coffee drinker, try substituting tea on occasion and see how you feel. I predict that we will see a great increase in tea drinking in our land, which I think will be a good thing. —**A.W.**

MATCHA (Japanese Powdered Green Tea)

Matcha is the special green tea used in the Japanese tea ceremony. It is my favourite tea, and I drink a bowl of it every morning. Along with the special utensils used to make it, matcha is becoming more available here. It comes in small cans, usually containing 20 or 40 grams of bright-green, finely powdered tea grown under special conditions. You can order it on the Internet or find it at better Japanese food shops. One source of high-quality matcha and kits for preparing it is www.drweil.com.

To reduce the possibility of the matcha powder forming lumps with the addition of hot water, it is best to pass it through a fine sieve (tea strainer). Sift the contents of the can onto greaseproof paper and then return the sifted powder to the can.

Bring a small quantity of purified water to the boil and remove from heat. Pour a small quantity of this water (about 120 ml/$1/2$ cup) into the tea bowl *(cha-wan)* to warm it. Soften the bamboo tea whisk *(cha-sen)* by immersing the end in the hot water for about 10 seconds, then remove it. Empty the bowl and dry it with kitchen paper.

Using the bamboo tea scoop *(cha-shaku)* place two heaping scoops (about 1 level teaspoon) of matcha powder in the bottom of the bowl.

Add approximately 80 ml (1/3 cup) of less-than-boiling water to the bowl. (By the time you have warmed and dried the bowl the water in the kettle should be about the right temperature.) Boiling water is too hot for matcha; it will damage the flavour of the tea.

Using the tea whisk, first incorporate any stray bits of powder into the water with slow circular or figure-of-8 strokes, then agitate the mixture vigorously with a back-and-forth motion of the wrist for approximately 15 seconds. The surface of the tea should be completely frothy. *Caution:* To protect the tea whisk, do not rub it or press it against the bottom or sides of the bowl. After each use, rinse it under running cold water. You can wipe the tea scoop clean with kitchen paper.

Drink the matcha immediately. In the tea ceremony, Japanese quaff a bowl in three audible slurps, but you can enjoy it at your own pace. It is pleasant to nibble on something sweet while sipping the tea.

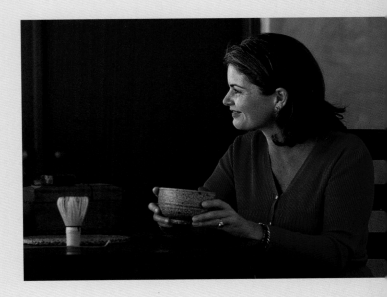

Yogurt-Lime Drink

This is a versatile beverage because you have the choice of making it with just yogurt; adding fruit and blending it just enough to transform the drink into a whipped, frothy, chunky fruit beverage; or adding frozen fruit to create a dessert drink. This drink is festive, yet the coconut milk flavoured with cinnamon and cloves gives it a mellow flavour.

SERVES 6

PER SERVING:

CALORIES 132.4

FAT 2.6 G
  SATURATED FAT
  2.4 G

(6% OF CALORIES
  FROM FAT)

PROTEIN 2.1 G

CARBOHYDRATE
  21.2 G

CHOLESTEROL 2 MG

FIBRE 0.1 G

80 ml (1/3 cup) fresh lime juice
250 g (1 cup) plain low-fat yogurt
115 g (1/3 cup) honey
480 ml (2 cups) purified water
1 tablespoon pure vanilla extract

1/8 teaspoon ground cloves
1/8 teaspoon grated nutmeg
1 x 400 g (14 oz) can light
  coconut milk
1/8 teaspoon ground cinnamon

Mix the ingredients together in a bowl. Chill for 2 hours. Pour into six glasses, sprinkle cinnamon on top, and serve.

Tips from Rosie's Kitchen

To create a low-fat tropical shake, add 500 g (2 cups) sliced frozen peaches or papaya, or use 170 g (1 cup) sliced fresh fruit – about 3 peaches or 1/2 papaya – and 240 ml (1 cup) ice. Use a blender to blend everything together. Garnish each glass with a sprinkling of cinnamon and a straw.

__Peach-Yogurt Lime Drink:__ For a different kind of fruit taste and some festivity, add 1 pitted peach, sliced in half, to the yogurt-lime drink and pulse it in the blender just enough to blend the fruit but maintain some chunks. Pour into 6 cups and serve. The delicate chunks of peach will colour the frothy coconut milk with hues of red, pink, and yellow.

ANDY SUGGESTS

I would substitute cashew milk (pages 34–5) for the coconut milk.

Low-Fat Vanilla Shake

I came up with this concoction when my diabetic niece was craving a sweet cool treat. The banana, honey, and ice are a good substitute for ice cream, as they thicken, sweeten, and chill this creamy dessert drink. This is a great way to satisfy a sweet tooth without all the fat and sugar you'll find in a regular shake. And this delicious delight is a great way to sneak some calcium, protein, and potassium into your kids, as well as yourself.

150 g (1 cup) peeled sliced banana (see Tips)
2 tablespoons pure vanilla extract
480 ml (2 cups) ice

480 ml (2 cups) skimmed milk (or prepared milk alternative)
2 tablespoons honey
2 tablespoons cocoa powder (optional)

Put the sliced banana, vanilla, ice, milk, and honey into the blender and blend until smooth. Pour into 6 glasses and add a straw – a shake just isn't complete without a fun straw!

SERVES SIX

PER SERVING:
CALORIES 98.3
FAT 0.3 G
SATURATED FAT 0.2 G
(3.1% OF CALORIES FROM FAT)
PROTEIN 3.2 G
CARBOHYDRATE 19.9 G
CHOLESTEROL 1 MG
FIBRE 0.9 G

Tips from Rosie's Kitchen

When you have more bananas than you know what to do with, don't throw them away! Just peel, slice, and freeze them while they're ripe and put each banana in its own sealed baggie. Not only does this buy you some time for using them all up, but frozen bananas are useful in chilling and thickening this shake and other blended drinks. If you would like a non-dairy drink, you can substitute 225 g (8 oz) silken tofu for the skimmed milk (if you do use this substitution, the maple syrup and cocoa combinations really hit the spot). The cocoa powder is a great way to tempt kids into this healthy drink, and if you love a maple flavour, you can substitute maple syrup for the honey in this recipe. Use your imagination and adapt this recipe here and there to suit your own tastes and preferences.

Raspberry Evening Spritzer

This simple blend of fruit, natural sweeteners, tea, and soda water is an ideal afternoon or evening drink for a casual gathering with friends or an afternoon surprise during the workweek.

240 ml (1 cup) purified water
180 g (6 oz) raspberries
1 teaspoon herbal or black tea
  leaves

340 g (1 cup) honey
1 small orange, washed and cut
  into 8 thin slices
2 litres (8 cups) chilled soda water

Bring the water to the boil in a saucepan and drop in the raspberries. Lower heat and simmer for 3 minutes. Remove from heat and sprinkle the tea into the pan. Cover and let steep for 2 minutes. Strain the warm liquid through a fine mesh strainer into a small saucepan, using the back of a large spoon to break up the pulp of the berries and push the liquid through. Add the honey. Stir for about 2 minutes, then chill in the refrigerator.

Place 1 orange slice at the bottom of 8 tall glasses. Pour 1 tablespoon of the chilled raspberry syrup and 240 ml (1 cup) of cold soda water into each glass. Stir, add ice, and serve immediately. If you wish, stick a couple of colourful straws in each glass for added colour and fun.

Starters

Chicken Satay with Peanut Dipping Sauce

Baked Vegetable Wontons

Mediterranean Stuffed Vine Leaves

Broccoli Griddle Cakes

Spanish Seafood Cocktail, Gazpacho Style

Steamed Alaskan Crab Legs

Smoked Fish with Horseradish Sauce

Horseradish Sauce

Thai Prawn Brochettes

Vegetable Nori Rolls

Spinach Toasts

Polenta Triangles with Roasted Peppers

Aubergine Dip

Miso Pâté

White Bean Spread

Goat's Cheese Toasties with Sun-dried Tomato and Basil

Stuffed Mushroom Caps with Couscous

OUTDOOR COOKING

Barbecues are more popular than ever, especially since the advent of efficient gas barbecues that are much easier to use than charcoal-burning devices. I love cooking food outdoors, and I can do it almost year-round in southern Arizona, where I live. But there are some health pitfalls to this kind of cooking.

The typical American barbecue emphasises large portions of meat and usually skimps on vegetables and whole grains. On my barbecue, you will find fish, vegetables, and mushrooms. And research findings have clearly established that high-temperature barbecuing (or grilling) of foods that contain fat and protein produces carcinogenic compounds called heterocyclic amines (HAs) that can raise the risk of colo-rectal cancer in those with a genetic predisposition for it. HAs probably increase risks of other cancers as well.

I have a number of recommendations for protecting yourself from exposure to them. First of all, use more vegetables and fish and less meat. Animal flesh is more likely to become carcinogenic when it is exposed to high heat. Second, try not to cook animal foods, including fish, to the point of charring. Blackened fish and other animal foods are popular but not healthful. If you are served food this way, try not to eat the blackened outer layer. Third, if you do use meats, choose leaner cuts, because the more fat, the likelier the fire is to smoke, and the smoke from burning fat is carcinogenic. (Don't inhale it!) Finally, be aware that marinating flesh foods before cooking them may help reduce the formation of HAs, probably because common marinade ingredients act as antioxidants. This is true of citrus juice and spices like turmeric, ginger, and garlic, for example.

Never use charcoal-lighter fluid or self-starting packages of briquettes in a charcoal grill. If you do, you will wind up with residues of toxic chemicals in your food. Instead, use an inexpensive chimney lighter that uses a small amount of newspaper to ignite a mass of charcoal in a large metal cylinder. Some chefs feel that charcoal grills give better results, but gas barbecues offer great convenience. They are much faster to light and heat and much less polluting of the atmosphere.

Barbecued vegetables can be terrific if they are well flavoured and well cooked – still crunchy but also tender and sweet. I can't get enough of thick slices of sweet onion, brushed with olive oil, salt, pepper, and maybe sprinkled with herbs, then cooked to perfection. Sweet peppers and mushrooms are also great. In fact, with a portion of barbecued salmon or tuna, a green salad, and maybe some rice, I find it hard to imagine a more satisfying experience of outdoor cooking.—**A.W.**

SERVES 6

PER SERVING:

CALORIES 34.4

FAT 0.4 G
SATURATED FAT
0.1 G
(10.2% OF CALO-
RIES FROM FAT)

PROTEIN 6.4 G

CARBOHYDRATE
0.5 G

CHOLESTEROL
16 MG

FIBRE 0 G

PEANUT DIPPING
SAUCE

SERVES 6

PER SERVING:

CALORIES 157.1

FAT 9.7 G
SATURATED FAT
1.7 G
(50.6% OF CALO-
RIES FROM FAT)

PROTEIN 6.6 G

CARBOHYDRATE
15.2 G

CHOLESTEROL 0 MG

FIBRE 8.4 G

Chicken Satay with Peanut Dipping Sauce

Satay, or bite-sized pieces of skewered meat or fish, originated in Indonesia. Traditionally, a peanut sauce is served with satay, but you can serve it with Pineapple Dipping Sauce (page 67) if you or your guests don't like nuts or peanut butter.

PEANUT DIPPING SAUCE

160 g (1 cup) chopped onions
2 cloves garlic, sliced
3 tablespoons toasted sesame oil
480 ml (2 cups) vegetable stock, (page 122)
2 tablespoons natural soy sauce (such as tamari)
1 tablespoon Thai chilli sauce or 1 tablespoon dried chilli flakes
1 tablespoon paprika
1 1/2 teaspoons ground cumin
3 tablespoons grated root ginger
1 tablespoon honey
130 g (1/2 cup) natural peanut butter

3 tablespoons chopped parsley
3 tablespoons chopped chives
1 tablespoon chopped fresh mint leaves

CHICKEN

4 boneless, skinless chicken breasts (fillets)
60 ml (1/4 cup) freshly squeezed orange juice
1 tablespoon red or green Thai curry paste or 1/8 teaspoon dried chilli flakes
12 x 15 cm (6 in) wooden skewers, soaked in water for 1 hour

Make the Peanut Dipping Sauce: sauté the onions and garlic in the sesame oil in a sauté pan over medium heat. Cook for 4 minutes, until the garlic turns golden brown. Add the vegetable stock, soy sauce, chilli sauce or flakes, paprika, and cumin and whisk until completely blended. Add the ginger, honey, and peanut butter, stir, and simmer for 10 minutes or until the sauce becomes thick. Remove from heat and add the parsley, chives, and mint. Pour 180 ml (3/4 cup) of the sauce into a bowl. Store the remainder in the refrigerator to use later with Slow-Baked Tofu with Stir-Fry or another dish.

Preheat grill or prepare the barbecue.

Cut each chicken breast into 3 sections by making 2 vertical slices through each one. Mix the orange juice and the curry paste or flakes together in a large bowl and drop in the chicken. Mix well with a spoon, coating the chicken pieces. Cover and refrigerate for 30 minutes.

After the chicken has marinated, secure 1 slice of meat on each skewer by puncturing 1 end of it with the point of the skewer. Sliding the meat down a bit on the skewer, puncture the other end of the meat and pull the chicken piece tight across the skewer. The chicken should lie flat on the skewer. (It is almost as if you are threading the chicken slices.) Repeat the process for all the skewers. Put the chicken on a baking tray and grill for 2 minutes on each side, or cook over medium heat on the barbecue, spooning a little sauce over each skewer.

Serve the chicken satay on a platter with a sprinkling of chopped mint and the bowl of the peanut sauce in the middle for dipping. Makes 12 skewers– 2 per person – with 1 tablespoon peanut sauce for each skewer.

Tips from Rosie's Kitchen

Wooden skewers come in varying lengths. You'll want 15 cm (6 in) skewers for this recipe, but sometimes it's hard to find this size (they seem to be the most popular), so you can buy larger ones and cut them in half. Soaking them in water keeps them from burning while exposed to the heat. When you are putting the chicken on the skewer, be sure to pierce the meat at the pointed end, not on the end that you cut.

This peanut sauce is a favourite dipping sauce of mine. I often serve it with a stir-fry tofu dinner. If you think the dipping sauce is too thick and you want to change the consistency to more of a dressing, add 60 ml (1/4 cup) rice vinegar. You can double the Peanut Dipping Sauce recipe so you'll have extra on hand in the fridge to top off your favourite stir-fry. It also goes well with Slow-Baked Tofu (page 193).

POULTRY

One of the differences in Rosie's style of cooking and eating and mine is that she uses chicken and turkey and I do not. Poultry is a popular and versatile animal food that offers one great advantage over meat: its fat is mostly external to muscle and can be removed by skinning. In terms of its effect on human hearts and arteries, skinned chicken is a more healthful choice than beef, veal, lamb, or pork, provided you cook it without a lot of added saturated fat. Simple grilling and baking are good ways to prepare it, and Rosie's recipes show you how to do this. Duck and goose have much more fat in them and are more challenging to turn into healthy fare, because the fat of these fowl is highly saturated and contains cholesterol. Wild fowl have much less fat, so little, in fact, that recipes often call for generous amounts of butter or bacon fat to keep their meat moist during roasting.

You will see that I suggest substituting baked tofu for the chicken and turkey in some of Rosie's creations. I do this to show that it is possible to make very acceptable vegetarian versions of them, which I enjoy. I avoid poultry for two reasons, one more personal than the other. I know that I live at the expense of other living things, both animal and vegetable. My daughter, a strict lacto-ovo vegetarian, says she will not eat anything that would run away from her. She will not eat fish because she identifies too much with them. I draw my own line between fish and fowl, recognising the arbitrariness of that decision.

Aside from the moral question of eating other creatures, I have a number of concerns about the health risks of commercially raised poultry. Free-range chickens and turkeys – those that are allowed to run around and peck for food – are more nutritious than birds that spend all of their lives caged, often in crowded, appalling conditions. The fat from free-range poultry has a better spectrum of fatty acids, and the flesh tastes better. Also, the common birds sold in supermarkets contain significant residues of drugs and hormones used to stimulate their growth. People who eat a lot of them increase health risks – for hormonally driven cancers, such as breast cancer, among others. If you are going to eat chicken and turkey, I urge you to buy organically raised birds that are certified to be free of drugs and hormones. These are more expensive, of course. They are also becoming more available at better supermarkets as well as from mail-order sources.—**A.W.**

Baked Vegetable Wontons

I serve these a lot as a starter or light finger food when I'm having a small, informal gathering of friends. They are light with barely a touch of crunch on the outside. Enjoy them with the simple Soy and Ginger Dipping Sauce described below or with the Pineapple Dipping Sauce (page 67). You can use it with the Chicken Satay (page 52) or with the fish from the Grilled Fish Tacos (page 210).

This is another great recipe in which to involve kids. Gather them in the kitchen after the preparation of the vegetables is complete and let them help you with the stuffing and folding. It is actually fun and it will make the process move faster.

SOY AND GINGER DIPPING SAUCE

240 ml (1 cup) purified water
60 g (1/2 cup) dried mango
1 tablespoon natural soy sauce (such as tamari)
2 tablespoons mirin (sweet rice wine)
1 tablespoon rice vinegar
1 teaspoon finely grated root ginger
1/4 teaspoon chilli paste

VEGETABLE WONTON FILLING

110 g (1 cup) grated carrot
100 g (1 cup) finely shredded Chinese leaves (about 1/4 head)

35 g (1/2 cup) thinly sliced shiitake, oyster or button mushrooms
2 tablespoons toasted sesame oil
30 g (1/4 cup) chopped spring onions
1/2 tablespoon grated root ginger
1/2 tablespoon curry powder
1 tablespoon mirin (sweet rice wine)
1 tablespoon natural soy sauce (such as tamari)
30 small, square wonton wrappers
60 ml (1/4 cup) toasted sesame oil (for brushing)

Make the Soy and Ginger Dipping Sauce first. Boil the water and pour over the dried mango. Soak for about 30 minutes or until the fruit softens. Strain the fruit-flavoured water and use 120 ml (1/2 cup) as the base for the sauce. Add the soy sauce, mirin, rice vinegar, ginger, and chilli paste.

Preheat oven to 190°C.

SERVES 10

PER SERVING:
CALORIES 101.8
FAT 8.4 G
    SATURATED FAT 1.2 G
(72.8% OF CALORIES FROM FAT)
PROTEIN 0.8 G
CARBOHYDRATE 6.7 G
CHOLESTEROL 0 MG
FIBRE 1.4 G

SOY AND GINGER DIPPING SAUCE
SERVES 20

PER SERVING:
CALORIES 19.3
FAT 0 G
    SATURATED FAT 0 G
(20% OF CALORIES FROM FAT)
PROTEIN 0.3 G
CARBOHYDRATE 4.4 G
CHOLESTEROL 0 MG
FIBRE 0.3 G

Brushing a border of sesame oil on each wonton wrapper

Filling and folding the wontons

Make the filling: sauté the carrots, Chinese leaves, and mushrooms in the sesame oil in a large sauté pan over medium heat, until limp, about 5 minutes. Add the spring onions and ginger. Sprinkle the vegetables with curry powder, then stir in the mirin and soy sauce. Remove from the heat.

Lay out 12 wonton wrappers at a time on a clean surface and with a pastry brush lightly brush all along the edges using some of the sesame oil (see illustrations). You will be folding the wrapper at an angle, so drop 1 tablespoon of the vegetable mixture a touch off the centre of the diagonal fold so that you can close the wonton. After the filling is in place, fold 1 corner of the wrapper over to the opposite corner. Press the 2 sides of the wonton down with a fork to seal it. Fold in the 2 pointed edges, which jut out from the folded side of the triangle. Brush the tops with sesame oil. Repeat this process for the remaining wonton wrappers. Put the stuffed wontons on a baking sheet lightly greased with olive or grapeseed oil and brush the tops of the wontons with the remaining sesame oil. Bake for 6 minutes, then turn them over and continue baking until the tops are brown, about another 6 minutes.

Serve the dipping sauce in a bowl in the middle of a platter with the wontons arranged around it. Makes 30 wontons—3 per person.

Sampling the baked wonton

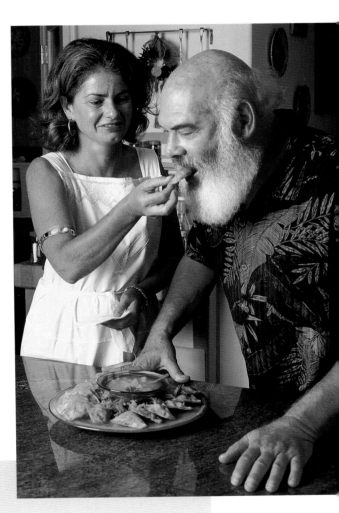

Left: Securing the seals with the back of a fork; below left: Brushing sesame oil on the filled wonton

Tips from Rosie's Kitchen

Wontons can keep in the refrigerator for up to 3 months. Wrap about 5 of them carefully in greaseproof paper, and then seal the package tight with cling film. They are good to have on hand. All you need to do is heat them up for a few minutes in the oven and eat!

SOY SAUCE: SHOYU AND TAMARI

'Shoyu' is the Japanese word for soy sauce, a universal condiment and ingredient in the cooking not only of Japan but also of China, Korea, and other countries of East and South-east Asia. Rosie and I both like to use soy sauce in our cooking, often using it in place of salt, but we are careful about the brands we buy.

Soy sauce is a traditional fermented food, made originally from soya beans, rice starter (koji), wheat, salt, and water. Good-quality Japanese soy sauce is still brewed traditionally from all-natural ingredients, but mass-produced Chinese and American soy sauce is made by a chemical process that results in a distinctly inferior product. Instead of saying 'naturally fermented' or 'naturally brewed', the imitations will list 'hydrolysed soya protein' as a main ingredient. It not only tastes bad, it may not be good for you; dangerous toxins have recently been found in popular Chinese brands.

The real soy sauce will usually be called shoyu or tamari, though the latter word is inaccurate. ('Tamari' properly refers to the liquid drained from vats of miso, a fermented soya bean paste; it is now used to indicate a high-quality shoyu brewed without wheat.) Be aware that soy sauce contains a lot of salt – too much for both Rosie's taste and mine. We prefer reduced-sodium varieties, with up to one-third less salt. Again, look for naturally brewed brands with only the ingredients listed above.

Soy sauce can be a base for dipping sauces and marinades, flavoured with vinegar, sugar, ginger, garlic, toasted sesame oil, or chilli. You can use it to deepen the flavour of soups and gravies or to season grain dishes. Add it carefully, always tasting to avoid making dishes too salty. You will find it to be a versatile and welcome addition to the kitchen.—A.W.

Mediterranean Stuffed Vine Leaves

Mediterranean Stuffed Vine Leaves

This easy, exotic Greek treat makes a fine starter, but it can also be enjoyed as a side dish with lunch or dinner. The raisins and mint give the rice a sweet and aromatic taste, and the simplicity of chive 'ribbons' wrapped around the vine leaves dresses them up a bit. For hors d'oeuvres, use 36 leaves and 1¹/2 tablespoons of filling for each leaf.

SERVES 12

PER SERVING:

CALORIES 110.9

FAT 4.4 G

SATURATED FAT
0.7 G

(34.4% OF CALO-
RIES FROM FAT)

PROTEIN 2.5 G

CARBOHYDRATE
16.6 G

CHOLESTEROL 0 MG

FIBRE 1.3 G

✳

FILLING

480 ml (2 cups) vegetable stock (page 122) or purified water
185 g (1 cup) brown rice
1 teaspoon salt
35 g (1/3 cup) grated radishes
40 g (1/3 cup) chopped spring onions
60 g (1/2 cup) finely chopped celery
45 g (3/4 cup) chopped fresh mint leaves
2 tablespoons olive oil
2 teaspoons white wine vinegar

2 teaspoons freshly squeezed lemon juice
50 g (1/3 cup) currants or sultanas
35 g (1/4 cup) pine nuts
1/4 teaspoon freshly ground black pepper
pinch of salt (optional)
1 tablespoon capers

36 vine leaves
1 bunch chives
1 teaspoon olive oil
1 tablespoon lemon juice

Bring the stock or water to the boil in a large pan. Add the rice and salt. Reduce heat and simmer, covered with a tight-fitting lid, for 45 minutes. All the water should be absorbed. Fluff the rice with a fork.

Mix together the rice and all the other filling ingredients in a large bowl, tossing thoroughly with a spoon. Rinse the vine leaves (see Tips). Spread the vine leaves out on the work surface and spoon 1¹/2 tablespoons of the filling on the end of each leaf, then roll up, folding the outer edges in. Take three 12.5 cm (5 in) long chives and dip briefly in boiling water to make them more pliable. Tie them around each stuffed vine leaf. Place the rolled stuffed leaves in a small casserole or ovenproof dish and drizzle 1 teaspoon olive oil and 1 tablespoon lemon juice over them. Cover with foil and bake for 10 minutes at 180°C. Serve warm or cold. Makes 36 grape leaves, 3 per person.

Tips from Rosie's Kitchen

Vine leaves are not readily available fresh, so you will have to buy them bottled or canned. They are packed in brine, a salty solution that you'll want to rinse off before using. Gently lift the leaves out of the jar, lay them in a bowl, and rinse them under a soft stream of water, letting the water completely drench the leaves. To dry, lay the leaves in a colander and let them drain, or lay them on a flat surface and pat dry with a clean cloth.

Broccoli Griddle Cakes

Even if your kids don't like broccoli, they will eat these little cakes. I serve them as a side dish with the Thai Prawn Brochette (page 67), alongside the Mock Soured Cream; however, they are certainly a meal on their own if you want to serve them as a main dish.

SERVES 10

PER SERVING:

CALORIES 88.3
(WITH MOCK SOUR
CREAM)

FAT 5.8 G
SATURATED FAT
0.7 G
(83.5% OF CALO-
RIES FROM FAT)

PROTEIN 2 G

CARBOHYDRATE
7.6 G

CHOLESTEROL 0 MG

FIBRE 1.3 G

1 large head broccoli
40 g (1/4 cup) coarsely chopped
  onion
1/2 green chilli or 1 teaspoon chilli
  paste
1 large garlic clove, peeled and
  sliced
60 ml (1/4 cup) vegetable oil
85 g (2/3 cup) wholemeal flour
1/8 teaspoon dried dill
pinch of salt
1 medium egg or 2 egg whites
60 ml (1/4 cup) semi-skimmed
  milk

Sprinkling of paprika

MOCK SOURED CREAM

245 g (1 cup) plain non-fat yogurt
1 tablespoon freshly squeezed
  lime or lemon juice
1/2 small onion or large shallot,
  finely chopped
1/2 teaspoon Tabasco sauce, or to
  taste
Sprinkling of chopped fresh dill

Cut the florets off the head of broccoli. Cut the large ones in half so they are all more or less the same size. Discard the stalks, or save them to use in soup or a vegetable stir-fry.

Bring 120 ml (1/2 cup) water to the boil in a medium pan, then drop in the broccoli florets. Cover and steam cook for 3 minutes. Drain in a colander.

Put the steamed broccoli, onions, chilli, and garlic in a food processor and pulse on and off to chop (do not purée the vegetables), or chop by hand. Transfer the chopped ingredients to a mixing bowl and stir in the oil, flour, dill, and salt. Add the egg or egg whites and milk and mix thoroughly with a wooden spoon.

Smear the bottom of a large, nonstick griddle or frying pan with 1/4 teaspoon of butter and set it over medium heat for about 1 minute. Drop tablespoonfuls of the batter onto the hot pan, placing them far enough apart so that the griddle cakes don't touch. They should be about 2.5 cm (1 in) in diameter.

Tips from Rosie's Kitchen

If you don't want to bother to make the Mock Soured Cream, plain low-fat yogurt is fine as a topping.

Cook over low to medium heat for about 1 minute. Turn the griddle cakes and cook the other side for 1 minute. Transfer them to a hot platter to keep warm while you continue making the rest until all the batter is used up.

Mix all of the ingredients for the Mock Soured Cream together and spoon 1 teaspoonful on top of each griddle cake, then top with a sprinkle of paprika.

Makes 20 little griddle cakes – 2 per person.

MOCK SOURED CREAM
SERVES 20

PER SERVING:
CALORIES 1
FAT 0 G
  SATURATED FAT
  0 G
(0% OF CALORIES
  FROM FAT)
PROTEIN 0 G
CARBOHYDRATE
  0.3 G
CHOLESTEROL 0 MG
FIBRE 0 G

Spanish Seafood Cocktail, Gazpacho Style

Peeled prawns are easy to cook and take no time at all. However, if you find yourself without time to spare, you can use peeled prawns that are already cooked. If you buy them raw, cook the prawns first and then toss the cocktail ingredients together while the prawns are chilling on ice. Cut the fruits and vegetables into bite-sized portions so you and your guests will easily be able to take a stab at a little bit of everything and taste all the flavours in one bite.

SERVES 6

PER SERVING:

CALORIES 300.8

FAT 8.1 G
  SATURATED FAT
  1.3 G
(23.8% OF CALO-
  RIES FROM FAT)

PROTEIN 33.7 G

CARBOHYDRATE
  24.8 G

CHOLESTEROL
  230 MG

FIBRE 3.7 G

PRAWNS

900 g (2 lb) medium-sized raw
  prawns, peeled and deveined
320 ml (1 1/3 cups) purified water

1 large grapefruit
180 ml (3/4 cup) pineapple juice
60 ml (1/4 cup) freshly squeezed
  lime juice
2 green chillies, finely chopped
1/8 teaspoon chilli powder

1/4 teaspoon salt
12 ripe avocados diced
240 g (2 cups) chopped celery
30 g (1/2 cup) chopped fresh
  coriander leaves
125 g (1 cup) finely chopped
  spring onions or red onion
60 g (1 cup) chopped leaf lettuce

GARNISH

2 limes

Fill a large pan with water. Steam the prawns in a steamer basket until they turn pink. Drain them in a colander and pour ice over them to chill them and stop the cooking. After the prawns are chilled, cut each one into 4 sections.

Peel the grapefruit and separate the segments. Cut the segments into bite-sized pieces. Put them in a large bowl with the pineapple juice. Toss to coat the grapefruit with the juice. Add the remaining ingredients except the lettuce and limes. Toss gently to mix everything together. Lay a bed of lettuce on the bottom of each of 6 martini glasses. Scoop an equal portion of the seasoned salad mixture on top of the lettuce. Cut the limes into 6 slices, and then cut a small slit in each so that you can insert a slice on the rim of each martini glass.

Steamed Alaskan Crab Legs

Alaskan crab is best when bought frozen. Keep it frozen until you are ready to use it, or defrost it overnight in the refrigerator. Crab has a sweet, mellow flavour, and it's light, so it makes a great late-night dinner served with mixed salad greens.

360 ml (1 1/2 cups) purified water
6 large frozen crab legs (approximately 900 g/2 lb)

GARNISH

6 lemon wedges
Cocktail sauce
Horseradish Sauce (page 66)

SERVES 6

PER SERVING:

CALORIES 127.1

FAT 0.9 G
SATURATED FAT 0.1 G

(6.9% OF CALORIES FROM FAT)

PROTEIN 27.7 G

CARBOHYDRATE 0 G

CHOLESTEROL 64 MG

FIBRE 0 G

Pour the water into a large pan with a steamer basket inside. Bring the water to the boil and lay the crab legs in the basket. If the legs are frozen, steam them for 16 minutes. If they have been defrosted, steam them for 7 minutes. Remove the legs from the pan using kitchen tongs and cool briefly, until you are able to touch them with your fingers. Cut them in half using clean kitchen scissors, then cut them down the leg for easy access to the meat. Serve 1 leg per person with lemon wedges and dishes of cocktail sauce and Horseradish Sauce on the side.

Tips from Rosie's Kitchen

You may come across a transparent cartilage inside the crab legs. Pull it out, and don't eat it.

SMOKED FISH WITH HORSERADISH SAUCE

If you have never dealt with a fresh horseradish root, be prepared for an experience. In the days before food processors, grating the root by hand was just like being exposed to tear gas. Freshly ground horseradish with vinegar and a little salt completely outclasses the prepared varieties sold in shops, and mixed with low-fat soured cream or reduced-fat crème fraîche, it becomes a wonderful condiment for fish, boiled or baked potatoes, and other vegetables.

SERVES 4

PER SERVING:

CALORIES 170

FAT 3 G
  SATURATED FAT
  2 G
(16% OF CALORIES
  FROM FAT)

PROTEIN 30 G

CARBOHYDRATE
  5 G

CHOLESTEROL
  47 MG

FIBRE 0.5 G

120 ml (1/2 cup) low-fat sour cream
  or reduced-fat crème fraîche
2 tablespoons Horseradish Sauce
  (recipe follows), or more to taste

Smoked fish, such as salmon or
  trout, 60–120 g (2–4 oz) per
  person
1 medium-sized sweet onion, finely
  chopped

Mix the soured cream with the horseradish.

Serve individual portions of smoked fish, accompanied by the chopped onion and creamed Horseradish Sauce.

Horseradish Sauce

110 g (1 cup) fresh horseradish root,
  peeled and cut into 1 cm (1/2 in)
  cubes (see *Note*)

60 ml (1/4 cup) white vinegar, or
  more if necessary
1/2 teaspoon salt

Put the horseradish cubes in a food processor and grind them to fine particles. This will take 3–4 minutes. Be careful not to inhale the very irritating fumes.

Pour the white vinegar onto the ground horseradish until it is thoroughly moist. Season with salt and mix well.

Store the prepared horseradish in the refrigerator in a tightly covered container and use it as a condiment.

Note: Horseradish roots are available in the produce sections of some supermarkets. Choose a root that is firm, not one that is shrunken, limp, or dried out. Use a vegetable peeler to remove the outer brown layer and a paring knife to trim out any remaining peel. Then cut the firm, white flesh with a heavy knife.

Thai Prawn Brochettes

There are many diverse flavours on the skewer in this recipe, but none of them competes. The fruit sweetness in contrast to the chilli gives this dish an exotic flair. The prawns can be served hot or cold.

MARINADE

80 ml (1/3 cup) toasted sesame oil
2 tablespoons Thai chilli paste
1/2 teaspoon salt
120 ml (1/2 cup) freshly squeezed
    lime juice
15 g (1/4 cup) finely chopped
    fresh coriander leaves

12 large raw prawns, shelled and
    deveined

BROCHETTE

1 green or yellow pepper, seeded
    and cut into 4 cm (11/2 in)
    pieces
1 red onion, quartered
2 small courgettes, cut into rounds

12 cherry tomatoes

PINEAPPLE DIPPING SAUCE

1 tablespoon cornflour
60 ml (1/4 cup) cold purified
    water
480 ml (2 cups) pineapple juice
30 g (1/4 cup) finely chopped red
    or green pepper
1/4 teaspoon dried chilli flakes
155 g (1 cup) finely chopped fresh
    pineapple

GARNISH

1/2 bunch washed fresh coriander,
    stalks discarded

SERVES 6

PER SERVING:
CALORIES 291
FAT 14 G
    SATURATED FAT
    2 G
(40.3% OF CALORIES FROM FAT)
PROTEIN 9.5 G
CARBOHYDRATE
    37 G
CHOLESTEROL
    40 MG
FIBRE 5.3 G

❀

Soak twelve 15 cm (6 in) wooden skewers in water for 1 hour.

Mix the marinade ingredients in a medium-sized mixing bowl. Put the prawns in another bowl, and all the vegetables in a third bowl. Use half of the sauce to coat the prawns completely, turning them with a spoon. Use the remaining half of the sauce to coat all the vegetables. On each skewer thread 1 piece of pepper, 1 prawn, 2 chunks of red onion, 1 courgette round, and 1 cherry tomato (feel free to make all-vegetable skewers if you have vegetarian guests). Discard the remaining marinade used to coat the prawns (to avoid contamination); use the vegetable-coating sauce to baste the brochettes while cooking, to keep everything extra moist and spicy. Lay the skewers on the barbecue, baste, and cook for 2 1/2 minutes. Turn them over, baste, and cook for an additional 2 1/2 minutes.

If you are using the grill, lay the brochettes on a baking tray and grill them under a medium heat. Follow the timings for cooking on a barbecue.

Meanwhile, make the Pineapple Dipping Sauce: mix the cornflour with the water in a small bowl until the cornflour is completely mixed in. Bring the pineapple juice, peppers, and chilli flakes to the boil in a small saucepan, then pour in the cornflour and water mixture. Stir with a whisk until

Tips from Rosie's Kitchen

You'll want to devein the prawns because the intestinal tract that runs along the back sometimes contains sand and grit. First, remove the shell by cutting down the back of the prawn and peeling it off. Remove and discard the dark vein that runs down the back, then rinse the prawns.

When you are cutting the vegetables, try to be consistent with the size of each piece. It's a good way to ensure that they cook evenly.

Prepare the barbecue fire 30–40 minutes before cooking, or preheat the grill at least 15–20 minutes in advance, so that the intensity of the heat is consistent.

You can use the same method as for the Thai Prawn Brochettes, using a variety of marinated vegetables and prawns, chicken, or tofu.

I prefer a different dipping sauce with the brochettes, like one of those Thai sweetened chilli sauces you can buy in most Asian food shops.

it thickens, about 3 minutes. Cool, then fold in the chopped pineapple.

Serve the skewers on a platter on top of a bed of coriander leaves, with the Pineapple Dipping Sauce alongside. This makes 12 skewers – 2 per person.

Here, Rosie is threading marinated prawns and aubergine on skewers, and Andy is preparing tofu, courgettes, and other vegetables.

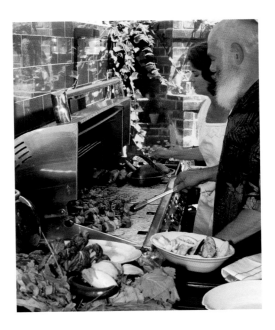

Cooking the brochettes on Rosie's barbecue

THE PLEASURES OF PEPPERS AND CHILLIES

Peppers and chillies belong to the genus *Capsicum* and are native to the New World. Most are green when unripe and go through various colour changes as they mature. Most end up bright red, some orange or yellow. Purple and chocolate-brown peppers are not fully ripe. Ripe peppers are sweeter, softer, and more digestible, with a high content of vitamins C and A. Chillies also contain variable amounts of capsaicin, the pungent principal ingredient that gives a sensation from a mild tingle to a searing burn. Birds cannot taste capsaicin, which may have evolved to deter animals other than birds from eating the fruits and chewing up the seeds. Birds excrete the seeds and help propagate the plants.

Despite the violent effect of capsaicin in the mouth, it has several health-promoting aspects that have led herbalists to recommend chillies for a number of conditions. Chillies stimulate blood circulation and sweating, increase metabolism, and actually promote healing of tissues in the mouth, oesophagus, and stomach. Capsaicin is also a long-acting local anaesthetic, now used in medicine, both as an injectable preparation and a topical cream (especially for the long-lasting pain that sometimes follows an attack of shingles). Eating chillies can cause an endorphin high that many people enjoy, and some take very seriously.

It is a common belief that spicy food upsets the stomach. Usually it is not the chillies that are responsible. It may be other spices, such as black pepper and mustard, that irritate, or too much fat, or poor preparation. I grow many varieties of hot chillies as well as sweet peppers in my garden, drying some of them to use in cooking throughout the year and turning others into hot sauces that I freeze. If I want to tame the heat, I remove the placental tissue (the whitish ribs to which the seeds adhere), which contains the most capsaicin. I always wear rubber gloves when handling very hot chillies and I am careful not to let any of the juice get in my eyes.

I don't like heat in my food just for the sake of heat. I find some varieties of chillies and some dishes made with them just too hot without any redeeming flavour. But I am a great fan of chillies and recommend them for health as well as pleasure. —**A.W.**

Vegetable Nori Rolls

Nori is dried, sweet-tasting seaweed that is used quite a bit in Japanese cuisine, such as in sushi. It is high in protein, calcium, and iron. This recipe is an example of how simple ingredients such as vegetables and rice, with a combination of just the right seasonings, can exceed our expectations. When that happens, inspiration kicks in and you start to think of additional ways to use what you already have in your kitchen.

SERVES 12

PER SERVING:

CALORIES 126.2

FAT 2 G
  SATURATED FAT
  0.3 G
(15.3% OF CALO-
  RIES FROM FAT)

PROTEIN 3.9 G

CARBOHYDRATE
  24.3 G

CHOLESTEROL 0 MG

FIBRE 3.4 G

480 ml (2 cups) purified water
185 g (1 cup) brown, white, or
  basmati rice
1 tablespoon rice vinegar
1 tablespoon mirin (sweet rice
  wine)
6 sheets nori
1/2 medium carrot, peeled and cut
  into thin strips
1/2 medium cucumber, seeded
  and cut into thin strips
1/2 avocado, thinly sliced

5 spring onions, cut into strips
2 tablespoons plum paste
2 tablespoons wasabi (hot, green
  horseradish paste)

GARNISH

1/2 red cabbage, shredded
225 g (2 cups) shredded white
  radish (mooli or daikon)
2 tablespoons natural soy sauce
  (such as tamari)

Bring the water to the boil in a medium pan. Add the rice, reduce heat, cover, and simmer. For brown rice, simmer for 45 minutes; white rice, 20 minutes; basmati, 25 minutes. Rice should be firm and all the water absorbed. Dump the rice into a bowl and add the vinegar and the mirin. Fluff the rice with a wooden spoon and leave to cool completely.

You will toast, fill, and roll each nori sheet one at a time. Hold the first sheet 25 cm (10 in) above a low flame, lightly waving it with your hand until it discolours slightly. Lay the nori sheet on top of a sushi mat. Using a flat wooden spoon, drop one-sixth of the cooled rice on one of the narrow ends of the toasted sheet, flattening the rice to create a slab. About 1 cm (1/2 in) up the rice slab, make a lengthways gutter or groove, using a chopstick or the dull edge of a knife, to cradle the vegetable strips

Tips from Rosie's Kitchen

You will need sushi mats, which can be found at kitchen shops or Asian markets.

If you have chopsticks, you can use the thick end of one to make the 'gutter' in the rice that cradles the vegetables. It makes a perfectly sized gutter. If you don't have chopsticks, the edge of a knife will work too.

When storing the other half of the avocado, leave in the stone, because that will help to keep the avocado fresh. Wrap it tightly with cling film and refrigerate.

so they don't roll off the rice. Lay a strip of each cut vegetable in the trench, then spread 1 teaspoon plum paste and 1 teaspoon wasabi across the vegetables. Roll the sheet up from the filled end. When you get to the other end of the roll, wet the inside edge of the sheet like an envelope, and seal in the contents. Wrap the roll tightly in cling film. Do not remove or cut it until you are ready to serve, or it will dry out. Repeat the process with the remaining 5 rolls. Refrigerate.

Right before serving, remove the rolls from the cling film and cut each one into six 2.5 cm (1 in) sections. Serve on a platter garnished with a bed of shredded red cabbage and white radish. Place a dish of natural soy sauce in the centre of the platter. Makes 6 rolls – 3 slices per person.

Spinach Toasts

Cooking spinach takes very little time, but you need to wash and drain it carefully, and remove tough stalks first, which may take 5 or 10 minutes. Plan accordingly.

The spinach on these little toasts is a great source of iron and vitamins A and C.

SERVES 12

PER SERVING:

CALORIES 115.5

FAT 3.3 G
  SATURATED FAT
  0.6 G
(24.2% OF CALO-
  RIES FROM FAT)

PROTEIN 4.4 G

CARBOHYDRATE
  18.8 G

CHOLESTEROL 1 MG

FIBRE 3 G

❈

180 ml (3/4 cup) purified water
900 g (2 lb) fresh spinach, thick
    stalks discarded
9 thin slices wholemeal bread
1 small onion, finely chopped
1 clove garlic, finely chopped
1 tablespoon grapeseed oil
160 g (2/3 cup) low-fat plain
    yogurt
1/8 teaspoon freshly grated
    nutmeg
1 tablespoon chopped fresh mint
Freshly ground pepper to taste
11/2 tablespoons chopped toasted
    walnuts (page 112)

GARNISH

1 red apple, cut into thin wedges

Preheat oven to 150°C.

Pour the water into a large stainless steel pan and bring it to the boil. Drop in the washed spinach and cook for 3 minutes, stirring several times. Drain the spinach in a colander over a pan to catch all the water, which you can save to make vegetable stock (page 122). Put a bowl or plate on top of the spinach, inside the colander, and press down to squeeze excess water from the leaves.

Trim the crusts from the bread slices. Cut each one on the diagonal to create 2 triangular pieces, then cut again to make 4 triangles. Put them on a baking sheet and bake until lightly toasted, about 5 minutes.

Meanwhile, sauté the onions and garlic in the grapeseed oil in a medium nonstick sauté pan over low heat until onions are softened, about 2 minutes. Remove from heat.

Put the spinach into a medium bowl, together with the onion and the garlic. Add the yogurt, mint, pepper, and walnuts and toss thoroughly with a fork.

Spread the spinach mixture on the toasts just before serving. Garnish with apple wedges. Makes 36 pieces – 3 triangles per person.

Tips from Rosie's Kitchen

Remove the stalks from the spinach leaves by holding the sides of the leaf and pulling the stalk upwards and off the leaf. Wash the spinach by dunking it in a large pan filled with water. Swish it around on the surface with your fingers to separate the leaves and loosen the dirt. Do this for about 5 minutes. Lift a few leaves at a time out of the water and shake off any excess water before dropping them into a bowl. If the leaves are still gritty, change the water and repeat the process.

Polenta Triangles with Roasted Peppers

Polenta is made from dried maize or corn kernels that have been ground into fine, medium, and coarse textures. It is cooked to a thick and moist consistency and either served hot right out of the cooking pot or cooled in a baking tray and then cut into shapes. Here it is cooked with cheese to give it added flavour. I find that the simple act of roasting peppers for the puréed spread gives them a sweet, smoky taste – just right for mild tasting polenta.

This dish makes not only a substantial starter, but it can also be eaten for breakfast, a snack, or lunch.

SERVES 6

PER SERVING:

CALORIES 111.6

FAT 10.4 G
  SATURATED FAT
  1.5 G

(82.5% OF CALO-
  RIES FROM FAT)

PROTEIN 0.8 G

CARBOHYDRATE
  4.2 G

CHOLESTEROL 0 MG

FIBRE 0.5 G

❉

POLENTA

720 ml (3 cups) purified water
125 g (1 cup) polenta
1 teaspoon salt
1 tablespoon finely chopped fresh basil
25 g (1/4 cup) freshly grated Cheddar or Parmesan cheese

ROASTED PEPPER PURÉE

3 large red peppers, seeded (about 675 g/1 1/2 lb)
1 1/2 tablespoons olive oil
1 tablespoon balsamic vinegar
1/8 teaspoon Tabasco sauce

2 shallots, peeled and roughly chopped
1/4 teaspoon salt
1/8 teaspoon freshly ground black pepper

GARNISH

2 tablespoons chopped parsley
1 1/2 tablespoons freshly grated Parmesan cheese
6 fresh basil sprigs

Prepare the polenta. Bring the water to the boil in a saucepan. Slowly pour in a continuous stream of polenta, stirring constantly. Add the salt. Reduce the heat to low and cook uncovered, stirring occasionally, until the polenta begins to pull away from the sides of the pan, about 20 minutes. Remove from the heat and stir in the basil and cheese. Working quickly, grease with olive oil a shallow ovenproof dish or tin that is about 23 x 17.5 cm (9 x 7 in). Pour in the polenta, spreading it out over the whole surface. Leave the polenta to set and cool for 1 hour.

Preheat oven to 200°C.

Prepare the Roasted Pepper Purée. Cut the red peppers into large pieces. Smear a little of the olive oil over the bottom of an ovenproof dish and lay the peppers inside. Cover and roast for 20 minutes until they become soft. Remove from the oven (leave the oven on to bake the polenta) and allow to cool. Put the peppers in a food processor and process until smooth. Add the remaining ingredients, except for 1 teaspoon of the remaining olive oil, and process until thoroughly blended. Scrape the dip into a serving bowl.

When the polenta has cooled completely, cut two vertical lines through it, so you have three rectangles. Make diagonal cuts from corner to corner of each rectangle to make an 'X', creating 4 triangles within each of the 3 rectangles. Smear some olive oil over a baking sheet. With a palette knife, remove each of the 12 triangles and arrange them on the sheet, leaving space around each one so that the edges can crisp. Bake on the top shelf in the oven for 15 minutes, or until browned.

To serve, pour 2 tablespoons of the Roasted Pepper Purée on each of 6 serving plates. Arrange 2 Polenta Triangles alongside, sprinkle some chopped parsley and Parmesan over them, and place a basil sprig on the side. Makes 12 triangles – 2 per person.

Tips from Rosie's Kitchen

If you plan to serve polenta as a side dish, spoon it out of the cooking pot immediately after it is removed from the heat. As a side dish it could be served as a bed for the Savoury Roasted Poussins with Roasted Garlic (page 150). If you are serving it as an appetizer, you must let it set for at least 1 hour before it is cut into individual servings. For leftovers, warm the remainders in a baking tin under the grill for a few minutes, then serve.

ANDY SUGGESTS

I prefer Parmesan to the Cheddar in the polenta – I think it gives a more authentic Italian flavour.

Aubergine Dip

Aubergine Dip has a great texture with a tangy, vinegary, seasoned taste that is mellowed with the pita. I also like to smear the dip inside warm pancakes (page 170) for a different kind of presentation.

1 aubergine (675 g/1 1/2 lb)
1/2 medium onion, grated or finely chopped
2 tablespoons capers
2 tablespoons freshly squeezed lemon juice
60 ml (1/4 cup) olive oil
1/2 teaspoon dried oregano
1/2 teaspoon salt or to taste

3/4 teaspoon freshly ground black pepper
1 tablespoon red wine vinegar
4 pita breads
1 tomato, peeled, seeded, and diced
1 tablespoon chopped fresh parsley

SERVES 8

PER SERVING:

CALORIES 169.3

FAT 7.3 G
   SATURATED FAT
   1 G
(38% OF CALORIES
   FROM FAT)

PROTEIN 3.8 G

CARBOHYDRATE
   23.1 G

CHOLESTEROL 0 MG

FIBRE 2.7 G

Preheat oven to 190°C.

Set the aubergine on a baking tin or dish and pierce it a few times with a knife. Bake it until it becomes soft, about 30 minutes; it should pierce easily with a fork. Remove it from the oven and cool. When completely cooled, peel the skin off and put the flesh into a blender or food processor. Add the onions, capers, and lemon juice. Turn on the machine, then gradually add the olive oil. Continue to blend until the aubergine mixture is smooth and creamy. Transfer to a bowl and stir in the oregano, salt, pepper, and vinegar.

Warm the pitas briefly on a baking sheet in the oven or under the grill, then cut each of them into 8 wedges. Arrange them on a plate or platter. Just before serving, stir the tomato and parsley into the dip. Makes 32 – 4 wedges per person.

Top: Goat's Cheese Toasties with Sun-Dried Tomato and Basil; front left: White Bean Spread; right: Polento Triangles with Roasted Peppers

MISO PÂTÉ

This starter is a bit more complicated than the other dishes I've devised for this book, but it's worth making for a special dinner. It's a vegetarian answer to chopped liver that will make the chickens thank you. It also happens to be a heart-healthy treat, since it has none of the saturated fat of pâté made from meat or poultry. The texture and flavour will develop as the mixture rests for a day after you put it together, so please resist the temptation to dig into it prematurely!

1 loaf good-quality wholemeal bread, sliced (OK if stale)
240 ml (1 cup) unsalted vegetable stock
240 ml (1 cup) tahini
1½ tablespoons red, mugi, or hatcho miso
1 tablespoon toasted sesame oil

2 cloves garlic, mashed
1 medium onion, finely chopped
30 g (½ cup) chopped fresh parsley
3 tablespoons dry sherry, more as needed
Pinches of dried thyme, sage or rosemary, and ground allspice
Freshly ground black pepper to taste

Preheat oven to 130°C.

Place the bread slices on a baking sheet and bake them until they are thoroughly dry, about 45 minutes. Allow the bread to cool, then break it into pieces. Put the bread and stock in a bowl and work it with your hands until evenly moist.

In a separate bowl, mix the tahini, miso, sesame oil, and garlic until well blended. Add to the moistened bread and work everything together well using your hands. Add the onions, parsley, and sherry. Season well with thyme, sage or rosemary, allspice, and pepper. Add a few more tablespoons of sherry if needed, and knead with your hands until pâté is well blended. Add a little more liquid (stock or water) if necessary, to make a moist, sticky consistency. Pack the pâté firmly into a small loaf tin or bowl. Cover and refrigerate for 24 hours. (This is important!)

Remove the pâté from the refrigerator at least half an hour before serving. Turn it out and serve with savoury biscuits.

SERVES 10

PER SERVING:

CALORIES 266

FAT 14.2 G
  SATURATED FAT
  2 G

(48% OF CALORIES
  FROM FAT)

PROTEIN 9 G

CARBOHYDRATE
  28 G

CHOLESTEROL 0 MG

FIBRE 5 G

White Bean Spread

Most of us love bread. When thinking of great taste accompaniments to bread, challenge the butter and olive oil and balsamic vinegar routine with this herby spread. What you have here is a versatile spread for toasted baguettes or warm pancakes. You can also use it as a dip made for thick chunks of French bread or pita sandwiches. Plan one day in advance in order to soak the beans overnight. Of course, you always have the option of using canned beans if you're really pressed for time, but I encourage you to prepare them from scratch. The difference is in the taste and the feeling you get when you've really made something yourself.

SERVES 12

PER SERVING:

CALORIES 156.1

FAT 4.1 G
 SATURATED FAT
 0.7 G
(23.1% OF CALO-
 RIES FROM FAT)

PROTEIN 8.6 G

CARBOHYDRATE
 22.3 G

CHOLESTEROL 1 MG

FIBRE 5.4 G

✳

2 cups dried haricot or cannellini
  beans, soaked overnight in
  1.4 litres (6 cups) of water with
  1 teaspoon bicarbonate of soda
1 bay leaf
1 teaspoon dried basil or pesto
  (page 160)
2 teaspoons freshly squeezed lime
  juice

1 clove garlic, coarsely chopped
1 teaspoon ground cumin
1 teaspoon salt
2 tablespoons freshly grated
  Parmesan cheese
3 tablespoons extra virgin olive oil
1 whole-grain
  baguette

Do not drain the water that the beans have been soaking in overnight. Bring it to the boil and cook for 45 minutes. The beans should be tender enough to be easily pierced with a fork.

Preheat the grill to medium.

Drain the cooked beans and transfer to a food processor or blender. Add the basil or pesto, lime juice, garlic, cumin, salt, Parmesan cheese, and 1 tablespoon of the olive oil, and process or blend until smooth. Cut the baguette into 2.5 cm (1 in) slices and brush the remaining tablespoon of olive oil over them. Grill until lightly browned.

Put the toasted baguette slices on a platter. Scrape the bean spread into a nice bowl, set it in the middle of the platter and serve.

ANDY SUGGESTS

I much prefer the pesto to the dried basil.

Tips from Rosie's Kitchen

As long as you are preparing beans from scratch, you could double the amount, using half to make White Beans and Fusilli (page 160).

CHEESE

I love cheese, and so do most people I know. We love it for its unctuous texture and complex range of flavours that include notes of earth, mushrooms, and, in stronger varieties, distinctly animal tones, which in other contexts might be disagreeable. I especially like cheeses from England, Ireland, France, Switzerland, and Italy. I'm afraid I'm not much of a fan of most of the anaemic varieties made for the American mass market. But I am encouraged by the growth of new artisanal and farmhouse cheeses made in the United States, some of them honest and robust enough to satisfy cheese lovers.

For years, I ate cheese sparingly and with guilt, because I was afraid of its effect on my cholesterol levels and cardiovascular health. My continuing study of nutrition has reduced my anxiety and given me confidence to make cheese a regular part of my diet. I'm encouraged that it occurs in the Mediterranean diet, which is associated with some of the best health on the planet, including low incidence of cardiovascular disease. Mediterranean peoples eat cheese often, but the cheeses they like are natural, not processed, and they do not favour varieties with an extremely high fat content, like Brie and triple crèmes. Furthermore, they eat cheese in the context of a diet rich in monounsaturated fat from olive oil and omega-3 fatty acids from fish. The Mediterranean diet also provides a wealth of antioxidants and other protective phytochemicals from an abundance of fresh fruits and vegetables of high quality. All of this neutralises any adverse impact of the butterfat in cheese.

Sometimes I make a meal of cheese with a green salad. I always have a wedge of Parmesan on hand, which I grate as a seasoning on many dishes. I keep other cheeses, like Gruyère, for snacking. And I often put several varieties out at the end of a meal, usually with fruit, instead of a sweet dessert.

Some people cannot tolerate dairy products. The protein in cow's milk (casein) may aggravate such conditions as asthma, eczema, bronchitis, sinusitis, allergies, and auto-immunity. Cheeses made from the milk of goats and sheep do not present that problem; they have a different kind of protein. I like most sheep's milk cheeses (Roquefort is probably the most famous) for their sharp, full flavours, and I believe that the fat in sheep's milk is less likely to raise levels of cholesterol in the blood than butterfat. Goat's cheese, in my experience, runs the gamut from luscious to nasty, depending on the breed of goat, the handling of the milk, and the age of the product. Once rare in America, it has now become popular, at least in trendy restaurants. Cheese substitutes, made from soya, rice, almonds, or hemp, bear little resemblance to the real thing; they may substitute for processed cheese slices, but why bother?

Good natural cheeses are available at speciality shops and better super-markets and, increasingly, on the Internet. Suppliers will usually provide information on their products and help you find ones you like. I encourage you to experiment and to enjoy good cheese without guilt.—A.W.

Goat's Cheese Toasties with Sun-Dried Tomato and Basil

This spread tastes pretty amazing on a warm, thick piece of French baguette. Sometimes if I don't have a baguette I spread it on bagel chips that I have in the cupboard. Goat's cheese definitely has a sharp flavour, but it doesn't fight with the distinct flavours of sun-dried tomato and basil.

13 dry-pack sun-dried tomatoes
60 g (2 oz) goat's cheese, at room temperature
2 tablespoons pesto (page 160)
1/2 French baguette or 1 small French stick
60 ml (1/4 cup) olive oil
1 clove garlic, crushed

Freshly ground black pepper to taste

GARNISH

1 red pepper, chopped
1 bunch fresh basil, finely shredded

SERVES 12

PER SERVING:

CALORIES 213.3

FAT 7.7 G
  SATURATED FAT
  2.1 G

(34.7% OF CALO-
  RIES FROM FAT)

PROTEIN 11.6 G

CARBOHYDRATE
  29.2 G

CHOLESTEROL 5 MG

FIBRE 2.5 G

❄

Preheat the grill.

Soak the sun-dried tomatoes in a bowl of hot water until they become plump and soft, about 20–30 minutes. When they are soft, chop them up. Mix them with the goat's cheese and pesto in a bowl until you have a paste like consistency.

Cut the baguette into 1 cm (1/2 in) slices. Mix the olive oil and garlic together in a small bowl. Season to taste with black pepper. Using a pastry brush, brush the baguette slices with the oil and garlic mixture. Grill for less than 1 minute. Remove slices from the heat.

Scatter the chopped red pepper and shredded basil on the bottom of a small shallow dish. Scoop up rounded tablespoons of goat's cheese spread and gently drop the scoops over the peppers and basil. Set the dish in the middle of a large platter and arrange the warm slices of bread on the platter around the dish. Makes 12 slices – 1 per person.

Tips from Rosie's Kitchen

If you don't want to use bread, serve this dip surrounded by chicory leaves. You can do the same with the Aubergine Dip (page 79). Put the Aubergine Dip or the goat's cheese, tomato, and pesto paste on the wide end of the chicory leaves and garnish with the chopped red pepper and basil.

Stuffed Mushroom Caps with Couscous

Couscous is a mildly nutty-tasting grain that comes from North Africa. It makes a great stuffing, especially for a small cavity like a mushroom, because it's so moist. When the stuffed mushrooms are baked, the full flavour of the couscous and the mushrooms really come through. These will go fast!

30 g (1/4 cup) chopped walnuts
2 tablespoons olive oil
2 cloves garlic, finely chopped
3 shallots, chopped
1 1/2 tablespoons natural soy sauce (such as tamari)
240 ml (1 cup) white wine
12 medium-sized button mushrooms, washed and stalks removed
120 ml (1/2 cup) chicken (page 124) or vegetable stock (page 122) or purified water
45 g (1/4 cup) couscous
Salt
Freshly ground black pepper
2 tablespoons chopped fresh basil
1 bunch fresh parsley, chopped
25 g (1/4 cup) freshly grated Parmesan cheese

SERVES 6

PER SERVING:

CALORIES 106.9

FAT 5.7 G
SATURATED FAT
0.9 G

(53.4% OF CALO-
RIES FROM FAT)

PROTEIN 2.6 G

CARBOHYDRATE
9.6 G

CHOLESTEROL
1 MG

FIBRE 1 G

Preheat the oven to 180°C.

Spread the walnuts on a baking sheet and toast them in the oven for 5 minutes, just until they turn slightly more brown. Pour them into a small bowl.

Set a large sauté pan with the olive oil over low heat for less than 1 minute. Drop in the garlic and the shallots. Add the soy sauce, wine, and mushrooms and simmer covered until the mushrooms are tender, about 10 minutes. Use a slotted spoon to shake the mushrooms so that the cooking liquid falls back into the pan, then transfer the drained mushrooms to a baking dish, arranging them hollow side up. Reserve the liquid in the pan.

Cook the couscous by bringing the stock or water to the boil in a separate pan. Pour in the couscous, lower the heat, and simmer covered for 2 minutes. Remove from the heat and leave, covered, for 10 minutes. All the liquid should be absorbed. Now, dump the couscous into the sauté pan with the reserved liquid, cover, and cook over low heat until all the liquid is absorbed.

Lightly salt and pepper the mushroom caps. Finish the stuffing by mixing the nuts, herbs, and Parmesan cheese into the cooked couscous. Using a tablespoon, pile a small mound of filling inside the cap of each mushroom. Bake for 10 minutes or until the stuffing is lightly browned on top. Makes 12 mushroom caps – 2 per person.

SNACKS

Snacks make up more and more of the typical diet, and sales of snack foods have made them very big business for manufacturers. Unfortunately, the kinds of foods we snack on are not terrific for our well-being. They tend to be calorie-dense processed foods that are high in the wrong kinds of fat, the wrong kinds of carbohydrate, salt, and additives, while not giving us the nutrients we need. The ultimate snack food is the crisp, a morsel of starch, usually with a high glycaemic index, that has been fried in partially hydrogenated vegetable oil containing trans fats and made attractive with salt and other chemicals, including artificial colours. Overconsumption of crisps and similar processed snack foods greatly contributes to the epidemics of obesity and type II diabetes in our society, particularly in children.

Americans now commonly eat all day long – on the street, in their cars, in airports, at sporting events. I'm not against snacking. In fact, I think many people need to eat throughout the day rather than eat three defined meals. But I am very concerned about what they eat.

Here are some of the snacks I can recommend:

- a piece of fresh fruit
- some dried fruit
- a small handful of raw, unsalted nuts – pistachios, cashews, or walnuts
- a flavourful piece of natural cheese
- a piece of dark chocolate
- a portion of leftover food.

Most commercial snack foods are simply not very good for you. So, while it is fine to snack, just choose foods to eat between meals with the same care you choose foods to eat at meals. And do your best to encourage kids to do the same.—A.W.

Salads

THE MEDITERRANEAN DIET

Many people talk up the Mediterranean diet these days. I myself am one of its champions, and many of the recipes in this book are consistent with the nutritional philosophy it represents. The Mediterranean diet is a composite of the traditional cuisines of Spain, southern France, Italy, Greece, Crete, and parts of the Middle East. All of them emphasise olive oil, fish above meat, and cheese above milk, and all include an abundance of high-quality fresh fruits and vegetables. People who follow it have low rates of heart disease and cancer and also get to enjoy food that is very flavourful, with enough fat to make it interesting.

Here are the features of the Mediterranean diet that recommend it to health-conscious people as well as food lovers:

- great variety, with tastes that appeal to people of many different cultures
- lots of whole-grain products as opposed to the refined carbohydrates in our typical diet, hence a reduced glycaemic load (see page xx)
- mostly monounsaturated fat and plenty of omega-3 fatty acids from fish, nuts, seeds, and vegetables
- little meat and poultry compared to our diet; more fish and pulses in place of them
- inclusion of some cheese and yogurt
- a great variety of fruits and vegetables, including low-glycaemic-index ones that provide fibre and protective phytochemicals (see page xxvii)
- an emphasis on fresh foods
- little processed food
- use of familiar ingredients and good adaptability to locally available ingredients
- relative ease of preparation compared to other cuisines.

The Mediterranean diet promotes health and is in no way a cuisine of deprivation. I should point out two qualifications about it, however. First of all, the traditional Mediterranean diet, like other traditional diets throughout the world, is changing. In Greece, Italy, and Spain, processed food and American fast food are appearing, as they are everywhere, and affluence is bringing with it greater consumption of calories and meat. We will have to wait to see the effects of these changes on the health of Mediterranean peoples. Also, the traditional Mediterranean diet is part of a whole cultural package that is good for health. People throughout the region get more physical activity than most of us, and they enjoy strong social and family bonds around meals. Eating together and taking pleasure in food are central to healthy living in Mediterranean cultures. It's not just the olive oil. —**A.W.**

Greek Salad with Mild Chilli Dressing

SERVES 6

PER SERVING:

CALORIES 374.7

FAT 18 G
  SATURATED FAT
  3.9 G
(38.7% OF CALO-
  RIES FROM FAT)

PROTEIN 15.5 G

CARBOHYDRATE
  49.3 G

CHOLESTEROL
  13 MG

FIBRE 11.5 G

❁

I love this salad because of all the prominent tastes in the dressing. Here, the dressing is tossed with fresh spinach leaves and topped with crumbly and tangy feta cheese, but you can toss this dressing on any mixed-green combination or vegetables and it would taste excellent!

CITRUS AND MILD CHILLI DRESSING

8 dry-pack sun-dried tomatoes
180 ml (3/4 cup) hot purified water
60 ml (1/4 cup) extra virgin olive oil or apple juice
1 teaspoon mild chilli powder
1 clove garlic
2 tablespoons orange juice concentrate
60 ml (1/4 cup) cider vinegar
1 teaspoon natural soy sauce (such as tamari) or low-sodium soy sauce

1/4 teaspoon freshly ground black pepper

SALAD

675 g (1 1/2 lb) fresh spinach, washed and stalks removed
90 g (3 oz) feta cheese, finely cubed
Freshly ground black pepper

GARNISH

12 Kalamata olives, pitted
2 tablespoons toasted sunflower seeds

Mediterranean olives and olive oil

Soak the sun-dried tomatoes in the bowl of hot water for 20–30 minutes until they become soft and plump. Pour the water and the tomatoes into a food processor and process until blended. Pour in all the remaining dressing ingredients and continue to process until creamy. Cover and refrigerate until you are ready to use it.

Toss the spinach leaves together with the dressing until the leaves are completely coated. Sprinkle over the feta cheese and pepper and serve. Garnish each salad with 2 olives and a sprinkle of sunflower seeds.

Tips from Rosie's Kitchen

Toast your own sunflower seeds by placing them in a medium sauté pan over low heat for 1 minute until browned.

Thai Prawn and Papaya Salad

The papaya in this salad gives it a subdued, sweet flavour and the prawns coated in chilli oil give it a lively kick.

PRAWNS

12 large raw prawns, shelled and deveined

1 tablespoon toasted sesame oil

1/4 teaspoon prepared chilli paste (optional)

SALAD

600 g (6 cups) washed and dried mixed baby salad greens

1/4 teaspoon salt

60 ml (1/4 cup) freshly squeezed lemon juice

60 ml (1/4 cup) olive oil

PAPAYA SALSA

1 bunch fresh coriander
140 g (1 cup) cubed papaya
30 g (1/4 cup) cubed red pepper
40 g (1/4 cup) diced red onion

1 green chilli , seeded and finely chopped (optional)
2 tablespoons freshly squeezed lime juice

Preheat the grill to medium high.

Meanwhile, put the prawns in a medium bowl and add the sesame oil and chilli paste. Toss with a spoon to coat the prawns completely and evenly. Lay the seasoned prawns on a baking tray and grill them for 1 minute. Turn them over and grill for 1 more minute or until they are cooked through. The prawns should be pink when they are done.

Toss the mixed greens with the salt, lemon juice, and oil, until all the leaves are thoroughly coated.

Pinch the leaves off the coriander stalks. Put the leaves in a small bowl with the remaining salsa ingredients and mix thoroughly with a spoon. Toss the prawns into the salsa and stir until they are all coated. Put the mixed greens on a platter and lay the prawns on top.

SERVES 6

PER SERVING:
CALORIES 188.2
FAT 14.3 G
  SATURATED FAT
  2 G
(65.1% OF CALO-
  RIES FROM FAT)
PROTEIN 7.8 G
CARBOHYDRATE
  9.4 G
CHOLESTEROL
  40 MG
FIBRE 2.3 G

ANDY SUGGESTS

Again, I prefer more spice here, so I would add some chilli paste to the dressing.

Simple Marinated Chicken Salad

You have a couple of cooking and serving options with this recipe. You can either barbecue or bake the chicken and serve it as part of a main course, or serve it as a main dish salad.

The marinated chicken is tossed with the greens in a perfectly seasoned dressing with punch from the garlic, lemon, and Worcestershire sauce, mellowed with smooth avocado and cool soured cream. The avocado adds a bit of good fat, too.

SERVES 6

PER SERVING:

CALORIES 263.9

FAT 19.2 G
  SATURATED FAT
  3.4 G
(66.2% OF CALO-
  RIES FROM FAT)

PROTEIN 15.6 G

CARBOHYDRATE
  8.3 G

CHOLESTEROL
  39 MG

FIBRE 1.2 G

4 boneless, skinless chicken
  breasts (fillets) 225 g (8 oz)
  Slow-Baked Tofu (page 193)

MARINADE

5 tablespoons freshly squeezed
  lemon juice
3 tablespoons natural soy sauce
  (such as tamari)
1/8 teaspoon black pepper
1 teaspoon dried basil
2 cloves garlic

DRESSING

1 ripe avocado, stoned

120 ml (1/2 cup) low-fat soured
  cream or reduced-fat crème
  fraîche
80 ml (1/3 cup) olive oil
80 ml (1/3 cup) freshly squeezed
  lemon juice
2 large cloves garlic, quartered
2 teaspoons black pepper
2 teaspoons Worcestershire sauce

SALAD

2 cos lettuces
2 tablespoons freshly grated
  Parmesan cheese

Tenderise each chicken fillet by laying it on a large piece of cling film on a cutting board. Cover it with another piece of cling film. Using a mallet, gently pound the surface of the chicken. Turn the chicken over and repeat. Put the tenderised chicken into a deep pan. Wash your hands, the knife, the cutting board, and anything else that came into contact with the raw chicken.

Mix together all the marinade ingredients. Pour over the

chicken, cover, and refrigerate for 30 minutes, or no longer than 2 hours.

Meanwhile, prepare the barbecue.

To barbecue the marinated chicken, lay it on the hot grill. You should hear the meat sear (otherwise, the fire may not be hot enough). Cook on each side for 4 minutes, basting with the remaining marinade while cooking. Be sure to cook the chicken completely, but don't overcook. You can check it with a knife by cutting it in the centre. It should be moist, but not pink on the inside. Remove from the heat and leave to cool.

To bake the marinated chicken, preheat the oven to 200°C. Put the marinated chicken on a baking tray and bake it on the lower shelf for 20 minutes, turning the chicken over after 10–12 minutes and basting the other side to keep it moist. Check the chicken by cutting into the centre to make sure there is no sign of pink flesh. Remove from the oven and cool.

Put all the ingredients for the dressing in a blender and blend until the garlic is puréed and the dressing is smooth.

When the chicken is cool, slice it at an angle. Tear the cos lettuce leaves into bite-sized pieces and toss them with the chicken in a large bowl. Pour in the dressing and toss until the leaves and the chicken are evenly coated. Garnish with Parmesan cheese and serve.

Tofu Variation

Per serving:

Calories 199.5

Fat 18.5 g
  Saturated fat
  3.3 g

(84.6% of calo-
  ries from fat)

Protein 2 g

Carbohydrate
  8.3 g

Cholesterol
  5 mg

Fibre 1.2 g

❈

BROCCOLI SALAD WITH AVOCADO

SERVES 4

PER SERVING:

CALORIES 177

FAT 15 G
   SATURATED FAT
   2 G

(76% OF CALORIES
   FROM FAT)

PROTEIN 4.6 G

CHOLESTEROL
   0 MG

FIBRE 4.8 G

❋

The contrasting textures of crunchy broccoli and creamy, soft avocado make this quick salad interesting and delicious. It is rich in monounsaturated fat and full of protective phytochemicals and fibre. Don't forget to use the broccoli stalks, which, if properly trimmed, are as good to eat as the florets. Cut a slice off the end of each large stalk and peel the stalks just below the outer fibrous layer to expose the tender, lighter-coloured flesh within.

450 g (1 lb) broccoli
1 ripe avocado
2 tablespoons extra virgin olive oil

2 tablespoons freshly squeezed lemon juice
1 tablespoon grainy mustard

Trim and wash the broccoli and cut it into bite-sized pieces. Steam or boil the broccoli in a large pan until it is just crunchy-tender and bright green, then drain it well, and cool.

Peel and stone the avocado, then cut it into small cubes. Fold the avocado into the broccoli.

Whisk the olive oil, lemon juice, and mustard together in a small bowl until well mixed.

Toss the broccoli and avocado with the dressing.

Tabbouleh Salad

Tabbouleh is a moist, light Turkish dish using bulgur, a form of wheat that has had some of the bran removed and then is baked and cracked. Bulgur wheat requires soaking for one hour before adding any seasonings, and at least three additional hours for complete absorption of both liquid and seasonings. So plan ahead – even one day in advance. Tabbouleh makes an excellent alternative to rice or potatoes, and the onions, tomatoes, parsley, and mint tossed into it create a colourful and savoury confetti.

80 g (1/2 cup) bulgur wheat
240 ml (1 cup) boiling purified water
80 ml (1/3 cup) freshly squeezed lemon juice
6 tablespoons finely chopped fresh spearmint
1 tablespoon salt
1 teaspoon black pepper
60 ml (1/4 cup) extra virgin olive oil
60–120 g (1–2 cups) finely chopped parsley
95 g (3/4 cup) chopped spring onions
3 large tomatoes, finely diced
2 cloves garlic, finely chopped
1 red leaf lettuce

Put the bulgur in a large bowl and pour the boiling water over it. Leave to soak at room temperature for at least 1 hour.

When the grain has absorbed all the water, mix the lemon juice, mint, salt, and pepper in a separate bowl and slowly stir in the olive oil. Pour the dressing over the bulgur wheat and mix with a large spoon until all the grains are coated. Stir in all remaining ingredients (except the lettuce) until they are thoroughly distributed throughout the grain. The hardest part about making Tabbouleh Salad is waiting for all of the tempting ingredients to set as the grain absorbs all of the liquid. Cover and refrigerate for at least 3 hours before serving, or overnight if you are preparing a day in advance. Fluff up with a fork and serve on a bed of red leaf lettuce. Serve as a side dish along with chicken or fish, such as Lemon Baked Halibut (page 185), or simply scoop up with some warm pita bread.

SERVES 6

PER SERVING:
CALORIES 154.8
FAT 9.5 G
    SATURATED FAT 1.3 G
(51.4% OF CALORIES FROM FAT)
PROTEIN 3.1 G
CARBOHYDRATE 17.1 G
CHOLESTEROL 0 MG
FIBRE 4.9 G

❀

ABOUT HERBS

Culinary herbs are the delicate green parts of aromatic plants: dill, thyme, marjoram, oregano, basil, parsley, and coriander among them. Most of us know them as dried ingredients in bottles, but in many parts of the world people have ready access to fresh herbs and make liberal use of them in cooking. Some herbs dry fairly well. I often use dried dill, oregano, marjoram, thyme, and bay leaves and am happy with their ability to flavour cooked dishes. But I can't bring myself to use dried parsley, coriander, or basil when I know how much better the fresh versions look and taste.

I lived for a while in South America (Colombia, Ecuador, Peru) and got in the habit of drinking herb teas there. The reason was that if I ordered peppermint, chamomile, or lemongrass, what I got was a pot full of the fresh herbs steeping in hot water. These infusions had more colour, aroma, flavour, and vitality than ones I knew made from tea bags. The experience spoiled me.

Many of these aromatic plants are extremely easy to grow; some, like dill, are truly weeds that can become invasive if you do not keep them in check. And you don't need much space to plant a garden of kitchen herbs that will be ready for clipping whenever you need them. You can even grow some herbs indoors. It is not hard to have a few basil plants, thyme, oregano, tarragon, and chives growing in pots on a kitchen windowsill.

As with other flavourings, learning to use herbs in your cooking takes practice. Become familiar with several, taste them, try them out in cooking, and note the combinations that appeal to you. You may discover that you like dill with cold salmon, coriander with beans, bay leaf in tomato sauce, parsley with potatoes, chives and basil in salad. Get to know these leaves with their distinctive odours and tastes. They will greatly add to the pleasure you get from both cooking and eating.—A.W.

A Corner of Andy's Herb Garden

1. Agave Cactus
2. Italian Large Leaf Basil (herb)
3. Chocolate Mint (herb)
4. Evolvulus 'Blue Daze'
5. 'Red Rubin' Basil (herb)
6. Purple Oregano (herb)
7. Spearmint (herb)
8. Elfin Thyme (herb)
9. Gerbera Daisy
10. Gerbera Daisy
11. Society Garlic
12. Rosemary (herb)
13. Rosemary (herb)
14. 'Purple Ruffles' Basil (herb)
15. Peppermint (herb)
16. 'Sweet Dani' Lemon Basil (herb)
17. Purple Thai Basil (herb)

Rosie's Tips
about Growing Herbs

I think you will be surprised by how little effort it takes to grow the fresh herbs that you need to make your cooking taste really good. It is wonderful to have the plants right at your fingertips when you need a sprig of fresh mint for a garnish or a big bunch of basil to make a delicious pesto. Moreover, you'll save a lot of money, because you pay a premium for the fresh herbs that are sold in little packets in supermarkets. And since they don't keep well, you often end up throwing out what you haven't used right away.

My herb garden isn't fancy. I simply chose a sunny space around my patio, planted the seeds in regular garden soil, and let them grow. If you don't have a backyard, you can grow herbs in pots on a sunny windowsill, as Andy suggests. Incidentally, kids love growing things and it helps them to appreciate fresh foods. They feel a pride in something they have nurtured themselves and it is a reminder for them of where things come from – a benefit that we could all share these days.

Basil, mint, and coriander are the herbs I use most frequently and that really make a difference when they are fresh in pasta, chicken, fish, and tofu dishes, and in soups and salads. I also use a lot of thyme, rosemary, and oregano, which are perfectly acceptable dried, too.

Just having your own fresh herbs available will encourage you to experiment, to add something special to many tried-and-true recipes, and to create lovely new combinations of flavours on your own. It is the mark of a good cook to know and appreciate the power of fresh herbs.

Mixed Greens with Potato Croutons and Tarragon Dressing

The potato croutons in this salad are so enjoyable that you can eat them alone. They also provide the complex carbohydrates that we sometimes feel are missing when eating a salad by itself. They help curb that feeling of deprivation that often causes us to grab for more bread or pile on more croutons. The red pepper, onion, and fennel add great flavour to the croutons and colour to the salad.

POTATO CROUTONS

60 ml (1/4 cup) olive oil
30 g (1/3 cup) very thinly sliced
    red pepper
1 small white onion, very thinly
    sliced
1 tablespoon balsamic vinegar
1/2 teaspoon crushed fennel seeds
1/2 teaspoon seasoned salt
Pinch of cayenne pepper
450 g (1 lb) waxy potatoes,
    scrubbed

TARRAGON DRESSING

120 ml (1/2 cup) raspberry vinegar
2 tablespoons finely chopped
    shallot
1 tablespoon freshly squeezed
    lemon juice
120 ml (1/2 cup) olive oil
1 tablespoon chopped fresh
    tarragon
1 teaspoon honey

900 g (2 lb) mixed salad greens
    (such as cos, rocket, watercress)
3 teaspoons goat's cheese

SERVES 6

PER SERVING:
CALORIES 259.6
FAT 18.8 G
    SATURATED FAT
    2.8 G
(60.7% OF CALO-
    RIES FROM FAT)
PROTEIN 3.6 G
CARBOHYDRATE
    23.8 G
CHOLESTEROL
    2 MG
FIBRE 2.5 G

Preheat the oven to 200°C.

Rub 2 baking trays with 2 tablespoons of the olive oil. Mix the red pepper, onion, vinegar, remaining olive oil, fennel seeds, salt, and cayenne pepper together in a medium bowl. Slice the potatoes very thinly by hand, or with a mandoline, if you have one, and add them to the red pepper, onion, fennel mixture. Toss well to incorporate all the flavours of the seasonings, onions, and peppers. Spread the mixture of red pepper, onion, fennel, and potato onto the baking trays and bake for 15 minutes. Turn them

over and bake for 5 to 15 minutes more, until the potatoes become crisp and the edges are browned.

Whisk the dressing ingredients in a medium bowl until the honey is dissolved and everything is thoroughly mixed.

Pour 80 ml (1/3 cup) of the dressing over the greens and toss thoroughly. Arrange on 6 salad plates, and then crumble 1/2 teaspoon goat's cheese over each salad. Garnish with equal portions of the baked potato crouton, red pepper, and onion medley. Pour the remainder of the dressing into a small bowl and serve it alongside.

Cobb Salad

Whether you anticipate a summer afternoon running errands or playing on the beach, this is a salad you'll look forward to eating. It's chilled, so you can prepare all the ingredients ahead and then arrange them on plates or in a big bowl, if you prefer, at the last moment. It's especially desirable on a hot day, and has a balance of assorted vegetables plus protein-packed tarragon-flavoured chicken. You can personalise this salad to suit your own tastes by eliminating or adding ingredients. For example, if you or your guests are vegetarian, omit the chicken and eggs and replace them with Slow-Baked Tofu (page 193). If artichoke hearts and hearts of palm seem pricey, omit them.

6 skinless, boneless chicken breasts (fillets), or 225 g (8 oz) baked tofu
60 ml (1/4 cup) white wine
1 tablespoon chopped fresh tarragon or 1 teaspoon dried
3 heads chicory
1 1/2 soft-leaf lettuces, shredded
55 g (1/2 cup) grated carrots

45 g (1/2 cup) shredded red cabbage
1 x 400 g (14 oz) can artichoke hearts or 6 hearts of palm (in water, not marinade or oil), drained and sliced (optional)
6 hard-boiled eggs, sliced
1 small avocado, diced
3 tomatoes, diced

Mixed Greens with Potato Croutons and Tarragon Dressing

SERVES 6

PER SERVING:

CALORIES 401.1

FAT 21.5 G
  SATURATED FAT
  4.1 G
  (47.4% OF CALORIES FROM FAT)

PROTEIN 32.9 G

CARBOHYDRATE
  20.7 G

CHOLESTEROL
  267 MG

FIBRE 10.1 G

❊

TOFU VARIATION

PER SERVING:

CALORIES 359.3

FAT 22.7 G

SATURATED FAT
4 G

(57.6% OF CALO-
RIES FROM FAT)

PROTEIN 23.6 G

CARBOHYDRATE
22.5 G

CHOLESTEROL
216 MG

FIBRE 11 G

DRESSING

3 tablespoons finely chopped
shallots
1 teaspoon honey
60 ml (1/4 cup) freshly squeezed
lemon juice

1 teaspoon salt
1 tablespoon balsamic vinegar
60 ml (1/4 cup) red wine vinegar
60 ml (1/4 cup) olive oil
Freshly ground black pepper to
taste

Preheat oven to 200°C.

Lay the chicken breasts in a baking tin and pour in the wine. Sprinkle the tarragon over the chicken and bake for 20 minutes. The chicken should be cooked through and not pink inside. Remove from the oven and leave to cool. When cool, cube the chicken.

Break the chicory leaves off the head by trimming the root and separating the leaves. Fan 6 chicory leaves on each of 6 plates so that the leaves are pointing outwards, creating a 'star' look. Mix together the lettuce, carrots, and cabbage and put equal portions around the inside of the chicory leaves on each plate. Spoon one-sixth of the chicken into the middle. On each plate, create separate piles of equal portions of the artichoke hearts or hearts of palm, hard-boiled eggs, avocado, and tomatoes, around the chicken.

Whisk all the dressing ingredients together in a small bowl. Drizzle some of the dressing over each salad and serve.

Tips from Rosie's Kitchen

If you want to make this a low-fat recipe, use soda water instead of olive oil to thin out the dressing.

If you didn't have a chance to make the slow-baked tofu for those who don't eat eggs or chicken, provide a hit of protein using sunflower seeds. Toss 35 g (1/4 cup) of raw sunflower seeds in a sauté pan over low heat until lightly toasted, about 2 minutes at the most. Serve on the side.

Cobb Salad

GREEN BEAN SALAD

This is one of my favourite vegetable dishes, delightful in its simplicity and perfection of flavours. It is not worth making with old, tough green beans nor with runner beans. Try to get some beautiful, slender, rich-green haricot beans from your own garden, a farmers' market, or a good greengrocer. Prepare the salad a few hours ahead so the flavours can develop and blend.

SERVES 4

PER SERVING:

CALORIES 105

FAT 7 G
  SATURATED FAT
  1 G

(60% OF CALORIES
  FROM FAT)

PROTEIN 2.5 G

CARBOHYDRATE
  12 G

CHOLESTEROL
  0 MG

FIBRE 4 G

450 g (1 lb) young tender green
   beans, preferably haricot beans
2 tablespoons extra virgin olive oil
2 cloves garlic, finely chopped

2 bay leaves
Salt to taste
1 lemon, preferably organic

Bring 2 litres (2 quarts) of water to the boil.

Trim the ends off the beans, then drop beans into rapidly boiling water. Boil them, uncovered, until they are bright green and just crunchy-tender. Taste one after 5 minutes. You do not want them overcooked.

Drain the beans and cover them with cold water to stop their cooking. Drain them again thoroughly, then dry them in a tea towel and toss them in a bowl with the olive oil, garlic, bay leaf, and salt to taste.

Use a vegetable peeler to remove 4 strips of yellow zest from the lemon. Add these to the beans, toss well, and leave them to stand, covered, at room temperature for several hours until the flavours merge.

Remove and discard the bay leaf, toss well, and serve.

WHY 'ORGANIC'?

In the recipes in this book we frequently call for ingredients that are 'preferably organic'. When I use the word 'organic', I mean produced without the use of toxic agrichemicals, especially pesticides, and without synthetic fertilisers. My main concern is the toxins. As a physician, I worry that the poisons used in growing conventional fruits and vegetables undermine long-term health, especially when people suffer cumulative exposure to many different agents. I believe that research will eventually link this exposure to increased risk of chronic disease, including cancer and degenerative diseases of the nervous system.

Until recently, the word 'organic' might or might not have meant anything depending where you lived. Some countries set and enforced standards that gave meaning to the term; others did not. Now we have better organic standards, and consumers can be more confident that when a packet of grapes, for example, carries an organic label, the fruit has been grown without toxic chemicals and with natural fertilisers.

It is still the case that in many parts of the country supplies of organic produce are uncertain, making it hard to get, very expensive, or past its prime by the time it reaches the market. Given a choice between limp, yellow-green organic broccoli in a health-food shop and a fresh, bright-green conventional variety in a supermarket, I would take the latter without hesitation.

Because it is often more difficult and more costly to shop organic, it is important to know which crops are most likely to carry significant residues of pesticides. In those cases I would avoid conventional versions or minimise consumption and try to buy organic. As I mentioned earlier, I do not eat conventional strawberries because they contain methyl bromide, a known cancer-causing pesticide, applied to the soil, taken up by the plant, and impossible to wash off the fruit. Other crops to be cautious about are apricots, peaches, cherries, winter grapes imported from Chile, celery, green beans, potatoes, and spinach. I try to use only organic flour, because conventional wheat is heavily treated with agrichemicals. And I prefer organic soya beans and products made from them, such as tofu. If you use the zest of citrus fruits, as called for in several of our recipes, try to get organic oranges and lemons, because the peel is the most likely part to be contaminated. (If you can't find them, at least scrub the fruit well with a soap-and-water solution.)

As consumer demand grows, the quality and availability of organic produce are improving, and in bigger markets, prices are coming down. There is even some research documenting claims of proponents of organic agriculture that its products are more nutritious and flavourful than conventional ones. Experiment for yourself and see if you can detect differences. In any case, know that by buying organic fruits and vegetables and supporting organic agriculture you are protecting your health and the health of your family.—**A.W.**

Celery, Artichoke, Hearts of Palm, and Prawn Salad

This salad is a big hit – people are always asking me for the recipe, so here it is. I like to serve this salad all year round.

Hearts of palm, also known as palmetto, come from the stalk of a palm tree that grows in tropical climates. There aren't many salads that have both artichoke hearts and hearts of palm in them, and if it has been a while since you've eaten either, you may find yourself using them more in salads of your own creation. If you have time, steam your own artichokes (see Tips).

SERVES 6

PER SERVING:

CALORIES 279.1

FAT 11.7 G
  SATURATED FAT
  1.7 G
(37.9% OF CALO-
  RIES FROM FAT)

PROTEIN 32.4 G

CARBOHYDRATE
  10.7 G

CHOLESTEROL
  230 MG

FIBRE 2.1 G

❀

900 g (2 lb) cooked peeled medium prawns, cut into bite-sized pieces
1 x 400 g (14 oz) can artichoke hearts in water, drained and sliced
240 **g** (2 cups) chopped celery

1 x 400 g (14 oz) can hearts of palm, drained
125 g (1 cup) sliced spring onions

BASIL VINAIGRETTE DRESSING

2 tablespoons pesto (page 160)
2 tablespoons freshly squeezed
  lemon juice
2 teaspoons salt
60 ml (1/4 cup) olive oil
1 teaspoon freshly ground black
  pepper

1 tablespoon chopped fresh basil
3 large shallots, finely chopped
1 teaspoon honey
1/8 teaspoon dried chilli flakes

GARNISH

2 sprigs parsley

Mix all the salad ingredients together in a big bowl.

Mix all the dressing ingredients in a large bowl, and pour over the salad. Toss thoroughly, making sure everything is evenly coated with the dressing. Garnish with the parsley. Cover and refrigerate until ready to serve.

Tips from Rosie's Kitchen

Peel the strings off the celery stalks with a vegetable peeler. Instead of throwing out the strings, you can refrigerate them in a sealed polythene bag and use them the next time you make vegetable stock.

If you buy raw prawns, see Spanish Seafood Cocktail, Gazpacho Style (page 64), for cooking instructions.

If you want to cook your own artichokes, buy 3. Cut 5 cm (2 in) off the top of the artichokes and lay them flat side down in a steamer basket. Lower the steamer basket into a large pan and fill the pan with enough water to reach the bottom of the steamer. Cover and steam the artichokes over medium-high heat for 1 hour, adding more water if necessary. Remove from heat and cool. When completely cooled, scoop out the furry choke with a spoon and discard. Remove the leaves and set them aside. Chop the artichoke hearts. Lay the artichoke leaves out on each of 6 plates to create a base for the salad. Arrange the salad on top of the artichoke leaves and serve.

LEBANESE SALAD

This dish has a classic Mediterranean look and taste, with its combination of freshly squeezed lemon juice, olive oil, mint, garlic, and onion. Don' t even think about using Californian black olives here; they are a pathetic imitation of the real thing. (Rosie, this means you!) You can add some cubed or crumbled feta cheese and even some broken pieces of toasted wholemeal pita bread at the last minute to make this a main dish and still retain its authenticity. Remember to prepare the salad a few hours ahead so that the flavours can mingle.

2 cucumbers, peeled and diced
4 plum tomatoes, diced
1 red onion, finely chopped
60 ml (¼ cup) freshly squeezed
   lemon juice
2 tablespoons extra virgin olive oil
1 clove garlic, finely chopped
3 tablespoons chopped fresh mint
   or 1 tablespoon dried mint

35 g (¼ cup) pitted, sliced black
   olives (Kalamata or oil-cured)
135 g (1 cup) cubed or crumbled
   feta cheese (optional)
Salt and freshly ground black
   pepper to taste

SERVES 4

PER SERVING:

CALORIES 287.7

FAT 19.6 G
   SATURATED FAT
   6.7 G

(58.1% OF CALO-
   RIES FROM FAT)

PROTEIN 9.4 G

CARBOHYDRATE
   22.4 G

CHOLESTEROL
   33 MG

FIBRE 5.3 G

Toss all the ingredients together in a salad bowl, adding salt and pepper to taste.

   After the ingredients are well mixed, chill the salad for at least 3 hours before serving it.

Walnut, Apple, and Celery Salad

This is a good salad for autumn, when you want a change from leafy salads. Don't limit the dressing to just your salads; you can use it as a mayonnaise on your favourite sandwich.

230 g (2 cups) cored and cubed
  apples
Juice from 1 lemon (about
  60 ml/1/4 cup)
240 g (2 cups) sliced celery
1 x 400 g (14 oz) can hearts of
  palm, drained and sliced
65 g (1/2 cup) chopped walnuts
1 soft-leaf lettuce or red leaf
  lettuce

DRESSING

125 g (1/2 cup) plain low-fat
  yogurt
60 ml (1/4 cup) cider vinegar
1 tablespoon grainy mustard
1 tablespoon roughly chopped
  shallots
1 tablespoon pesto (page 160) or
  1 clove garlic and 1 tablespoon
  fresh basil leaves

SERVES 6

PER SERVING:

CALORIES 219.8

FAT 8 G
  SATURATED FAT
  1.3 G
(28.4% OF CALO-
  RIES FROM FAT)

PROTEIN 8 G

CARBOHYDRATE
  37.1 G

CHOLESTEROL
  5 MG

FIBRE 4.6 G

Toss the apples (immediately after cubing) with the lemon juice in a small bowl so they don't turn brown. Put the celery, hearts of palm, and walnuts in a big bowl, then mix in the apples and toss.

Put all the dressing ingredients together in a blender and blend until smooth. Pour the dressing over the salad ingredients and toss until everything is thoroughly coated. Tear 6 leaves off the lettuce and lay 1 leaf on each of 6 salad plates. Spoon equal amounts of the salad on the lettuce leaves and serve.

Tips from Rosie's Kitchen

If you'd like to use the dressing as a mayonnaise alternative in tuna salad or on sandwiches, just double the dressing ingredients and store half in a covered plastic container. This dressing also goes well with Scrambled Tofu (page 10) to make an egg-salad style sandwich.

NUTS

Nuts are totally taboo in spa cuisine, relegated to the list of off-limits ingredients, along with olives and avocados, because of their fat content. It is true that most nuts are high in fat, but in most cases it's the kind of monounsaturated fat that's best for our bodies and comes along with a number of key micronutrients, including vitamin E, trace minerals, fibre, and, in the case of walnuts, vital omega-3 fatty acids. I love nuts, eat them frequently, and also use them in my cooking. But there is information about them you need to know.

Except for chestnuts, which are best considered a starchy vegetable, and coconuts, which contain a lot of saturated fat, nuts are rich in protein as well as the best kinds of fat. (Remember that peanuts are legumes, not nuts, and have a less desirable fatty-acid profile.) The oil in nuts is good for health and often delicious in food, as long as you do not heat them. For example, both walnut and hazelnut oils are wonderful in salad dressings.

I use mostly raw, unsalted nuts, and I store them in the refrigerator until I need them. Unsaturated nut oils oxidise quickly on exposure to heat, light, and air, creating rancidity that should immediately offend your senses of smell and taste. Roasted chopped or ground nuts go rancid much more quickly than whole raw ones. In any case, smell nuts before eating them or adding them to recipes, and discard any that smell rancid. It is easy enough to toast nuts yourself as you need them by stirring them about in a dry frying pan over medium-high heat or putting them in a 180°C oven on a baking sheet and tossing them occasionally until they are done to your liking.

I use freshly ground nuts – walnuts especially – as a base for spreads and dips and often use nut milk (recipe on pages 34–5) in place of cream – in soups and desserts, for example.

If you have avoided nuts because you thought they were fattening, please renew your acquaintance with them. In moderation, nuts of good quality are a delightful component of the optimum diet.—A.W.

Warm Chicken and Asparagus Salad

There will be days when you'll just want to serve a light meal, and salads are the answer. Tossing together various herbs and greens gives you the confidence to be creative and experiment with other ingredients. Eating salads helps you get some of your greens in for the day, and eating a really, really good salad is a simple joy. If you're not convinced, this salad may change your mind.

12 baby red potatoes, cut in half
6 boneless, skinless chicken breasts (fillets) or Slow-Baked Tofu (page 193)
1/2 teaspoon freshly ground black pepper
1/2 teaspoon salt or to taste
60 ml (1/4 cup) white wine
1 tablespoon chopped fresh basil
1 tablespoon chopped parsley
1 bunch fresh asparagus
200 g (2 cups) mixed salad greens

LEMON DILL VINAIGRETTE

1 large shallot, finely chopped
2 cloves garlic, finely chopped
2 tablespoons freshly squeezed lemon juice
3 tablespoons balsamic vinegar
3 tablespoons rice vinegar
60 ml (1/4 cup) olive oil
2 tablespoons white wine
2 tablespoons chopped fresh dill
1/4 teaspoon salt or to taste

GARNISH

6 radishes, cut into rosettes

SERVES 6

PER SERVING:
CALORIES 405.6
FAT 10.8 G
 SATURATED FAT
 1.7 G
 (25.4% OF CALO-
 RIES FROM FAT)
PROTEIN 26.3 G
CARBOHYDRATE
 45.1 G
CHOLESTEROL
 51 MG
FIBRE 4.5 G

❋

Preheat oven to 170°C.

Steam the potatoes by putting them in a large pan with about 5 cm (2 in) of boiling water. Cover the pan and steam the potatoes until tender, approximately 30 minutes. Drain and transfer the potatoes to a large bowl.

Put the chicken into a baking dish, season with salt and pepper, and add the wine, basil, and parsley. Bake for 30 minutes. Make 2 diagonal slices across each chicken breast, creating 3 pieces of chicken per breast.

Meanwhile, cut 5 cm (2 in) off the bottom of each asparagus

spear and blanch the spears in a pan of boiling water, just until they are tender, about 2 minutes. Lay the asparagus on a platter and leave them to cool at room temperature. When they are cool, cut lengthways down the centre of each spear.

Whisk together thoroughly all the dressing ingredients in a large bowl.

Arrange some mixed greens on each of 6 plates and lay 6 or 7 of the halved asparagus spears on top of the lettuce, spaced apart, with the tips pointing outwards, creating a 'fan'. Lay 3 pieces of chicken between the asparagus pieces.

Pour half of the dressing over the potatoes and mix gently with a spoon so they are completely coated with the dressing. Place 4 potatoes in the centre of each asparagus arrangement and drizzle 1 tablespoon of the remaining dressing over the top. Garnish each plate with a radish rosette.

Tips from Rosie's Kitchen

When choosing asparagus, I always look for bright green, thin spears. Sometimes a bundle of thin spears will yield more asparagus than thicker spears. If you can't find good-looking asparagus, steamed green beans are a perfectly fitting alternative.

Transforming simple radishes into blooming roses sounds tough, but is in fact very simple. It's a garnish idea that you can steal for other recipes. Your guests will certainly notice them. Once they are cut, the radishes must sit in iced water for 2 hours to achieve the look of blooming flowers, so make them before you prepare the rest of the dish.

First, wash the radishes well. Using a small paring knife, cut the tops and bottoms off the radishes so both ends are flat. Following the illustrations on page 209, start at the top of the radish and make a small cut into the bulb, going in only about 5 mm (1/4 in). Make another cut, spaced a little bit apart from the first cut. Picture these cuts as 'flaps' that will spring out from the bulb when iced, to create the look of open flower petals. Continue to cut all the way around the radish, then start another row of small cuts below this first one.

Warm Chicken and Asparagus Salad

Jicama and Carrot Salad

Jicama comes from Mexico and it doesn't really taste like any other vegetable. Its white, crunchy flesh has a texture similar to an apple and it tastes somewhat like a mixture of apple and potato. Like carrots, jicama can be easily munched on alone. Pak choy is similar to celery and, like the other vegetables in this salad, has a lot of flavour and crunch. It takes no time at all to cut up some carrots, jicama, and tomatoes and mix up the dressing, so you'll probably rely on this salad a lot when you need a quick solution to a light meal.

SERVES 6

PER SERVING:

CALORIES 98.8

FAT 6.7 G
  SATURATED FAT
  0.8 G
(56.1% OF CALO-
  RIES FROM FAT)

PROTEIN 2.9 G

CARBOHYDRATE
  8.8 G

CHOLESTEROL
  0 MG

FIBRE 2.6 G

❁

20 g (1/2 cup) sunflower sprouts (optional)
2 tomatoes, diced
1/2 large jicama, peeled and grated or cut into matchsticks
2 carrots, grated or cut into matchsticks
2 heads pak choy, chopped
1 soft-leaf lettuce

DRESSING

80 ml (1/3 cup) freshly squeezed lime juice

60 ml (1/4 cup) apple juice
1 teaspoon mild chilli powder
1 teaspoon salt
2 shallots, finely chopped
2 cloves garlic, finely chopped
2 tablespoons Dijon mustard
80 ml (1/3 cup) olive oil

GARNISH (OPTIONAL)

Radish rosettes (page 209) or edible flowers (page 303)

Toss the salad ingredients together, except the lettuce, in a large bowl. In a separate bowl, whisk together the dressing ingredients thoroughly. Pour the dressing over the salad ingredients and toss well. Arrange the lettuce leaves on plates and scoop the salad onto the lettuce. If you wish, garnish with radish rosettes or edible flowers.

Tips from Rosie's Kitchen

Cutting vegetables into matchsticks, or 'julienne', adds a bit of flair to the traditional look of cut-up vegetables. Following the illustrations, first, cut the peeled jicama and carrots on the diagonal or at a slant to make thin slices. Note how you should hold your bent fingers on the vegetable so you don't risk cutting the fingertips. Now make a stack of the thin slices and cut them into thin sticks. Again note the way the hand holding the stack of vegetables has the fingers tucked under and is moved back a little after each slice.

Holding the carrot with the bent fingers of one hand so that the knuckles are flush with the blade of the knife, Rosie slices at an angle, moving her fingers back a little with each slice.

To julienne, she makes a stack of slices and cuts down at about 3 mm (1/8 in) intervals to make matchstick slices.

Soups

THE PROS AND CONS OF SALT

Salt brings out the flavours of food and is indispensable in cooking. How much to use is an important question, because taste varies from person to person, and medical authorities continue to try to convince us that salt is not good for our health.

Sodium in sodium chloride is an essential mineral, used by the body to regulate water content of tissues and normal functioning of nerves and muscles. Yet the amount we need each day is probably no more than that in a gram of table salt – about a quarter teaspoon. Most people eat much more than that, not only by way of the salt shaker but especially as a result of consuming processed foods, many of which are very high in sodium.

What happens if you eat more salt than you need? Most people probably do not have to worry. Their bodies eliminate the excess in sweat and urine. But a minority of people are salt-sensitive: too much makes them retain water, increasing blood volume and blood pressure and the workload on the heart. African-Americans and people with family histories of hypertension are more likely to be in this category.

I use salt in cooking but never add it at the table. I have learned to avoid foods with visible salt on them, preferring unsalted nuts, for example, and unsalted crisps if I eat them. I like olives and capers and Parmesan cheese and often use them in food or cooking in place of added salt. I have found it easy to change my taste away from liking very salty foods; as a result, I often find restaurant food to be oversalted.

In cooking I prefer to use high-quality sea salt or earth salt, meaning brands that are free of chemical additives. I add salt until a dish tastes right to me. Some of my guests may find my cooking undersalted; they are free to add salt at the table. No one ever complains that my cooking is oversalted.

Rosie and I both feel that most people eat too much salt, and we tend to add it to our recipes with a light hand. We specify an amount of salt to use in some. More often we tell you to put in 'salt to taste'. You can learn to like less salt by cooking as we do – using as many fresh foods and as few processed ones as possible. **—A.W.**

Rosie's Vegetable Stock

I think of stock as the gold in my refrigerator. Many of my recipes, and Andy's too, call for vegetable stock, and you'll find that your refrigerator probably holds most of what is needed to make this versatile and essential ingredient. When vegetables become wilted, don't throw them away – throw them in the cooking pot. When you are pinching leaves off coriander, basil, or parsley, keep the stalks and use them too. This is one of the most undemanding and useful recipes you will make.

2.4 litres (10 cups) purified water
220 g (2 cups) coarsely chopped carrots (about 4 carrots)
2 medium potatoes
55 g (1/2 cup) chopped parsnips
55 g (1/2 cup) chopped turnip or swede
120 g (1 cup) chopped celery (about 4 sticks)
2 medium onions with skin, quartered

4 cloves garlic
2–3 sprigs parsley
2 tablespoons salt
1–2 bay leaves
1/2 teaspoon dried thyme
1/4 teaspoon freshly ground black pepper
Pinch of cayenne pepper

MAKES ABOUT
2 LITRES (8 CUPS)

PER SERVING:

CALORIES 91.8

FAT 0.6 G

SATURATED FAT
0.1 G

(5.3% OF CALO-
RIES FROM FAT)

PROTEIN 3.7 G

CARBOHYDRATE
20.2 G

CHOLESTEROL
0 MG

FIBRE 5.4 G

Put all the ingredients in a stockpot filled with water. Bring it to the boil, then reduce the heat and simmer for 3 hours. Strain the stock through a fine sieve or colander. Store in an airtight container and refrigerate for 3 to 5 days, or freeze.

Tips from Rosie's Kitchen

Parsnips, swede, and turnips are winter root vegetables and may not be as readily available in the warmer seasons. So use mushroom stalks, courgettes, and an extra potato in the summertime. Whatever the season, you're in for a treat!

ANDY'S VEGETABLE STOCK

Vegetable dishes and soups will be much better if you make them with a vegetable stock instead of water. It is convenient to produce a quantity of stock and freeze it in batches for later use. If you have none on hand or do not have time to make your own stock, use instant vegetable bouillon powder (preferably low-sodium).

1 tablespoon extra virgin olive oil
2 leeks, white and light green parts only, well washed and chopped
4 medium onions, chopped
6 large carrots, peeled and chopped
3 sticks celery, chopped
1 small bunch parsley stalks

2 teaspoons dried marjoram
1/2 teaspoon dried thyme
3 bay leaves
5.7 litres (1 1/2 gallons) cold purified water

Heat the olive oil over medium heat in a stockpot. Add the vegetables and stir-fry to brown lightly. Add the marjoram, thyme, bay leaves, and cold water. Bring to the boil, then reduce the heat, cover, and simmer for 1 hour.

Strain the stock through a fine sieve or a muslin-lined colander. Press or squeeze the vegetables to extract their liquid. Discard the vegetables.

Use the stock as called for in recipes or chill and freeze it for later use.

MAKES ABOUT 4.8 LITRES (20 CUPS)

PER SERVING:
CALORIES 36
FAT LESS THAN 1 G
   SATURATED FAT
   0 G
   (LESS THAN 30%
   OF CALORIES
   FROM FAT)
PROTEIN LESS
   THAN 1 G
CARBOHYDRATE
   7 G
CHOLESTEROL 0 G
FIBRE 2 G

Chicken Stock

MAKES 2.9 LITRES
(12 CUPS)

PER SERVING:

CALORIES 52.1

FAT 0.6 G
    SATURATED FAT
    0.1 G
(9.8% OF CALO-
    RIESFROM FAT)

PROTEIN 5.2 G

CARBOHYDRATE
    7.9 G

CHOLESTEROL
    7 MG

FIBRE 3.6 G

Stocks are an excellent base for soups, sauces, and gravies. They are rich in flavour but not in extra calories or sodium. Any vegetables can be added to stock except cabbage, broccoli, or cauliflower, because these have a tendency to turn the stock bitter. When you make a big batch of stock, don't worry that you won't use it fast enough; it will keep for up to 2 days, covered, in the refrigerator. After 2 days, freeze it. It will keep for up to 3 months. Use it to punch up the flavour of soups or pour it over warm rice or grains, vegetables, or meat.

900 g (2 lb) chicken bones
450 g (1 lb) skinless chicken
    pieces, cubed
2 medium onions with skin,
    quartered
2 carrots, coarsely chopped
2 sticks celery, coarsely chopped

4 cloves garlic, unpeeled
6 sprigs parsley
1 teaspoon dried thyme
1–2 bay leaves
3.4–3.8 litres (14–16 cups)
    purified water

Put all the ingredients in a stockpot and bring to the boil. Reduce the heat to low and simmer for 4 hours. Strain the stock through a fine sieve and skim off any fat. Store in a covered, airtight container and refrigerate, or freeze.

MAKES ABOUT
1 LITRE (4 CUPS)

PER SERVING:

CALORIES 53.3

FAT 0.2 G
    SATURATED FAT
    0 G
(5.4% OF CALO-
    RIES FROM FAT)

PROTEIN 0.8 G

CARBOHYDRATE
    6.7 G

CHOLESTEROL
    0 MG

FIBRE 1.3 G

Fish Stock

Like Vegetable Stock or Chicken Stock you can use Fish Stock as a base for soups or sauces, or a flavouring over cooked grains or rice. It's likely that most of the ingredients called for are already in your refrigerator.

450 g (1 lb) bones and trimmings
    of any white fish, chopped
115 g (1 cup) sliced onion
120 ml (1/2 cup) dry white wine

2 tablespoons freshly squeezed
    lemon juice
1 litre (4 cups) purified water
1–2 bay leaves

Put all the ingredients in a heavy saucepan and bring to the boil. Skim the froth that collects on the surface and discard. Reduce the heat and simmer for 30 minutes. Strain the stock through a fine sieve. Pour it into an airtight container and store in the refrigerator for up to 2 days, or in the freezer for up to 3 months.

Miso Soup

This is a light yet fortifying soup made with miso, a highly nutritious food made from soya beans. Miso is rich in protein and vitamin B. Miso's colour variations are due to the amount of soya bean and salt that are used. I always use light yellow miso because it has the right amount of texture and flavour.

480 ml (2 cups) vegetable stock (page 122)
1 litre (4 1/2 cups) purified water
120 ml (1/2 cup) chopped dried wakame seaweed
1/4 package silken tofu, finely cubed

60 ml (1/4 cup) light yellow miso (soya bean paste)

GARNISH

180 ml (3/4 cup) chopped tofu
3 spring onions, chopped

SERVES 6

PER SERVING:
CALORIES 43.4
FAT 0.9 G
  SATURATED FAT 0.1 G
(6.1% OF CALORIES FROM FAT)
PROTEIN 2.9 G
CARBOHYDRATE 7.7 G
CHOLESTEROL 0 MG
FIBRE 2.1 G

❄

Bring the vegetable stock and all but 120 ml (4 fl oz) of the water to the boil in a large saucepan. Reduce the heat and simmer. Add the wakame and the tofu and continue to simmer for 5 minutes.

Mix the miso with the reserved water in a large bowl and stir it with a spoon to make a paste. Add a ladleful of soup to the miso paste and mix, then return it to the soup pan.

Ladle soup into small bowls and sprinkle 2 tablespoons of tofu and 1 tablespoon of spring onions into each bowl.

BEANS, BEANS

Beans are a superlative food – nutritious, satisfying, versatile, and inexpensive. They are full of fibre, protein, and the kind of carbohydrate you want to eat and, except for soya beans and peanuts, contain almost no fat. They provide folic acid, a B vitamin that most people do not get enough of, as well as iron for people on plant-based diets.

I much prefer to start with dried beans than to use canned ones (except for canned baked beans, which I find convenient). It is not that difficult to soak them overnight and boil them. Adding bicarbonate of soda to the water softens the skins and shortens the cooking time of larger varieties like chickpeas and kidney beans. It does not significantly lower the nutritional value. People often make the mistake of cooking beans insufficiently. They have the best flavour and texture when they are quite tender and begin to melt into the liquid. Lower the heat and keep an eye on them in the final stages, stirring frequently to avoid burning the bottom layer.

Some people object to the wind-forming properties of beans. The solution to the problem is to select varieties that contain lower amounts of the indigestible sugars that cause it. Black beans and Anasazi beans are relatively innocuous, for example, whereas pink beans and soya beans can be problematical.

Cooked beans can be turned into hearty soups, dips and spreads, salads, main-dish combinations with grains, and even desserts. (The most common Japanese sweets contain a paste of red beans mixed with sugar.) —**A.W.**

Mixed Bean Minestrone Stew

This Italian vegetable soup with pasta and beans is a great way to warm and fill you up during the cold winter months. You can always exchange other vegetables for the ones listed or leave a few out and give your minestrone your own accent. After all, the greatest soups are simply medleys of whatever's on hand in your kitchen! This Mixed Bean Minestrone Stew is an ample lunch or supper main dish with slices of Wholemeal Baguette with Sun-Dried Tomatoes and Herbs (page 255).

400 g (2 cups) mixed dried beans (haricot, kidney, and chickpeas are good)
1 teaspoon bicarbonate of soda
1 bay leaf

160 g (1 cup) chopped onions
3 carrots, peeled and sliced
120 g (1 cup) chopped celery
3 garlic cloves, sliced
60 ml (1/4 cup) olive oil
1 tablespoon Italian seasoning herbs
1/8 teaspoon dried chilli flakes
1 teaspoon dried rosemary
1 teaspoon salt
80 g (1 cup) peeled and cubed aubergine (or cabbage, pumpkin, broccoli)

720 g (4 cups) chopped fresh tomatoes, or 2 x 400 g (14 oz) cans
1 large floury potato, cubed
1.4 litres (6 cups) purified water (or vegetable stock for added flavour – and see Tips)
120 g (1 cup) chopped green beans or frozen peas
235 g (1 1/2 cups) pasta for soup or prepared barley (see Tips)

GARNISH

Fresh cracked pepper (optional)
75 g (3/4 cup) freshly grated Parmesan cheese
60 ml (1/4 cup) pesto

Soak the beans overnight in a large pan with 1.4 litres (6 cups) of water and the bicarbonate of soda. Add the bay leaf to the pan, place over medium-high heat, and boil the beans for 45 minutes until tender (they should pierce easily with a fork). Meanwhile, you can prepare the vegetables.

MAKES 12 CUPS, SERVES 6

STEW WITHOUT GARNISH

PER SERVING:
CALORIES 449
FAT 10.7 G
  SATURATED FAT 1.6 G
  (21.6% OF CALORIES FROM FAT)
PROTEIN 0 G
CARBOHYDRATE 18.2 G
CHOLESTEROL 0 MG
FIBRE 17.2 G

STEW WITH GARNISH

PER SERVING:
CALORIES 571
FAT 33.2 G
  SATURATED FAT 5.3 G
  (27.1% OF CALORIES FROM FAT)
PROTEIN 24.6 G
CARBOHYDRATE 75.4 G
CHOLESTEROL 11.8 MG
FIBRE 17.5 G

In a separate large pan, sweat the onions, carrots, celery, and garlic in the olive oil on low heat for about 10 to 15 minutes, stirring occasionally to bring out the natural vegetable juices as a base for the soup. Stir in the Italian seasoning, chilli flakes, rosemary, and salt, along with the aubergine, tomatoes, potatoes, and any other vegetables you'd like to use, then pour in the water or stock and continue to cook for 20 minutes. Add the cooked beans, green beans or peas, and pasta or cooked barley to the soup and cook on medium heat for another 15 minutes.

Serve in large soup bowls and sprinkle with fresh cracked pepper (optional) and 1 tablespoon Parmesan cheese each. Or you could add a small dollop pf pesto, if you have some on hand.

Tips from Rosie's Kitchen

This recipe uses a cooking technique known as sweating, which means cooking something over low heat in a little oil in a covered pan or the oven in order to bring out the juices without browning.

You can use the already cooked pearl barley remaining from the Cranberry Barley Tonic (page 38) along with the pasta in this recipe. For additional flavour you can use vegetable stock, if you have it on hand, instead of water. If you really want to add some flair, add 60 ml (1/4 cup) pesto to the soup right before you're ready to serve.

Cooled leftover soup should be stored in small airtight containers or ziplock bags in the freezer to make it easy to take to work. It will keep for up to 3 weeks.

COURGETTE SOUP

This is another easy, flavourful soup that can either be a first course or a main course with salad, bread, and cheese. Eat it right away; the fresh taste of the vegetables is what makes it appealing.

1 medium leek, preferably organic
450 g (1 lb) courgettes, preferably organic
2 tablespoons extra virgin olive oil
Salt and freshly ground black pepper to taste
1 litre (4 cups) vegetable stock

1 tablespoon chopped fresh marjoram or 1 teaspoon dried marjoram
2 tablespoons artichoke purée (see *Note*)

GARNISH
Freshly grated Parmesan cheese

SERVES 6

PER SERVING:
CALORIES 24
FAT 0.2 G
    SATURATED FAT
    0 G
(5.8% OF CALO-
    RIES FROM FAT)
PROTEIN 1.2 G
CARBOHYDRATE
    5.3 G
CHOLESTEROL
    0 MG
FIBRE 1.3 G

Remove the root end and green top part of the leek. Wash the white part of the leek well to remove any dirt, then chop it into fine pieces.

Wash and trim the courgettes and cut into medium-sized pieces.

Heat the olive oil in a frying pan over medium heat. Add the chopped leek and sauté it until it is translucent. Add the courgettes and sauté, stirring, until they soften, about 10 minutes. Season with salt and pepper.

Add the stock and marjoram, heat to boiling, cover, reduce heat, and boil gently for 30 minutes. Add the artichoke purée and mix well.

Pour the soup into a food processor and process into a coarse purée. Serve the soup in warm bowls with freshly grated Parmesan cheese to garnish.

Note: Artichoke purée is available in delis and other speciality food shops. You can also make your own simply by draining a jar of water-packed baby artichokes and grinding them in a blender or food processor. Store any leftover purée in the refrigerator and use it as a base for a pasta sauce or a dip for raw vegetables.

Clam Chowder

The two types of clam chowder are Manhattan clam chowder, using tomatoes, and New England, using milk and cream. It is simply a matter of taste as to which one you choose to make. Ideally, clam chowder should be made with fresh clams, but you also can make it with canned clams.

160 g (1 cup) chopped onions
2 cloves garlic, chopped
1 tablespoon butter or olive oil
60 g (1/2 cup) chopped celery
1 teaspoon dried thyme
30 g (1/4 cup) unbleached plain flour
720 ml (3 cups) purified water
225 g (11/2 cups) peeled, cubed potatoes
480 ml (2 cups) half cream *or* 360 g (2 cups) chopped fresh tomatoes

900 g (2 lb) fresh clams or mussels or 1 x 400 g (14 oz) can minced clams
360 ml (11/2 cups) white wine
1 teaspoon Worcestershire sauce
1/8 teaspoon Tabasco sauce (optional)
1/4 teaspoon freshly ground black pepper

GARNISH

2 tablespoons chopped parsley

Put the onions, garlic, and butter or olive oil in a big, heavy pan. Sauté on low heat for 2 minutes. Add the celery and thyme and cook for 3 minutes, stirring occasionally. Sprinkle the flour on top of the vegetables. Pour the water in slowly and use a whisk to break up the clumps of flour. Add the potatoes, then turn up the heat to medium-high until mixture comes to the boil. Boil for 10 minutes, then turn down the heat.

Add the half cream or tomatoes, depending on which style chowder you are making. Simmer, covered, for 20 minutes or until the potatoes are cooked completely.

Meanwhile, if you are using fresh shellfish, soak the clams or mussels in a large basin of cold water for 5 minutes. Scrub the shells with a vegetable scrubber or the abrasive side of a clean

Manhattan Clam Chowder

SERVES 6

MANHATTAN CLAM CHOWDER

PER SERVING:
CALORIES 268.3
FAT 4.2 G
  SATURATED FAT 0.5 G
(16.4% OF CALORIESFROM FAT)
PROTEIN 22.4 G
CARBOHYDRATE 25.9 G
CHOLESTEROL 51 MG
FIBRE 2.7 G

❀

NEW ENGLAND CLAM CHOWDER

PER SERVING:
CALORIES 449.9
FAT 23.9 G
  SATURATED FAT 12.9 G
(52% OF CALORIES FROM FAT)
PROTEIN 23.8 G
CARBOHYDRATE 25.9 G
CHOLESTEROL 121 MG
FIBRE 21 G

sponge to remove any seaweed or mud. Put the clams or mussels and the wine in a large, lidded pan with enough space to hold them without them being cramped. Steam until the shellfish open up, about 10 minutes. Discard any shellfish that remain closed. Take the shellfish out of the pot and reserve the cooking liquid. Remove the clams from their shells, setting aside a few to garnish each bowl, if you wish, and add the clam meat and the reserved liquid to the rest of the soup. Cook the soup for an additional 5 minutes. Season with the Worcestershire sauce, Tabasco sauce, and black pepper. Garnish with fresh parsley and (optional) clams in their shells.

Tips from Rosie's Kitchen

In almost every American fishing town, local restaurants serve a fish stew special. It usually is a chowder-based soup made with a fresh, white fish, such as halibut. The addition of fresh fish to clam chowder is optional, though it adds a mild, yet richer, fish taste. With or without the fresh fish, this is a full-bodied soup.

BLACK BEAN SOUP

Black bean soup is a staple of Mexican and Caribbean cuisines. It turns up in many different versions that vary in texture and spicing. With coriander and chillies, this recipe has an authentic Latin American character. If you wish, you can garnish it with low-fat soured cream or reduced-fat crème fraîche, finely chopped sweet onions, or a bit of grated cheese, such as a mature Cheddar.

340 g (2 cups) dried black beans
2.9 litres (12 cups) purified water
2–4 large cloves garlic, peeled and mashed
Salt to taste
2 tablespoons extra virgin olive oil
1 medium onion, chopped

2 large, mild green chillies, such as anchos or Anaheims, seeded and chopped
2 hot green chillies, seeded and chopped
60 g (1 cup) chopped fresh coriander

SERVES 8

PER SERVING:

CALORIES 287

FAT 5.5 G
    SATURATED FAT
    1 G
(17% OF CALO-
    RIES FROM FAT)

PROTEIN 15 G

CARBOHYDRATE
    46.5 G

CHOLESTEROL
    0 G

FIBRE 11 G

Pick over the beans to remove any foreign objects. Wash and drain the beans and place them in a large pan with the cold water. Bring to the boil, and continue boiling for 3 minutes. Stir well, then cover, remove from the heat, and leave to soak for 1 hour.

Return the beans to the boil, then reduce the heat, cover, and simmer gently, stirring occasionally, until they are tender, about 2 hours. Add the garlic and leave to cool for 30 minutes.

Transfer the beans, in batches, to a food processor and process them into a coarse purée – don't overdo. The mixture should still have texture. Return the purée to the pan and add salt to taste. If the soup seems too thick, add water until the consistency is to your liking.

Heat the olive oil in a frying pan over medium-high heat, add the onions and chillies, and sauté, stirring frequently, until the vegetables are softened and the onions are beginning to colour, about 10 minutes.

Add the sautéed onions and chillies to the beans and heat the soup to the simmer. Simmer for 15 minutes. Add the chopped coriander, cook for a few minutes more, and serve in warm bowls.

Cold Cucumber Soup

Early summer, when cucumbers are cheap and plentiful, is the best time to make this soup. It is so easy that you'll be making it a lot on warm afternoons or when you feel you want to eat something less than a complete meal. When I have guests for a late-evening meal, I serve this soup, along with Steamed Alaskan Crab Legs (page 65), and mixed salad greens, because it is so light. The crab legs and the salad round out the meal.

You can make this soup ahead of time and chill it, covered, in the refrigerator until ready to use.

SERVES 6

PER SERVING:

CALORIES 168.3

FAT 3.7 G
  SATURATED FAT
  1.9 G
(18.1% OF CALO-
  RIES FROM FAT)

PROTEIN 7.9 G

CARBOHYDRATE
  29.8 G

CHOLESTEROL
  11 MG

FIBRE 6.1 G

3 leeks, washed and sliced into
  rounds
480 ml (2 cups) vegetable stock
  (page 122)
480 ml (2 cups) milk
6 cucumbers, peeled, sliced, and
  seeded
3 tablespoons chopped fresh dill
1 tablespoon freshly squeezed
  lemon juice
2 tablespoons chopped spring

onions or chives
1 teaspoon salt
1 teaspoon freshly ground black
  pepper

GARNISH

Mock Soured Cream (page 62), or
  low-fat soured cream or
  reduced-fat crème fraîche
2 tablespoons capers

Cook the leeks in the stock in a large saucepan for 10 minutes. Add the milk and cucumbers. Pour small batches at a time into a blender and purée until smooth. Add the dill, lemon juice, spring onions or chives, salt, and pepper. Stir once or twice. Chill, covered, in the refrigerator for 3 hours. Pour into 6 bowls, garnish each with a dollop of Mock Soured Cream, and sprinkle a few capers on top.

Tips from Rosie's Kitchen

If you want to cut down on the fat from the milk, use skimmed milk instead.

ESCAROLE SOUP

This almost-instant soup couldn't be easier. The Parmesan cheese is indispensable for giving the soup body and flavour. I use a good-quality powdered vegetable bouillon if I do not have any stock on hand. The soup should be served and eaten as soon as it is made; it does not keep.

1 head escarole
1 litre (4 cups) vegetable stock
   (page 123)
1 tablespoon extra virgin olive oil
Salt and freshly ground black
   pepper to taste

GARNISH
100 g (1 cup) freshly grated
   Parmesan cheese

Trim the escarole, removing and discarding the outer leaves. Wash it, shake it dry, and chop it coarsely.

Bring the stock to the boil in a large saucepan. Stir in the olive oil and season to taste with salt and black pepper. Add the escarole to the stock. Mix well, and remove from the heat.

Serve immediately in warm bowls with freshly ground pepper and the grated Parmesan cheese.

SERVES 4

PER SERVING:
CALORIES 173
FAT 9.4 G
   SATURATED FAT
   4 G
(48% OF CALO-
   RIES FROM FAT)
PROTEIN 20 G
CARBOHYDRATE
   3 G
CHOLESTEROL
   16 MG
FIBRE 3.5 G

Mexican Chicken Soup

SERVES 6

PER SERVING:

CALORIES 486

FAT 15.2 G
   SATURATED FAT
   2.7 G

(28.2% OF CALO-
RIES FROM FAT)

PROTEIN 8.9 G

CARBOHYDRATE
25.2 G

CHOLESTEROL
24.4 MG

FIBRE 7.1 G

❋

I find the smell of this soup alone soothing. I love the scent and flavour of thyme, and it is prominent here. I also love to taste the Spanish rice with every bite. Nurture yourself with this soup when you've come down with a cold. It makes you feel nourished, and it's just the right amount of food.

SPANISH RICE

1 tablespoon olive oil
40 g (1/4 cup) chopped onion
30 g (1/4 cup) chopped celery
30 g (1/4 cup) chopped carrots
180 g (1 cup) chopped tomatoes
1/8 teaspoon cayenne pepper
1 tablespoon paprika
280 g (11/2 cups) brown rice
720 ml (3 cups) chicken stock
   (page 124) or vegetable stock
   (page 122)
1/2 teaspoon salt

SOUP

160 g (1 cup) chopped onions

110 g (1 cup) cubed carrots
120 g (1 cup) chopped celery
3 tablespoons olive oil
2 litres (8 cups) chicken stock
150 g (1 cup) cubed potatoes
1/4 teaspoon dried thyme
1 bay leaf
1 tablespoon salt
2 boneless, skinless chicken
   breasts (fillets), cubed
3 sweetcorn cobs, cut in half

GARNISH

180 ml (3/4 cup) Salsa (page ■■)
1 ripe avocado, cubed

To make the rice: heat the olive oil in a big saucepan over low heat, add the onions, celery, carrots, and tomatoes, and sauté, stirring, for 3 minutes. Add the spices, rice, stock, and salt. Cover and bring to the boil, then reduce heat and simmer, covered, for 45 minutes.

To make the soup: put the onions, carrots, and celery in the olive oil in a large sauté pan. Cook over low heat until they become limp. Add the stock, potatoes, thyme, bay leaf, and salt and bring to the boil. Reduce heat and simmer, covered, for 30 minutes. Add the chicken. Cook for 15 more minutes and add the sweetcorn. Continue to cook for 5 more minutes.

Put 2 tablespoons of rice into each of 6 soup bowls. Ladle the soup into each bowl along with 1/2 cob of sweetcorn. Garnish with 2 tablespoons of salsa and 1 tablespoon of avocado.

BARLEY AND VEGETABLE SOUP

Barley is a grain that is unfamiliar to some of us. The round, chewy kernels are delightful in soup, especially in a well-flavoured vegetable broth. Barley and mushrooms are used together in many dishes from central and eastern Europe.

150 g (3/4 cup) pearl barley
2.6 litres (11 cups) vegetable stock
   (page 123)
3 tablespoons extra virgin olive oil
240 g (1 1/2 cups) chopped onions
110 g (1 cup) chopped carrot
70 g (1 cup) mushrooms (shiitake,
   chestnut, or button), thinly sliced

60 g (1/2 cup) chopped celery
Salt and freshly ground black
   pepper to taste
120 ml (1/2 cup) dry sherry or
   vermouth

GARNISH

15 g (1/4 cup) chopped fresh parsley

Rinse the barley and place it in a saucepan with 720 ml (3 cups) of the stock and a pinch of salt. Bring to the boil, then reduce heat, cover, and simmer until the liquid is absorbed, about 1 hour. Remove from the heat and fluff the barley with a fork.

Meanwhile, heat the olive oil over medium heat in a large pan and add the onions, carrots, mushrooms, and celery. Cook the vegetables for 5 minutes, stirring constantly, until they begin to soften.

Add the remaining stock and salt and pepper to taste, and bring to the boil. Reduce heat, cover, and simmer for 30 minutes.

Add the cooked barley and sherry or vermouth, mix well, and simmer for 5 minutes more. Correct the seasoning. Garnish with the chopped parsley.

SERVES 8

PER SERVING:

CALORIES 331

FAT 7 G
   SATURATED FAT
   1 G
   (19% OF CALO-
   RIES FROM FAT)
PROTEIN 25 G
CARBOHYDRATE
   39 G
CHOLESTEROL
   0 MG
FIBRE 13 G

Brown Rice Soup with Asparagus

This soup is chunky and thick with vegetables and rice so it can stand on its own with no real need for a side dish. And it's healthy. I serve soups with a warm baguette.

140 g (3/4 cup) brown rice
40 g (1/4 cup) wild rice
2 teaspoons salt or to taste
1 bunch asparagus
1 tablespoon olive oil
2 celery sticks, finely chopped
1/2 onion, finely chopped
1 small carrot, finely chopped
1/2 teaspoon dried thyme
1.4 litres (6 cups) vegetable stock (page 122)
2 tablespoons finely chopped spring onions

1 tablespoon chopped fresh parsley
1 tablespoon natural soy sauce (such as tamari)
1/2 teaspoon Tabasco sauce
Freshly ground black pepper (to taste)

GARNISH
Parsley sprigs

Put the rice with the salt in 720 ml (3 cups) of water in a medium saucepan. Bring it to the boil, then reduce the heat, cover, and simmer until the rice is tender and the water is absorbed, about 45 minutes.

Trim the tough ends off the asparagus spears and discard. Steam the asparagus until tender yet crisp, about 2 minutes. Drain it in a colander, then rinse under cold water. Leave the asparagus to cool for a few minutes. When completely cooled, cut into 2.5 cm (1 in) pieces, reserving the tips for garnish.

Coat the bottom of a large pan with the olive oil. Add the celery, onion, carrot, and thyme. Cover and cook over low heat for 4 minutes, stirring occasionally, until tender. Add the vegetable stock and cooked rice and bring to the boil. Reduce the heat, cover, and simmer for 10 minutes. Remove from the heat and allow to cool a bit.

Carefully transfer small batches to a blender and blend until smooth. Return all the blended mixture to a clean pan. Stir in the asparagus, spring onions, parsley, soy sauce, Tabasco sauce, and ground pepper. Return to a simmer for 2 minutes. Ladle into bowls and garnish with the reserved asparagus tips and parsley sprigs.

Tips from Rosie's Kitchen

I usually use a combination of wild rice and brown rice for this soup. It is sold together and you can find it at most super-markets, or mix your own. You may discover that you have some rice on the shelf that you haven't cooked yet and making this soup gives you an opportunity to use it up. If you want to use only brown rice, cook 185 g (1 cup) rice in 480 ml (2 cups) of water with 1 tablespoon of salt and olive oil, for 45 minutes. Or you can use leftover cooked rice (you'll need about 290 g/2 cups; just skip the first step of the recipe in that case).

If asparagus is out of season, or if you don't want to use it, you can substitute broccoli and make this soup a year-round favourite.

TOMATO, SWEETCORN, AND BASIL SOUP

Normally, I would have thought of this as a soup for summer, when you can get wonderful fresh sweetcorn and tomatoes. But I am very impressed with the quality of the new frozen supersweet corn, and I find canned, organic tomatoes to be very flavourful and convenient. So as long as you can get fresh basil, you can make this satisfying soup any time of year. It is very easy to make.

SERVES 4

PER SERVING:

CALORIES 191

FAT 8 G
  SATURATED FAT
  1 G
(38% OF CALO-
  RIES FROM FAT)

PROTEIN 5 G

CARBOHYDRATE
  31 G

CHOLESTEROL 0 MG

FIBRE 4 G

235 g (1 cup) finely chopped onion
2 tablespoons extra virgin olive oil
3–4 cloves garlic, finely chopped
800 g (28 oz) tomato passata, preferably organic
240 ml (1 cup) purified water

480 g (3 cups) fresh sweetcorn kernels cut from the cob, or 450 g (1 lb) frozen sweetcorn
Salt and freshly ground black pepper to taste
60 g (1 cup) chopped fresh basil

Sauté the onions in the olive oil in a saucepan over medium-high heat until they just begin to brown. Add the garlic and sauté for a minute, stirring constantly. Pour in the tomatoes and cook, stirring occasionally, until they give up their juice. Cover and continue cooking about 5 minutes more.

Add the water and sweetcorn to the soup and cook until the sweetcorn is soft and the kernels lose their raw taste, about 5 minutes. Season to taste with salt and pepper. Stir in the basil, mix well, remove from heat, and serve immediately.

CHICKPEA SOUP

This is a hearty soup that could be the centrepiece of a meal when combined with a salad and some good, grainy bread. It provides protein, healthful carbohydrate, fibre, and other micronutrients associated with pulses. The crispy onions provide a great flavour and texture complement to the smooth richness of the soup.

450 g (1 lb) dried chickpeas
2 litres (8 cups) cold purified water
2 teaspoons bicarbonate of soda
Salt and freshly ground pepper to
    taste
1 large onion, coarsely chopped
2 tablespoons extra virgin olive oil
4 cloves garlic, finely chopped
1½ tablespoons ground cumin
1½ tablespoons ground coriander
1½ teaspoons ground allspice

GARNISH

1 medium onion, sliced
1 teaspoon extra virgin olive oil
15 g (¼ cup) chopped fresh parsley

SERVES 8

PER SERVING:

CALORIES 265.7

FAT 7.9 G
    SATURATED FAT
    0.9 G
    (25.7% OF CALO-
    RIES FROM FAT)

PROTEIN 11.8 G

CARBOHYDRATE
    39.4 G

CHOLESTEROL 0 MG

FIBRE 10.6 G

❈

Wash and drain the chickpeas and put them in a large pan with the cold water. Stir the bicarbonate of soda into the water. Leave to soak at room temperature for 8 hours or overnight.

Bring the chickpeas in their soaking water to the boil over high heat. Skim off the first batch of foam that accumulates, stir well, then reduce heat, cover, and boil gently until the chickpeas are tender, about 45 minutes.

Preheat oven to 120°C.

Meanwhile, prepare the garnish: toss the sliced onion with the 1 teaspoon of olive oil and season them with salt and pepper. Place the onion slices on a non-stick baking sheet, making sure they are separated as much as possible, and bake until lightly browned, about 45 minutes. Remove and set aside.

Sauté the chopped onions in the 2 tablespoons of olive oil on medium heat, stirring frequently, until the onions are translucent. Add the garlic and sauté, stirring, for another minute. Add the cumin, coriander, allspice, and black pepper to taste. Stir-fry the mixture for another minute, then add it to the chickpeas, mixing well.

Simmer the chickpeas, covered, for 20 minutes. Working in batches, ladle out the chickpeas with their cooking liquid into a food processor and process into a smooth purée. Return the purée to a pot and add salt to taste. Bring it to a simmer. Correct the seasoning and serve the soup in warm bowls. Garnish with the crisp onions and chopped parsley.

ROASTED BUTTERNUT SQUASH AND APPLE SOUP

I think this rich soup is a show-stopper. See if conversation doesn't come to a halt when people taste it at your table. Roasting brings out a striking depth of flavour in the squash, and the combination with apples and onions is irresistible. The Coriander Walnut Pesto puts it over the top. I dream about this soup. And you will be delighted to find how easy it is to make. You get all sorts of goodies here: antioxidant carotenes from the squash, omega-3 fatty acids from the walnuts, and plenty of vitamins, minerals, and fibre.

SERVES 4

PER SERVING:

CALORIES 274

FAT 8 G
   SATURATED FAT
   1 G
(26% OF CALORIES
   FROM FAT)

PROTEIN 17 G

CARBOHYDRATE
   40 G

CHOLESTEROL 0 MG

FIBRE 11G

1 large butternut or kabocha squash (about 1.1 kg/2¹/2 lb), peeled, seeded, and cut into 5 cm (2 in) pieces
2 medium onions, peeled and quartered
3 cloves garlic, peeled
2 tart, firm apples, peeled, cored, and quartered
2 tablespoons extra virgin olive oil
Salt and mild chilli powder to taste
1–1.2 litres (4–5 cups) vegetable stock (page 123)

Preheat oven to 200°C.

In a large roasting tin, toss the squash, onions, garlic, and apples with the oil to coat. Season well with the salt and chilli powder. Roast, stirring every 10 minutes, until the vegetables are fork-tender and lightly browned, about 40 minutes.

Put half of the vegetables with 480 ml (2 cups) of the stock in a food processor and purée until smooth. Repeat with the remaining vegetables and stock. Return puréed mixture to the pan. If the soup is too thick, add more stock. Correct the seasoning and heat to a simmer.

Serve in warm bowls with dollops of Coriander Walnut Pesto (page 144).

Roasted Butternut Squash and Apple Soup

CORIANDER WALNUT PESTO

SERVES 16

PER SERVING:

CALORIES 50

FAT 4.7 G
 SATURATED FAT
 0.4 G

(84.2% OF CALORIES
 FROM FAT)

PROTEIN 1.2 G

CARBOHYDRATE
 1.7 G

CHOLESTEROL
 0 MG

FIBRE LESS THAN
 1 G

125 g (1 cup) walnut pieces
90 g (2 cups) coriander leaves,
  stalks removed
1 green chilli, seeded and chopped
1/2 teaspoon salt, or to taste

1 tablespoon cider vinegar
60 ml (1/4 cup) purified water
  (approximate)

Put the walnuts in a food processor and grind them until fine. Add the coriander, chilli, salt, vinegar, and 2–3 tablespoons of water and blend. Blend in a little more water if necessary to make a thick sauce. Taste and correct the seasoning, adding more salt if necessary.

Keep any leftover pesto in the refrigerator in a tightly covered container and use as a dip or spread.

DIETARY SUPPLEMENTS

Millions of people take dietary supplements. Sales of vitamins, minerals, and related products are in the billions of dollars. Is it really necessary to take them? Shouldn't your diet provide you with everything your body needs?

Ideally, yes. If we all ate high-quality fresh foods prepared in healthful ways and, especially, got a variety of fruits and vegetables at every meal, our nutritional needs would be satisfied and there would be no need to supplement. But that's not the case for most of us. I'm not always in control of my diet. When I travel, for example, I am rarely able to eat optimally. Furthermore, some dietary supplements may offer specific preventive or therapeutic benefits that are worth considering.

A common mistake is to think that supplements are substitutes for whole foods, that taking a multivitamin makes up for not eating fruits and vegetables, for example. That is not the case. Whole foods contain large arrays of compounds beneficial to health; pills provide a limited selection of them. For example, we know that foods containing beta-carotene, the principal member of the carotenoid family of pigments that give colour to yellow and orange fruits and vegetables and also occur (less visibly) in dark, leafy greens, are highly cancer-protective. Many people assume that taking isolated beta-carotene in pill form gives the same protection. It does not. In fact, evidence suggests that supplemental beta-carotene may actually raise cancer risks in some people (smokers, for example). It is the whole family of carotenoids, taken together, that does the trick. Some supplements now contain mixed carotenoids; still, they do not provide the whole spectrum of these pigments in the same balance that nature does, and I would not count on them as substitutes for the natural sources.

A better way to think of supplementation is as insurance against gaps in the diet, to compensate on those occasions when your intake of micronutrients is less than ideal, or to provide for increased needs that result from stress or exposure to environmental toxins.

I take a multivitamin and multimineral supplement every day because I want to be sure I'm getting enough folic acid and vitamin E. Folic acid, a B vitamin that occurs in beans, leafy greens, and orange juice, regulates many metabolic reactions and many of us do not get enough of it – deficiency of it can raise risks of many chronic diseases, including heart disease and cancer. There is also some evidence that the body can use supplemental folic acid even better than some of the food sources of it. I recommend taking 400 microgrammes a day in addition to whatever you may be getting from your diet. As for vitamin E, studies indicate that 400 to 800 international units a day gives maximum antioxidant protection. To get that amount from food, you would have to eat 450 g (1 lb) or so of nuts and seeds, taking in much too much fat in the bargain. My multivitamin provides 400 IU of the natural form of vitamin E, which I prefer.

My bottom line is this: I make an effort to eat an optimum diet, and for the most part I eat the kinds of food described in this book. I do not go overboard on supplements, but I use some of them judiciously to cover those days when I may not be getting all the micronutrients I need to maintain optimum health.

—A.W.

Main Dishes

Savoury Roasted Poussins with Roasted Garlic

Cold Vegetable Pasta Primavera

Linguine with Steamed Clams and Mussels

White Beans and Fusilli

Aubergine Rollatini with Spinach and Cheese Filling

Vegetable Lasagne

Roasted Pepper Turkey with Orange Liqueur

Savoury Lobster and Mushroom Crêpes

Fish with Spinach *en Papillote*

Grilled Fresh Sardines

Seared Salmon with Orange Glaze

Grilled Tuna with Coriander Ginger Sauce

Duxelles-Stuffed Sole

Grilled Salmon with Mustard Sauce

Lemon Baked Halibut

Grilled Fish with Tropical Relish

Baked Curried Sea Bass with Lentils

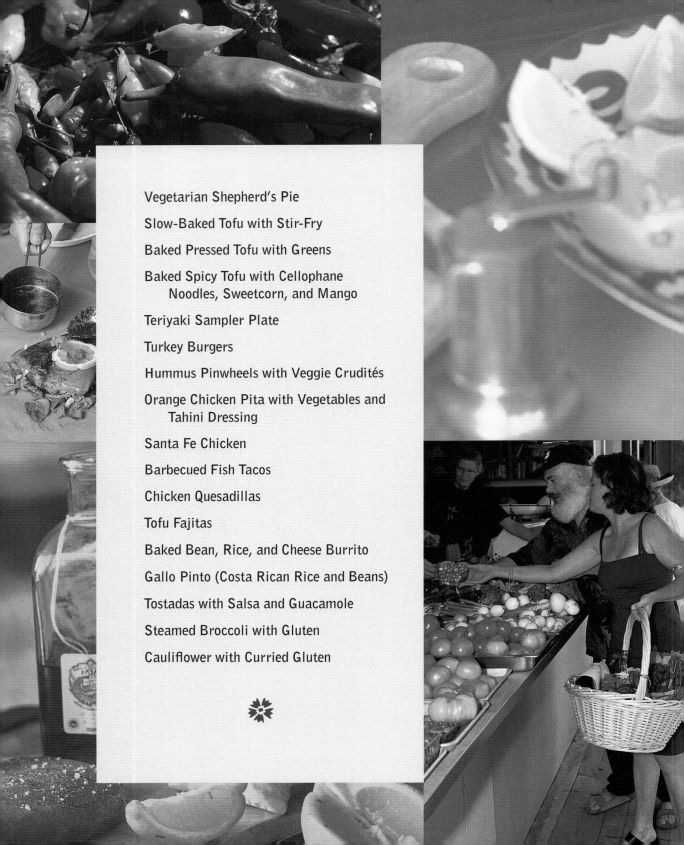

MEAT AND MEAT SUBSTITUTES

This book does not have any recipes for red meat but does have several that call for tofu and gluten, which some people think of as meat substitutes. Rosie and I avoid red meat for a number of reasons, primarily because of concerns for our health and the health of the planet. Meat certainly provides protein that the body can easily use, but it also gives us a great deal of saturated fat and toxins. The toxins represent pollutants in the environment that large animals tend to concentrate in their tissues as well as residues of drugs and hormones used in the commercial raising of animals for food. If you do eat meat, we recommend that you try to use drug-and-hormone-free, organically raised products. Even so, we worry that the large-scale raising of animals for food is terribly wasteful of resources – the grain they consume would be much better used to feed people directly. And our methods of raising them cause serious pollution of groundwater, soil, and the atmosphere.

Epidemiological studies consistently reveal that populations that eat more meat have decreased longevity and poorer health than populations that eat less. The impact of meat eating on cardiovascular health may account for much of the difference. People who eat less meat also tend to eat more fish and vegetables, which have beneficial effects on health. Neither Rosie nor I am a militant vegetarian. I eat fish, and Rosie likes to cook with chicken. But we both want to demonstrate the possibilities for creating satisfying main dishes without using meat.

Many vegetarians eat less-than-optimum diets. They eat a lot of macaroni cheese or meatless lasagne, for example, which are high in fat and low in many of the nutrients we need. They would do better to explore the range of vegetarian dishes from ethnic cuisines, such as those of India, China, South-east Asia, and the Middle East.

Some vegetarians – to the puzzlement of others –gravitate towards imitations of familiar dishes: veggie burgers and veggie sausages, for example, or even 'tofurkeys', which are holiday tofu roasts complete with stuffing and gravy. Actually, the tradition of 'facsimile food' has a long history in the Buddhist temple cuisine of China and Japan, where monks developed meat substitutes that enabled them to copy classic dishes without violating their religious beliefs. There are Chinese restaurants today that serve these creations: everything from sweet-and-sour 'pork' to Peking 'duck', all made without animal products.

The meat-like proteins used in these dishes are ingenious derivatives of soya beans and wheat. For example, the skin that forms on the surface of a pan of soya milk can be dried, soaked, and deep-fried to produce a tasty facsimile of the crisp skin of a roasted duck or chicken. A flour-and-water dough can be kneaded under water until all the starch washes out, leaving the pure wheat protein – gluten. Gluten is a rubbery, neutral-tasting product that can be flavoured, then braised, baked, or fried to yield a range of tasty, chewy morsels that closely reproduce the qualities of meat in stir-fries and stews.

We have given some examples of this kind of cooking in these pages – recipes using baked tofu and prepared gluten. Try them to see if you like these meat substitutes as much as we do. I prefer to think of them not as substitutes but rather as delicious foods in their own right that extend the range of creative possibilities in the kitchen. Whether you come to use them or not, it is worth knowing how to turn out meatless dishes that are good enough not to leave guests wondering when the main course is coming. —A.W.

Savoury Roasted Poussins with Roasted Garlic

Poussins are small, baby chickens. Try to get free-range poussins, if possible. These are raised with room to move about both indoors and outdoors as opposed to being raised in a cage. If organically reared, they will be free of growth hormones and antibiotics. Because of this some people believe organic birds have a richer flavour.

The roasted garlic head tastes wonderful squeezed onto slices of crusty French bread, making a good accompaniment to the poultry. Or you could squeeze the bulbs over Mashed Potatoes and Parsnips (page 231) and serve this alongside.

*Savoury Roasted Poussins with
Roasted Garlic*

SERVES 8

PER SERVING:

CALORIES 376.1

FAT 14.4 G
 SATURATED FAT
 4.2 G

(35.4% OF CALO-
 RIES FROM FAT)

PROTEIN 30.8 G

CARBOHYDRATE
 28.2 G

CHOLESTEROL
 153 MG

FIBRE 2.5 G

4 poussins, preferably free-range
 and organic
120 ml (1/2 cup) freshly squeezed
 lemon juice
4 teaspoons lemon pepper
Salt
700 g (4 cups) quartered plum
 tomatoes or whole cherry
 tomatoes
8 large shallots, quartered
4 large cloves garlic, peeled and
 left whole
1 small bulb fennel, chopped
1/2 teaspoon salt
30 g (1/2 cup) chopped fresh basil
240 ml (1 cup) red wine
4 bay leaves
4 lemon slices
4 sprigs fresh rosemary

ROASTED GARLIC

8 whole garlic bulbs
1 teaspoon olive oil
3 tablespoons water

GARNISH

8 sprigs fresh rosemary
1 lemon, cut into 8 slices

Rinse the poussins thoroughly, letting the water gush inside each cavity and drain back out. Rub the lemon juice, lemon pepper, and a little salt over the birds and leave to marinate for 1 hour or overnight. Put the tomatoes, shallots, garlic, fennel, a pinch of salt, the basil, and red wine together in a medium bowl and stir until everything is thoroughly mixed.

Preheat oven to 190°C.

Place 1 bay leaf, 1 lemon slice, 1 rosemary sprig, and equal portions of the tomato mixture inside each poussin. Each cavity should be full. Spoon the remaining mixture over the bottom of a roasting tin. Set the birds on top, spacing them evenly apart, spoon the lemon marinating juice over them, then sprinkle a little salt over them. Roast for 11/4 hours. The skins will be golden brown, and the juices will run clear when they are done.

Meanwhile, prepare the roasted garlic: Cut 1 cm (1/2 in) off the top of each garlic bulb so that the cloves can be easily squeezed out after roasting. Put the olive oil and water in the bottom of a 23 cm (9 in) baking tin. Arrange the garlic bulbs in the pan, cut side up. Cover the tin with a lid or foil. After the poussins have been roasting for 30 minutes, place the garlic dish in the oven and bake for 45 minutes.

Remove the poussins from the oven to a platter or board and allow them to rest at room temperature for 15 minutes. When they are cool, scoop the filling out of them and put it into the roasting tin with the remaining filling. Remove all the bay leaves and discard. Set the tin over low heat and simmer, stirring and scraping up the browned bits, for 3–4 minutes.

Split each poussin in half by cutting directly down the middle of the spine, slicing completely through to the other side. If you wish, remove and discard the skins. Place all the poussins on a serving dish, or half a poussin on each of 8 plates, with the breasts lying flat, and spoon the warm filling on top. You can put everything in the oven for a couple of minutes to keep warm until ready to serve. Garnish with a sprig of rosemary and a slice of lemon. Serve with slices of warm crusty bread to squeeze the roasted garlic onto.

Tips from Rosie's Kitchen

If you have time, marinate the poussins in the lemon juice, pepper, and salt overnight. It is worth it, because the flavours of the marinade are sealed into the meat, and then baked in it, along with the meat's own juices. What you get is juicier and more flavourful meat. Just stuff the birds as directed, put them in a large dish, cover, and refrigerate.

If you want to remove the bones of the poussins before serving, open the cavity slightly and pull them out gently. Discard the bones and repeat this process for the remaining 3 hens. I usually pull the bones out, but if you find this to be a hassle, leave them in.

Polenta (page 76) is also a great accompaniment to this dish. Spoon the hot polenta onto individual serving plates, top with a poussin half, and serve immediately.

GARLIC

For centuries, people have esteemed garlic as a remedy as well as a powerful flavouring agent; some even claim it's an aphrodisiac. Chinese cooks add garlic to dishes as much for its health benefits as for its taste; doctors in the West are just starting to learn about those benefits. Garlic not only lowers blood pressure and cholesterol, it also thins the blood (reducing risk of heart attack) and counteracts the growth of yeast and many kinds of bacteria. It's hard for me to imagine cooking without garlic. If I smell it in a kitchen, I feel right at home.

When you buy garlic, look for heads that are plump and firm, not dry or shrunken. Big cloves are easier to deal with than little ones. There are many ways of preparing the cloves, from smashing them with the broad side of a knife to putting them through a garlic press. However you do it, be aware that the medicinal virtues of garlic develop only when the flesh is exposed to air and dissipate under the influence of heat. When garlic is cut or crushed, an oxidation reaction quickly turns an inactive precursor into allicin, the main compound responsible for the medicinal properties. Allicin also creates much of garlic's pungency. Cooking tames that quality and also destroys much of the therapeutic effect. Therefore, to get the maximum benefit, let finely chopped or crushed garlic stand for a few minutes before adding it to food, use some raw (as in salad dressings), and add it near the end of cooking when possible to preserve allicin content. (Baked garlic, recently popular as a starter to be eaten with bread or with bread and cheese, is not the best way to get real garlic flavour and power.)

Some people are afraid of garlic because they think it will make them smell bad to others. I have never minded that smell, and I have also found that by starting with small amounts of garlic, eating it regularly, and gradually working up, most people can learn to digest it without problems of breath or body odour. If you are timid about garlic, I urge you to make friends with it. For me, food without it is so drab. —**A.W.**

ABOUT SHELLFISH

Shellfish are of two types: crustaceans and molluscs. Crustaceans include crabs, crayfish, lobsters, and prawns. Their flesh contains cholesterol but little fat and provides high-quality protein. I eat prawns occasionally, the others very rarely. My concerns about them have to do with their feeding habits. Crustaceans are scavengers and bottom feeders; they live in places where toxic pollutants accumulate. These creatures can be farmed, and if farmers take care to give them clean water, their value as protein foods is much higher. Prawn farming, however, is a major contributor to environmental pollution, and most of it goes on in developing countries. If you eat prawns, look for trap-caught prawns as an alternative to the farmed varieties.

Be aware that crustaceans spoil quickly once they die. Pay attention to freshness and quality of any that you cook. Also, you should know that crustacean allergies are not uncommon and that the reactions can be severe.

Molluscs include clams, mussels, oysters, and scallops – all 'filter feeders' that actually clean the water they live in. It is especially important to get them from unpolluted waters because of the risk of toxic contamination. Eating raw molluscs is additionally risky because of the possibility of viral and bacterial infection. Serious diseases like hepatitis and cholera can be acquired from these foods, and other shellfish-borne infections that would not bother most of us can be life-threatening for those with compromised immune systems (patients on immunosuppressive drugs and people with AIDS).

Bottom line: exercise caution with shellfish. Find out where they come from and pay particular attention to freshness and quality. —**A.W.**

Cold Vegetable Pasta Primavera

Cold pasta dishes are often overlooked, perhaps because we are used to seeing them looking tired in a deli counter. When the noodles are made fresh and tossed with seasoned, pan-grilled vegetables and home-made sauce, it makes all the difference.

Serves 6

Per serving:

Calories 696.5

Fat 28.1 g
    Saturated fat
    6.8 g

(34.9% of calo-
ries from fat)

Protein 19.9 g

Carbohydrate
97.8 g

Cholesterol
22 mg

Fibre 14.6 g

✽

SEASONING

60 ml (1/4 cup) olive oil
1 tablespoon Italian seasoning
   herbs
1/8 teaspoon cayenne pepper
1/4 teaspoon salt
1/8 teaspoon cracked black pepper

GRILLED VEGETABLES

3 courgettes, preferably 1 green
   and 2 yellow, cut lengthways
   into slices 1 cm (1/2 in) thick
4 Japanese aubergines, cut
   lengthways into slices 1 cm
   (1/2 in) thick
1 onion, cut into 1 cm (1/2 in)
   thick slices
1 red pepper, seeded and cut
   lengthways into 2 cm (3/4 in)
   thick slices

PASTA SAUCE

1 tablespoon finely chopped garlic
3 tablespoons finely chopped
   shallots or onions
60 ml (1/4 cup) lemon juice
60 ml (1/4 cup) balsamic or red
   wine vinegar
60 ml (1/4 cup) olive oil
1 kg (6 cups) peeled, seeded, and
   diced tomatoes
1 teaspoon salt
450 g (1 lb) fusilli
1 teaspoon grated lemon zest
1/2 teaspoon black pepper
20 fresh basil leaves, shredded
1 kg (1 cup sliced green or black
   olives
45 g (1/4 cup) capers
125 g (1 cup) cubed feta cheese

Mix all the seasoning ingredients together in a large bowl, then put in the sliced vegetables and toss until all the vegetables are completely coated. Spread out the vegetables on a hot ridged grill pan and cook for 11/2 minutes on each side.

Make the sauce: mix the garlic, shallots, lemon juice, vinegar, and 3 tablespoons of the olive oil together in a bowl. Purée the tomatoes in a blender or food processor, then add them to the bowl. Cover and refrigerate.

Bring a large pan of water and 1/2 teaspoon of the salt to a boil and cook the pasta until it is al dente. Drain in a colander. Transfer the pasta to a large bowl and toss with the remaining 1 tablespoon of olive oil. Add the grated lemon zest, pepper, the remaining 1/2 teaspoon salt, and the grilled vegetables and toss again.

Remove the sauce from the refrigerator just before you are ready to serve, and mix in the shredded basil leaves until they are evenly distributed throughout the sauce. Pour the sauce over the pasta and grilled vegetables, add the olives and capers, and toss until all the strands of pasta and the vegetables are evenly coated. Top with sprinkles of feta cheese and serve.

Tips from Rosie's Kitchen

You can cook the vegetables under the grill, if you prefer, or barbecue them outdoors.

The grilled vegetables alone make a wonderful first course if you don't want to make the pasta. Or you can just make the pasta and serve it with the sauce, hot or cold.

I always find it handy to know how to mix my own seasonings. If you don't have Italian seasoning herbs on hand and wish to mix it yourself, follow the recipe for Rosie's Italian Seasoning: 1/4 teaspoon dried sage, 1 teaspoon dried thyme, 1 teaspoon dried basil, and 1 teaspoon dried oregano.

Linguine with Steamed Clams and Mussels

SERVES 6

PER SERVING:

CALORIES 494.1

FAT 8.3 G
SATURATED FAT
1.2 G

(16.1% OF CALO-
RIES FROM FAT)

PROTEIN 29.3 G

CARBOHYDRATE
67.9 G

CHOLESTEROL
47 MG

FIBRE 2.5 G

✤

Although this pasta dish consists of fairly basic and quick cooking ingredients, you can give it a formal presentation. I steam just the clams or mussels if I'm serving this as a starter, or I pair the dish with a tossed green salad and warm slices of Wholemeal Baguettes with Sun-Dried Tomatoes and Herbs (page 255) for a full meal.

900 g (2 lb) mussels or clams, or
   450 g (1 lb) of each
450 g (1 lb) linguine
1 teaspoon salt
240 ml (1 cup) white wine
120 ml (1/2 cup) purified water
3 cloves garlic, sliced
3 shallots, chopped
360 g (2 cups) chopped tomatoes
2 tablespoons chopped fresh basil
1/4 teaspoon salt

1/2 teaspoon freshly ground black
   pepper
1/8 teaspoon dried chilli flakes
   (optional)
2 tablespoons olive oil
60 ml (1/4 cup) lemon juice
1 teaspoon grated lemon zest

GARNISH

2 tablespoons chopped fresh
   parsley

Soak the clams or mussels in a pan full of cold water for 5 minutes. Scrub the shells to remove any seaweed or mud using a vegetable scrubber or the abrasive side of a clean sponge.

Bring a large pan of water to the boil. Drop the linguine into it, add the salt, and cook until it is al dente.

Meanwhile put the clams or mussels in a large, lidded pan with enough space to hold them without them being cramped. Add the white wine, water, garlic, and shallots. Cover and cook over high heat until the shellfish open, about 10 minutes, shaking the pan occasionally.

Drain the pasta in a colander. Add it to the shellfish and toss the shellfish and pasta together. Add the tomatoes, basil, salt, pepper, chilli flakes, and olive oil, and toss again. Squeeze the lemon over everything, toss in the zest, and garnish with parsley. Serve immediately.

ANDY SUGGESTS

In order to get a more intense flavour, I would increase both the garlic and chilli flakes.

PASTA

Who does not like pasta? People all over the world love noodles, but some of us shun them because we fear they will make us fat. There is no question that many pasta dishes are fattening, fettucine Alfredo being a case in point – with all the butterfat in it, it is not good for the cardiovascular system, either. But pasta remains a nourishing and satisfying food that can be very good for you if you follow a few suggestions.

First of all, buy high-quality pasta made exclusively with hard (durum) wheat. It has more protein and less starch. Experiment with pasta that contains some whole wheat. To my taste most wholemeal pastas are terrible: gritty and lacking in the elastic quality I like. Japanese udon noodles are wonderful, however, as are some Italian shaped pastas made with a mixture of wholemeal and semolina. I'm also fond of Japanese soba noodles, prepared from a mixture of buckwheat and wheat flours. I like them in low-fat hot soups and also cold, dipped into a richly flavoured, non-fat sauce. Get to know South-east Asian rice stick noodles and Chinese cellophane noodles, made from mung beans rather than grain and therefore much higher in protein and lower in starch.

Next, learn to cook pasta properly. One of the best pieces of news to come out of research on carbohydrate foods is that pasta has a significantly lower glycaemic index than bread and so has less of an impact on blood sugar. The reason is that digestive enzymes take longer to get to the starch in pasta because it is more compact than that in bread, which offers much greater surface area for enzymatic action. For the many of us who are carbohydrate sensitive, that means we can enjoy pasta in moderation, even if we ought to minimise consumption of bread (especially the fluffy white sort). You should know that the glycaemic index of pasta is still lower when it is cooked al dente, and so even more resistant to quick digestion. Many people find the pasta of Italy underdone on first meeting it, but if, like so many of us, you can learn to prefer it this way, you will be eating more healthily as a result.

Another obvious suggestion is to find ways of eating pasta without drowning it in fat, especially butter, cream, and cheese. I recommend looking to the cuisines of Asia for inspiration here rather than to Italy. Asians eat noodles in flavourful, low-fat soups or stir-fry them with vegetables and protein foods in small amounts of unsaturated oils. If you want an Italian preparation, pasta is delicious with a fresh tomato sauce made with a small amount of olive oil and topped with a modest amount of freshly grated Parmesan cheese. Not only will you get the health benefits of olive oil in this dish, you will get a good helping of lycopene, the red pigment from tomatoes with anti-cancer properties. Lycopene is available from cooked tomatoes, not raw, and needs fat to be absorbed, so this is a perfect way to include it in your diet. —A.W.

White Beans and Fusilli

This makes a great lunch as well as a main dish for dinner. I make it with dried white beans because they provide a bit of protein. Serve with a green salad and a sliced French baguette brushed with olive oil and toasted.

SERVES 6

PER SERVING:

CALORIES 538.3

FAT 4.1 G
 SATURATED FAT
 0.6 G
(6.9% OF CALORIES
 FROM FAT)

PROTEIN 26 G

CARBOHYDRATE
 100.1 G

CHOLESTEROL 0 MG

FIBRE 12.8 G

WHITE BEANS

200 g (1 cup) dried haricot or
 cannellini beans, soaked
 overnight in 720 ml (3 cups)
 of water with 1/2 teaspoon
 bicarbonate of soda
1 bay leaf
720 ml (3 cups) vegetable stock
 (page 122)

PESTO

125 g (1/2 cup) chopped walnuts
225 g (5 cups) fresh basil leaves
5 large cloves garlic, peeled
25 g (1/4 cup) freshly grated
 Parmesan cheese

2 tablespoons olive oil

PASTA

450 g (1 lb) fusilli or pasta shells
1/2 teaspoon salt
1 small onion, chopped
2 cloves garlic, chopped
1 head escarole, chopped
1/2 teaspoon dried rosemary
1 tablespoon olive oil
Salt to taste

GARNISH

1 lemon, sliced

Drop the bay leaf into the pan of water that the beans have been soaking in overnight. Bring the water to the boil, pour in the vegetable stock, and cook for 45 minutes or longer. The beans should be able to be easily pierced with a fork.

Make the pesto: put all the pesto ingredients, except the oil, in a food processor and blend. Slowly add the oil and continue to process until it becomes a smooth paste. Set aside.

Bring a large pan of water with the salt to the boil. Add the pasta and cook until it is al dente.

Meanwhile, sauté the onions, garlic, escarole, and rosemary in 1 tablespoon of olive oil until limp. Add salt to taste and mix with the beans.

Drain the pasta in a colander and pour it into a large bowl. Add about 80 ml (1/3 cup) of the pesto, or more to taste, and toss well until it is distributed evenly and the strands of pasta are coated.

Serve the pasta in 6 individual pasta bowls and ladle the white beans on top. Garnish each with a slice of lemon.

Tips from Rosie's Kitchen

Store any leftover pesto in ice cube trays, then cover and freeze. Pesto is wonderful tossed with warm noodles or mixed with béchamel or white sauce and tossed with pasta. Check the index for other recipes that include pesto.

Aubergine Rollatini with Spinach and Cheese Filling

The tomato sauce is always best when it's fresh, but it can be made up to one day in advance if necessary.

Partner this dish with some freshly steamed broccoli, a crunchy green salad, and warm slices of whole grain baguette.

SERVES 6

PER SERVING:

CALORIES 309.9

FAT 18.2 G
  SATURATED FAT
  4.1 G
(53.1% OF CALO-
  RIES FROM FAT)

PROTEIN 14.5 G

CARBOHYDRATE
  26.4 G

CHOLESTEROL
  11.7 MG

FIBRE 8.1 G

Tomato Mushroom Sauce (page 256)
450 g (1 lb) spinach, stalks removed
2 large onions, finely chopped
2 large cloves garlic, finely chopped
5 tablespoons olive oil
55 g (2 oz) feta cheese
225 g (1 cup) low-fat cottage cheese
2 tablespoons finely chopped walnuts
2 egg whites
30 g (1/2 cup) fresh wholemeal breadcrumbs
2 tablespoons chopped parsley
1 teaspoon salt
1 teaspoon freshly ground black pepper
1/4 teaspoon grated nutmeg or mace
1/2 teaspoon ground fennel or cumin
2 medium aubergines, washed

GARNISH

6 Kalamata olives, pitted and sliced
2 tablespoons freshly grated Parmesan cheese
15 g (1/4 cup) chopped fresh parsley

Prepare the Tomato Mushroom Sauce so it will be ready when you put together the dish.

Preheat oven to 190°C.

To cook the spinach, set a steamer basket inside a large pan and fill it with enough water so that it barely touches the bottom of the basket. Put the spinach leaves in the basket, cover the pan, and steam for 2 minutes, maximum. Drain the spinach in a colander and leave it to cool. When it is completely cooled, squeeze the excess water from the leaves by wrapping the spinach in a tea towel and squeezing gently. Alternatively, put a bowl or plate directly on top of the spinach, inside the colander, and press down gently.

Sauté the onions and garlic in a sauté pan in 2 tablespoons of the olive oil until soft. Add the cooked spinach, feta and cottage cheeses, walnuts, egg whites, breadcrumbs, parsley, and spices. Stir with a wooden spoon until all the ingredients are thoroughly blended.

Slice the aubergines lengthways into thin slices and lightly brush them with the remaining olive oil, using a pastry brush. Grill them on a baking sheet just until lightly browned, about 3 minutes. Remove the aubergines from the grill and cover the baking sheet with cling film to allow them to steam, then cool. Once they are cool, arrange 2–3 tablespoons of the spinach filling at the narrow end of each slice and roll it up. Arrange the rolls in a baking dish, seam side down. Pour the tomato sauce over the top of each rollatini and bake until the sauce is bubbling, about 20–25 minutes. Garnish with the olive slices and a sprinkling of Parmesan cheese and parsley.

Vegetable Lasagne

What I love about this lasagne is that most of it can be made ahead of time and the lasagne noodles that I use don't need to be boiled, which saves a lot of time.

This lasagne has two sauces in it, but you have the option of making it with just one of them. The white sauce should be made fresh, but the red sauce and the filling can be made a day in advance and refrigerated.

When children want to participate in the kitchen, it usually involves making a dessert, but this is a savoury dish that children can

help make. I think laying the noodles down and pouring sauce or
spreading filling on top can be fun for kids and will make them feel
that a substantial meal was successfully completed due to their efforts.

MARINARA SAUCE

160 g (1 cup) chopped onion

3 cloves garlic

55 g (1/2 cup) chopped carrots

3 tablespoons olive oil

120 ml (1/2 cup) red wine

1/2 teaspoon dried oregano

1 teaspoon dried basil

16 plum tomatoes, peeled and
seeded, or 2 x 400 g (14 oz)
cans peeled whole tomatoes

35 g (1/2 cup) chopped button
mushrooms

1 tablespoon honey or sugar

1/2 teaspoon salt or to taste

1 tablespoon Italian seasoning
herbs

AUBERGINE

1 medium aubergine, sliced
lengthways 1 cm (1/2 in) thick

Salt to taste

Pinch of cayenne pepper

2 tablespoons olive oil

SPINACH

450 g (1 lb) spinach, stalks
removed

150 g (5 oz) goat's cheese or
ricotta cheese

1 tablespoon olive oil

80 g (1/2 cup) chopped onion

2 cloves garlic, sliced

1/8 teaspoon freshly ground black
pepper

2 tablespoons chopped fresh basil

BASIC WHITE SAUCE

(page 169)

LASAGNE

12 sheets precooked lasagne
noodles

240 ml (1 cup) purified water

190 g (11/2 cups) coarsely grated
mozzarella

10 Kalamata olives, pitted and
halved

SERVES 12

PER SERVING:

CALORIES 583.6

FAT 18.9 G
SATURATED FAT
5.9 G
(29.1% OF CALO-
RIES FROM FAT)

PROTEIN 20.5 G

CARBOHYDRATE
83.1 G

CHOLESTEROL
25 MG

FIBRE 6.3 G

Make the marinara sauce: sauté the onion, garlic, and carrots in
the olive oil in a medium saucepan over low heat for 3 minutes.
Add the red wine, oregano, and basil, and cook for an additional
5 minutes until the wine is reduced by half. Add the tomatoes,
mushrooms, honey or sugar, salt, and Italian seasoning, and
continue to cook until the mushrooms become limp, about 15
minutes.

Vegetable Lasagne

Tips from Rosie's Kitchen

If you want to cook your own lasagne instead of buying oven-ready ones, don't add the water when you are laying the cooked lasagne in the dish. The water is poured over the pre-cooked lasagne before baking only to add some moisture.

Preheat the grill.

Brush both sides of the aubergine slices with olive oil, salt lightly, sprinkle on a little cayenne, and spread out on a baking tray. Grill for 3 minutes until the aubergine slices turn brown. Remove from the heat and leave to cool.

Prepare the spinach: steam the spinach for 1 minute in a pan with 120 ml (1/2 cup) purified water. Remove from the heat, drain in a colander and allow to cool. Squeeze the spinach, with clean hands, to remove excess water.

Put the softened goat's cheese or ricotta in a medium bowl. Add the spinach and mix together thoroughly with a fork.

Put the olive oil, onions, and sliced garlic in a small sauté pan over low heat. Sauté for 2 minutes until the onions turn light golden brown. Remove from the heat and cool. Add to the softened cheese and spinach and mix. Add the pepper and the fresh basil and mix again until all the ingredients are thoroughly blended in.

Make the white sauce.

Preheat oven to 190°C.

To assemble the lasagne: cover the bottom of a deep baking dish with 120 ml (1/2 cup) marinara sauce. Lay 4 of the lasagne noodles on top. Spoon the spinach filling over the noodles and spread it around until all of them are covered. Pour the white sauce on top, cover-

A serving of the Vegetable Lasagne

ing all the noodles. Lay 4 more lasagne noodles on top of the white sauce. Lay the aubergine slices lengthways over the noodles. Sprinkle the mozzarella cheese on top. Pour 240 ml (1 cup) of marinara sauce over the cheese. Lay another 4 lasagne noodles over the sauce. Slowly pour the water over the lasagne. Pour the remaining marinara sauce on top of the noodles. Sprinkle the top with the remaining mozzarella cheese and the olives. Cover with foil and bake for 1 1/2 hours. When the lasagne is completely cooked, remove from the oven and allow to cool for 5 minutes. Cut into squares to serve.

Getting kids to help with lasagne – making a layer of aubergine and sprinkling with cheese

Roasted Pepper Turkey with Orange Liqueur

I make this for a holiday dinner or when I'm planning to have a large group of friends and family over.

The outside of the turkey is encrusted with a baked-on pepper rub. Inside, the meat is juicy and tender. This is great served with the Serrano Chilli and Coriander Cornbread Muffins (page 253), a bowl of Pear Relish (page 252) or Fresh Apple Sauce (page 249), and/or Steamed and Roasted Baby Red Potatoes (page 242).

SERVES 12,
WITH LEFTOVERS

PER SERVING:

CALORIES 185.9

FAT 6.9 G
  SATURATED FAT
  2.1 G

(7.4% OF CALORIES
  FROM FAT)

PROTEIN 182.8 G

CARBOHYDRATE
  11.1 G

CHOLESTEROL
  58 MG

FIBRE 1.8 G

❉

1 x 4.5–5.4 kg (10–12 lb) turkey
120 ml (1/2 cup) white wine

PEPPER RUB

11/2 teaspoons dried basil
11/2 teaspoons dried oregano
1 teaspoon cayenne pepper
1 tablespoon paprika
11/2 teaspoons salt

3 tablespoons Grand Marnier

SEASONING

5 cloves garlic
2 small onions, sliced
2 carrots, cut in rounds
1 bay leaf
2 orange slices

Preheat oven to 180°C.

Remove the neck and other giblets from the turkey cavity and reserve to make stock at a later time. Rinse the turkey in the sink and let the water gush inside the cavity.

Mix all the ingredients for the rub together with the Grand Marnier. Spread it over the outside of the turkey, reserving 1 tablespoon. Spoon the 1 tablespoon into the cavity of the turkey. Stuff the cavity with all of the seasoning ingredients.

Set the turkey in a roasting tin and pour in the wine. Cover the turkey with foil and roast. After 2 hours, uncover the turkey and baste with the cooking juices. Continue to baste the turkey with the juices every 20 minutes for the next 11/2 hours, until it is done. Total roasting time should be about 31/2 hours.

Allow the turkey to cool for 15 minutes before carving.

Tips from Rosie's Kitchen

Save the turkey bones to make stock!

Invariably with a good-sized turkey, there are leftovers, and that's part of the pleasure.

Turkey Sandwiches: *This is the time to make sandwiches spread with an impressive mayonnaise made by combining the Mock Soured Cream recipe (page 62) and the Pesto recipe (page 160). Serve the sandwiches on dense wholemeal bread, topped with crunchy lettuce and cold tomato slices. If you can't eat up all the leftovers within a few days, store the meat in airtight zip-lock bags or plastic containers in the freezer for up to 3 weeks. When you are ready to eat it, defrost the meat slowly in the refrigerator.*

Savoury Lobster and Mushroom Crêpes

The powerful flavours of lobster, saffron, and mushrooms all wrapped together in a freshly made, tarragon-flavoured crêpe create a very elegant dish. Even though it is rich, it doesn't overwhelm the taste buds. I like to serve this dish with a salad and the Lemon Dill Vinaigrette (page 113).

BASIC WHITE SAUCE MADE WITH OLIVE OIL

2 tablespoons olive oil

480 ml (2 cups) warm milk

2 tablespoons unbleached plain flour

25 g (1/4 cup) freshly grated Parmesan cheese

30 g (1/4 cup) thinly sliced spring onions

1/8 teaspoon nutmeg, preferably freshly grated

1/8 teaspoon cayenne pepper

3/4 teaspoon salt

MAKES 12 CREPES
SERVES 6

PER SERVING:

CALORIES 552.4

FAT 27.5 G
  SATURATED FAT
  11.7 G
(46.5% OF CALO-
  RIES FROM FAT)

PROTEIN 38.4 G

CARBOHYDRATE
  32.9 G

CHOLESTEROL
  220 MG

FIBRE 1.1 G

CREPE BATTER

125 g (1 cup) unbleached plain
  flour
1 egg
480 ml (2 cups) milk
1/8 teaspoon grated lemon zest
3/4 teaspoon salt
70 g (5 tablespoons) melted butter
1 tablespoon chopped fresh
  tarragon, or 1 teaspoon dried

LOBSTER FILLING

3 large lobster tails, defrosted if
  frozen (about 450 g/3 cups
  uncooked lobster meat) (see
  Tips), or 375 g (3 cups) white
  crab meat

60 ml (1/4 cup) white wine
1/2 teaspoon saffron threads
  (optional)
2 tablespoons olive oil
35 g (1/2 cup) chopped button
  mushrooms, or 140 g (2 cups)
  chopped shiitake or oyster
  mushrooms (see Tips)
120 ml (1/2 cup) white wine
225 g (1 cup) finely chopped
  shallots
1/8 teaspoon dried chilli flakes

GARNISH

15 g (1/4 cup) chopped fresh
  parsley

Make the white sauce: pour the olive oil into a medium
saucepan over low heat. Put the milk in a separate saucepan
over low heat only until it becomes warm; do not let it boil.
Gradually stir the flour into the warm oil, stirring constantly.
Cook for about 1 minute to make a brownish roux. Slowly add
60 ml (1/4 cup) of the warm milk, whisking to blend it in. Pour in
the remaining milk, continuing to whisk. Allow the sauce to
simmer for about 2 minutes, just to thicken slightly, then
remove from the heat. Mix in the cheese, spices, and salt. Cover
the sauce with cling film and set aside until ready to use.

Make the crêpe batter: put the flour in a large bowl and in
the middle make a small well big enough to hold the egg. Crack
the egg into the well. Pour the milk around the flour. Add the
lemon zest, salt, butter, and tarragon. Whisk everything together
until the batter is smooth. Leave the batter to rest at room temperature, covered, for 1 hour.

Set a medium (about 15 cm/6 in diameter) non-stick crêpe
pan over medium-high heat for a few seconds until it starts to
get hot. Pull the pan away from the heat, and pour 3 tablespoons
of batter into the pan. With the pan still away from the heat, roll

it around so that the batter spreads evenly across the bottom. Set the pan back on the heat until the edges of the batter curl up and bubbles appear on the surface, then flip the crêpe over and cook on the other side for about 1 minute. Remove each crêpe when done and continue with the rest of the batter. Let the crêpes cool before you stack them, or they will become mushy. When completely cooled, stack them with greaseproof paper between each one. Set aside until ready to use.

Make the lobster filling: using kitchen scissors, cut the lobster tails lengthways through the cartilage to remove the lobster meat. Cut down the centre of the lobster tail to remove the pink digestive tract and discard. Cut the lobster meat into fairly large cubes.

Heat the white wine in a small saucepan until it comes to a low boil. Remove from the heat and, if using, add the saffron threads. Set aside to steep for a few minutes.

Meanwhile, pour the olive oil into a large sauté pan, and set over medium-high heat. Add the raw lobster meat and stir with a fork a few times. Turn the lobster, slowly browning it, for about 2 minutes. Add the mushrooms, the white wine, shallots, chilli flakes, and, if you are using it, the saffron and its soaking liquid. Cook until the wine reduces by half and the vegetables are tender. (If using crab meat, add it along with the vegetables rather than before, since it is already cooked).

Tips from Rosie's Kitchen

Lobster tails vary in size depending on where they're from, so if the lobster tails you find are on the smaller side, you might want to add an extra one to yield the required amount of meat.

For a low-fat version of the white sauce, use evaporated skimmed milk instead of the whole milk.

The key to making the white sauce is proper preparation of the olive oil and flour mixture, which is a form of roux. Roux is a thickener or base for white sauce that usually involves butter and flour. Here, I am using olive oil because it gives the roux a good flavour. It is very important to add the milk slowly to the oil and flour mixture. It will thicken right after the initial 60 ml (1/4 cup) of milk is poured in, but if you keep an eye on it and stir constantly, you will have an excellent white sauce.

With the lobster, white sauce, and mushrooms, this recipe is quite full-bodied. You have the option of making it with or without the lobster. If you don't use the lobster, try the more exotic, flavourful mushrooms, such as shiitake, portobello, chestnut, or oyster. If you are using the lobster, the smaller quantity of button mushrooms will be fine to balance the intensity of the lobster and the white sauce.

Add 300 ml (1¼ cups) of the white sauce and heat through gently, stirring once or twice. Heat the rest of the white sauce in its saucepan. Place an equal quantity of the lobster and mushroom filling on each crêpe. Fold over into a half moon. Drizzle 1 tablespoon of the hot white sauce on top of each crêpe, and sprinkle with ½ teaspoon chopped parsley. Serve immediately.

Fish with Spinach *En Papillote*

MAKES 6
PAPILLOTES

PER SERVING:

CALORIES 248.3

FAT 1.8 G
  SATURATED FAT
  0.4 G
(7.7% OF CALO-
  RIES FROM FAT)

PROTEIN 40.1 G

CARBOHYDRATE
  13.4 G

CHOLESTEROL
  149 MG

FIBRE 1.5 G

❋

In cooking terms, papillote *is the French word for a paper bauble that is used to adorn the bones on chops or ribs.* En papillote *means food that is wrapped and baked inside baking parchment, not only for the presentation but to seal in and heighten the flavour of the food. In this recipe, tuna is the fish of choice, but mahimahi would work just as well. It is best to use thin slices, so butterfly each thick steak (see Tips for how to do this).*

Make the marinade first, because the fish will need to sit in the liquid for 30 minutes before it can be sealed in the baking parchment parcel. You can marinate it for up to one day, if you want to.

This recipe is fun to make – the cutting of the heart-shaped parchment is reminiscent of cutting shapes out of construction paper that we did in grammar school, only here the end product is edible, savoury, and elegant. Papillotes offer cooks a unique way of presenting food, and the cleanup is easy.

The heart-shaped baking parchment

MARINADE

240 ml (1 cup) low-sodium soy
    sauce
1 green chilli, seeded and finely
    chopped
2 tablespoons grated root ginger
60 ml (1/4 cup) freshly squeezed
    lime juice
1 bunch fresh coriander, stalks
    discarded, reserving 6 sprigs for
    garnish

6 x 165 g (5 1/2 oz) fresh tuna
    steaks, butterflied (see Tips)

FILLING

600 g (6 cups) spinach leaves,
    tough stalks removed (page 75)
    and chopped
35 g (1/2 cup) sliced oyster mush-
    rooms or red pepper strips
1/4 teaspoon grated orange zest

3 tablespoons grated root ginger
85 g (3/4 cup) thinly sliced red
    onion
1 lemon, cut into 6 slices (ends
    discarded)
1 egg white, slightly beaten

Tips from Rosie's Kitchen

*To butterfly a tuna steak, cut it in half
horizontally, cutting until just before you
get to the other side, then open the steak up
like a book and lay it face down on the bed
of spinach filling. Cutting the fish steaks
this way will enable you to close the baking
parchment over the filling.*

Whisk all the ingredients for the marinade together in a bowl.
Coat the tuna steaks with the marinade by turning them over in
the bowl a couple of times to completely moisten both sides.
Cover and refrigerate for 30 minutes or up to 1 day.

Cut 6 squares of baking parchment that each measure
approximately 32.5 x 45 cm (13 × 18 in). Fold each square in
half and cut out the shape of one half of a heart. When you open
up the parchment, you will have a complete heart-shaped piece.

Preheat oven to 180°C.

Remove the fish from the refrigerator. To make the filling,
toss the chopped spinach, mushrooms or peppers, orange zest,
ginger, and onions together in a bowl.

Open up a heart-shaped piece of parchment and lay one-
sixth of the spinach mixture a little off-centre on the heart. Place
a butterflied tuna steak on top of the spinach. Drizzle 1 table-

Top left: putting the filling on one side of the heart-shaped parchment; top right: folding the parchment over the filling; bottom left: pleating the edge all around; bottom right: the papillotes *ready for the oven*

spoon of the fish marinade over the tuna and add a slice of lemon. Brush the outer edges of the parchment heart with the egg white, using a pastry brush. Fold the other half of the heart over the filling to meet the opposite edge. Seal by making small folds in the edge, starting at the top and continuing all around, twisting the paper at the pointed end. Repeat for the remaining baking parchment hearts, fish and spinach filling.

Put the *papillotes* on a baking sheet and bake for 15 minutes. When cooked, the parchment parcels will puff up with steam.

Before serving, allow the *papillotes* to deflate a bit. If you try to open them immediately after cooking, you will get burned by the steam escaping from inside. Unseal the *papillotes* along the outer edge to reveal the tuna and spinach filling inside. Garnish with coriander sprigs before serving.

Fish with Spinach En Papillote

FISH

In 1970 I changed from an omnivore to a lacto vegetarian. I gave up eating all foods of animal origin except dairy products, mostly yogurt and cheese. That diet agreed with me, kept me healthy and strong, and gave me pleasure and variety. But after fifteen years of it, I decided I needed a change. As an experiment I cut back on dairy products and started to eat fish. Not only did I enjoy the change, it gave me greater freedom when travelling (to Japan, for example, where being a lacto vegetarian is a challenge) and dining out. Furthermore, my nutritional research convinced me of the health benefits of fish.

Populations that eat fish regularly live longer and have less chronic disease than populations that do not. Whether this is because fish displaces meat or because it has positive attributes of its own is not clear. Certainly, fish provides high-quality protein without the saturated fat present in meat and poultry. And some kinds of fish – specifically, oily fish from cold northern waters – also provide omega-3 fatty acids, the special, unsaturated fats our bodies need for optimum health. Salmon, mackerel, herring, and sardines are rich in them, as is, to a lesser extent, albacore tuna. Omega-3 sources other than fish are few: walnuts, linseeds, hemp seeds, and the oils extracted from them, and, to a lesser extent, soya and canola oils and specially fortified eggs.

Most people are deficient in omega-3s and as a result are more likely to develop cardiovascular disease, cancer, inflammatory disorders, and mental and emotional problems. Recent research suggests that supplementing the diet with omega-3 fatty acids not only can reduce these risks but can also help treat depression, bipolar disorder, autism, and attention deficit hyperactivity disorder. Fish is, indeed, a brain food.

The healthful qualities of fish can be neutralised by unhealthful ways of cooking it. Fish that is battered and fried, slathered with butter, or blanketed in creamy sauces becomes just another vehicle for putting saturated fat and excess calories into the body. I prefer fish that is raw (sashimi and sushi), marinated (ceviche), steamed, grilled, or smoked (as in salmon and trout). I much prefer fresh fish to frozen, and I often eat it in restaurants, where the quality is usually better than I can get to cook at home. (That may not be the case for all readers.)

Despite my enthusiasm for fish, I have two serious concerns about recommending that people eat more of it. The first is its content of environmental toxins, the result of pollution of lakes, rivers, and oceans. The second is the possibility of losing fish as a natural resource by overfishing those same bodies of water.

Take salmon as an example. Almost all of the salmon served today is farmed. Farmed salmon has less flavour, less protein, and more fat than wild salmon, and its content of omega-3 fatty acids may not be as high. It may also contain residues of antibiotics and other drugs used to control diseases that occur when fish are crowded together in the pens of fish farms. Those diseases may escape and decimate wild populations of salmon. Most people assume that fish farming is a way of protecting an endangered resource. Few know that it takes several pounds of feed fish to produce one pound of salmon. The net result of salmon farming is greatly accelerated depletion of the numbers of fish in the oceans. If you can get wild salmon, use it for the salmon recipes in this book. It tastes better and is more nutritious, and eating it does not have the environmental impact of eating farmed salmon.

As for other fish, be aware that larger, more carnivorous fish are more likely to contain dangerous levels of toxins. I avoid swordfish, marlin, shark, and bluefish for that reason. The safest and best fish for omega-3 fatty acids is probably the sardine. I love fresh sardines, grilled with nothing but salt and lemon juice, and I'm happy to see them increasingly available. (I used to be able to get them only in better Greek and Italian restaurants.) I also buy water-packed canned sardines and mash them up with mustard and onion as a spread. Give that a try; it's an easy way to get some safe oily fish into your diet.

I avoid grouper, black sea bass, rockfish, and most snapper because those species are endangered from overfishing. Cod, pollock, flounder, halibut, sole, and plaice are still relatively abundant in the Pacific but seriously depleted in the Atlantic. Finally, skate, Chilean sea bass, and orange roughy are threatened, because they do not spawn until they are old – thirty years in the case of orange roughy – and unless they are managed well, they will be overfished to depletion. Species that are still abundant and well managed include striped bass, Alaskan salmon, herring, sardines, anchovies, mackerel, mahimahi, Alaskan halibut, and Pacific albacore tuna. Try to keep these distinctions in mind if you want to continue enjoying fish. —**A.W.**

Grilled Fresh Sardines

SERVES 4
(450 G (1 LB)
SARDINES)

PER SERVING:

CALORIES 116

FAT 13.8 G
  SATURATED FAT
  1.4 G
(64.9% OF
  CALORIES FROM
  FAT)

PROTEIN 13.8 G

CARBOHYDRATE
  2.9 G

CHOLESTEROL
  0 MG

FIBRE 0.3 G

Fresh sardines are becoming more widely available. They taste completely different from any canned sardines you have ever tried. Cut the heads off if you wish and rinse them under cold water. Brush the sardines with olive oil and sprinkle lightly with salt. Place them on a barbecue or under a hot grill. Cook them about 2 minutes per side until the flesh is just firm and the skin lightly browned. Serve immediately with fresh lemon wedges.

Tips from Rosie's Kitchen

Searing meat or fish is a way to lock in the juices by exposing it to very high temperature. The correct way to sear is in a hot frying pan, or ridged grill pan, for a very short amount of time, and then to slowly finish cooking in the oven. Be careful not to get the pan too hot too fast or the sesame oil will burn.

If you want to serve this dish for lunch, serve half of a fillet with a side salad.

Seared Salmon with Orange Glaze

Not an ounce of flavour escapes this dish! The salmon is seared, trapping its rich flavour, briefly baked, and then drizzled with a thick, lightly fragranced orange and ginger glaze – a balanced companion for a fish as flavourful as salmon. Salmon provides ample amounts of protein, B vitamins, vitamin A, and omega-3 oils.

6 x 170 g (6 oz) salmon fillets
1 tablespoon toasted sesame oil
1 tablespoon low-sodium soy
   sauce
60 ml (1/4 cup) white wine
240 ml (1 cup) freshly squeezed
   orange juice

1 teaspoon grated orange zest
3 tablespoons dry sherry
1/2 teaspoon grated root ginger
2 slices orange

SERVES 6

PER SERVING:
CALORIES 271.8
FAT 8.2 G
  SATURATED FAT
  1.3 G
(29.8% OF CALORIES FROM FAT)
PROTEIN 34.3 G
CARBOHYDRATE
  9.7 G
CHOLESTEROL
  88 MG
FIBRE 0.2 G

Preheat oven to 200°C.

Sear the fish fillets in the sesame oil in a large, very hot frying pan for 1 minute on each side. You should hear the fish sizzle. Remove fillets from the heat and transfer them to a glass baking dish or baking tin. Drizzle the soy sauce and the wine over them and bake for 10 minutes.

Meanwhile, heat the orange juice, zest, sherry, and ginger together in a small saucepan over medium-high heat until reduced by half. Add the orange slices, and stir once or twice until the sauce becomes thick. Remove from heat, drizzle the sauce over the fish, and serve.

GRILLED TUNA WITH CORIANDER GINGER SAUCE

Grilled tuna satisfies all of my remaining carnivorous cravings. I like it cooked rare to medium-rare, and while I understand that some people prefer it well done, tuna that is cooked through is as uninteresting to me as a well-done steak must be to most beef lovers. The coriander ginger sauce is a snap to make and provides a depth of flavour that easily stands up to the taste and texture of the tuna.

2 x 115–170 g (4–6 oz) tuna steaks, about 2.5 cm (1 in) thick
2 teaspoons extra virgin olive oil
Salt and freshly ground black pepper to taste

SAUCE

1 tablespoon grapeseed oil
2 tablespoons finely chopped root ginger

60 g (1 cup) chopped fresh coriander
2 tablespoons shoyu or other natural soy sauce
1 tablespoon light soft brown or demerara sugar
60 ml (¼ cup) purified water

SERVES 2

PER SERVING:
CALORIES 349.9
FAT 16.6 G
 SATURATED FAT
 3 G
(43.4% OF CALO-
 RIES FROM FAT)
PROTEIN 41.3 G
CARBOHYDRATE
 7.6 G
CHOLESTEROL
 65 MG
FIBRE LESS THAN
 0.8 G

Rinse the tuna steaks under cold running water and pat them dry. Rub them with the olive oil and season them with salt and pepper.

Preheat the grill or barbecue.

Meanwhile, prepare the sauce: heat the grapeseed oil in a small frying pan over medium-high heat and add the ginger. Stir-fry for 1 minute, then add the coriander and stir-fry for another minute, until the coriander is bright green. Mix in the soy sauce, sugar, and water and cook for 1 minute over high heat. Remove the pan from heat.

Grill the tuna steaks until cooked to your taste; for medium-rare, this will be about 2–3 minutes per side. Spoon the sauce over the fish and serve immediately.

Andy seasoning his Grilled Tuna

Duxelles-Stuffed Sole

Duxelles is a mixture of finely chopped mushrooms and shallots some-times cooked with a little brandy; it is used primarily in stuffings or sauces. Here, thin fish fillets are stuffed with it and rolled up. The strong flavour of the duxelles coupled with the delicate and choice taste of sole makes it a complete meal. Serve this dish with steamed broccoli and a warm baguette.

SERVES 6

PER SERVING:

CALORIES 167

FAT 3.8 G

SATURATED FAT
0.3 G

(22% OF CALORIES
FROM FAT)

PROTEIN 21.1 G

CARBOHYDRATE
9.5 G

CHOLESTEROL 0 MG

FIBRE 1.6 G

❄

1 tablespoon olive oil
170 g (3/4 cup) finely chopped
   shallots
1 tablespoon brandy
210 g (3 cups) finely chopped
   mushrooms
1 teaspoon salt
1/8 teaspoon white pepper
1 tablespoon chopped parsley
6 x 70 g (21/2 oz) lemon sole or
   plaice fillets

1/4 teaspoon paprika
Pinch of cayenne pepper
60 ml (1/4 cup) white wine
1 tablespoon grated orange zest
120 ml (1/2 cup) freshly squeezed
   orange juice
1 tablespoon capers

GARNISH

1 sprig parsley

Preheat oven to 180°C.

   To make the duxelles, heat the olive oil in a small sauté pan. Slowly add the shallots and sauté them over medium heat for 2 minutes. Add the brandy and chopped mushrooms and sauté until the mushrooms have released their liquid and start to brown, about 4 minutes. Sea-son with salt, pepper, and pars-ley and remove from the heat to cool.

   Lay the sole fillets on a sheet of greaseproof paper and sprinkle them with the paprika and cayenne pepper. Drop 2 tablespoons of the duxelles at the end of each fillet and roll them up. Insert a wooden skewer through each to hold

ANDY SUGGESTS

As a change from fruit top-pings on fish, prepare this dish with a Dijon mustard sauce, such as the one for my grilled salmon (see the next recipe).

them together. Arrange the rolled fillets in a layer in a glass or ceramic baking dish and pour in the wine. Cover and bake for 15 minutes or until fish has visibly steamed through. Fish should be firm and white.

Pour off the baking juices into a small pan. Add the orange zest and juice and simmer for 3 minutes. Drop in the capers. Pour the sauce over the hot fish, garnish with parsley, and serve.

Tips from Rosie's Kitchen

The secret to making this dish successfully is in using thin fillets; they roll up more easily. Flat fish fillets such as sole tend to be thin. If you'd like larger portions, serve 2 per person.

Make extra duxelles while you're at it and store it in the freezer either in a covered container or packed into ice cube trays. It is a home cook's treasure. Use a little to invigorate the flavour of a sauce. For example, add 1 tablespoon of duxelles to 120 ml (1/2 cup) of any cream-based pasta sauce, or pop out a few cubes from the ice tray and toss them in with chicken soup while it's cooking. Duxelles also makes a wonderful coating for vegetables, such as green beans or asparagus, or as a stuffing for the courgette boats below.

Courgette Boats

Buy three 15 cm (6 in) courgettes. Make a cut lengthways on one side, about 5 mm (1/4 in) deep. Scoop out the seeds to create a cavity and pack about some duxelles into each cavity. Bake covered in the oven at 180°C for 15 minutes. Allow them to cool and then cut them in half. Serves 6.

GRILLED SALMON WITH MUSTARD SAUCE

SERVES 4

PER SERVING:

CALORIES 236

FAT 8.5 G
  SATURATED FAT 1 G

(32% OF CALORIES
  FROM FAT)

PROTEIN 36 G

CARBOHYDRATE
  3 G

CHOLESTEROL
  88 MG

FIBRE 1 G

❋

Here is simple grilled salmon dressed up with a strongly flavoured sauce that complements the natural oiliness of the fish. And unlike many sauces recommended for fish, this one is very low in fat. (Salmon is full of healthful omega-3 fatty acids and certainly does not need to be cooked with butter or served with any additional fat.) I much prefer salmon fillets to bony salmon steaks, and I like them to be moist when cooked, never dry.

4 salmon fillets (about 170 g/6 oz each)
1 lemon, cut in half
Salt and freshly ground black pepper to taste

SAUCE

125 g (1/2 cup) Dijon mustard
1 teaspoon extra virgin olive oil
3 tablespoons chopped fresh dill, or 1 tablespoon dried dill
1 handful chopped fresh basil

Rinse the fillets under cold running water and pat them dry. Squeeze the juice from one half of the lemon over the fillets, then season them with salt and pepper.

Preheat the grill or barbecue.

Meanwhile, prepare the sauce: whisk together the mustard, olive oil, and dill in a small bowl. Add the basil and the juice from the other half of the lemon, mixing well.

Grill the fish until it is cooked to your taste, but do not overcook. Spoon the sauce over the fish and serve immediately.

Lemon Baked Halibut

The mellow flavour of this low-fat fish comes from marinating it in vigorous spices. After cooking, it is topped with home-made salsa rich with the flavour of tangy onions, fiery chillies, and cool papaya.

Make the salsa first, before you start preparing the fish. It is also best to make the marinade far enough in advance so that the flavours can blend together for at least 2 hours before you actually marinate the fish in it for 30 minutes. Keep this in mind when deciding what time you want to serve this dish.

I couple this with an accompaniment of Steamed and Roasted Potatoes (page 242).

PAPAYA SALSA

25 g (1/2 cup) fresh coriander leaves
165 g (1 cup) cubed papaya
30 g (1/4 cup) diced red pepper
40 g (1/4 cup) diced red onion
1 green chilli, seeded and finely chopped
2 tablespoons freshly squeezed lime juice

MARINADE

3 tablespoons freshly squeezed lemon juice
1 tablespoon grated lemon zest
1 tablespoon olive oil
1 tablespoon grated root ginger
3/4 teaspoon freshly ground black pepper
30 g (1/2 cup) finely chopped fresh coriander

6 x 170 g (6 oz) halibut steaks, butterflied (page 173)
3 medium bulbs fennel, sliced
160 ml (2/3 cup) purified water
9 black or white peppercorns

Make the salsa: put all the ingredients in a small bowl, mixing with a spoon until everything is thoroughly blended. Cover and refrigerate until you are ready to serve.

Make the marinade: stir together the lemon juice, zest, oil, ginger, pepper, and coriander in a bowl. Cover and chill for at least 2 hours to allow the flavours to mingle.

After the 2 hours, put the fish in a baking dish, pour the marinade evenly over it, and leave for 20–30 minutes, covered, in the refrigerator.

Preheat oven to 200°C.

Meanwhile, cook the fennel in the water with the peppercorns in a large, flameproof sauté pan, covered, over high heat for about 6–8 minutes, until just tender, adding liquid if necessary. Remove from the heat.

Remove the halibut steaks from the refrigerator and bake them for 5 minutes on each side. The halibut should be flaky and white.

Arrange equal portions of the fennel on each of 6 plates, put the halibut on top, and spoon 1 tablespoon of Papaya Salsa on the fish.

Tips from Rosie's Kitchen

Zest is the aromatic, coloured top skin of the citrus. The oils in the zest are what intensifies the flavours of food. The zest can be peeled off with a zester or a sharp paring knife.

Red snapper and sea bass are excellent alternatives to halibut. Buy the same amount of these fish fillets if you are substituting, but because these fillets are thinner, you don't need to butterfly them.

GRILLED FISH WITH TROPICAL RELISH

The tropical relish in this recipe is more to my liking than a pure fruit topping because the sweetness of the mango is offset by the robust tartness of the capers, vinegar, and salsa, and the basil provides an unexpected, spicy note.

4 fish fillets, such as cod or halibut, about 170 g (6 oz) each
1 teaspoon extra virgin olive oil
Salt and freshly ground black pepper to taste

RELISH

1 ripe mango, peeled, stoned, and finely chopped

1 sweet onion, finely chopped
1 red pepper, seeded and finely chopped
1 bunch fresh basil, chopped
1 tablespoon capers, drained
1 teaspoon balsamic vinegar
1 tablespoon salsa

Rinse the fish fillets under cold running water and pat them dry. Brush them with the olive oil and season them with salt and pepper.
Preheat the grill or barbecue.
Meanwhile, prepare the relish: stir together the mango, onions, peppers, basil, capers, vinegar, and salsa in a bowl. Grill the fish for about 2–3 minutes per side or until cooked to your taste. Spoon the relish over the fish and serve.

SERVES 4

PER SERVING:

CALORIES 227

FAT 9 G
SATURATED FAT 1 G

(35% OF CALORIES FROM FAT)

PROTEIN 36.5 G

CARBOHYDRATE 13 G

CHOLESTEROL 54 MG

FIBRE 2 G

✳

Baked Curried Sea Bass with Lentils

SERVES 8

PER SERVING:

CALORIES 187.6

FAT 3.9 G
  SATURATED FAT
  0.5 G

(17.6% OF CALORIES
  FROM FAT)

PROTEIN 12.3 G

CARBOHYDRATE
  28.3 G

CHOLESTEROL
  0 MG

FIBRE 12.7 G

❈

Sea bass is a firm white fish with a buttery taste. Here it is lightly coated with ground almonds and spices, quickly sautéed, then baked. I would serve this with the Warm Tomatoes Stuffed with Quinoa and Courgette (page 236).

CURRIED LENTILS WITH VEGETABLES

780 ml (3¼ cups) purified water
1 bay leaf
190 g (1 cup) lentils
1 tablespoon Cajun seasoning
115 g (1 cup) sliced onion
2 cloves garlic, thinly sliced
70 g (1 cup) sliced shiitake or
  button mushrooms
50 g (¹/2 cup) broccoli florets
60 g (¹/2 cup) diced yellow or red
  pepper
2 tablespoons olive oil
160 ml (²/3 cup) nutritional yeast

1 teaspoon salt
¹/8 teaspoon curry powder
1 tablespoon cornflour

SEA BASS

50 g (¹/2 cup) ground almonds
1 teaspoon salt
Pinch of cayenne pepper
1 tablespoon curry powder
4 x 170 g (6 oz) sea bass steaks,
  cut in half
2 tablespoons olive oil
3 tablespoons freshly squeezed
  lemon juice

Bring 720 ml (3 cups) of the water to the boil in a large saucepan. Add the bay leaf and the lentils and cook for 40–45 minutes or until tender. Remove from heat and allow to cool briefly. Drain off any liquid and stir in the Cajun seasoning.

Sauté the onions, garlic, mushrooms, broccoli, and peppers in the olive oil until the onions are translucent and limp, about 4 minutes. Add the yeast, salt, and curry powder and stir until everything is blended in. Add to the cooked lentils. Mix the cornflour with the remaining water and stir it into the lentils and vegetables. Continue to cook for 3 minutes, until the mixture thickens. Remove from the heat.

Preheat oven to 200°C.

Mix the ground almonds, salt, cayenne pepper, and curry powder on a plate and flip both sides of the fish steaks on it until they are coated with the mixture. Heat the olive oil in a large sauté pan and lay the fish in the pan. Sauté over medium heat, turning once, for 5 minutes on each side. Drizzle the lemon juice over the fish. If you aren't using an ovenproof pan, transfer the fish to a baking dish. Put the lentil and vegetable mixture around the fish, cover with foil, and bake for 10 minutes to cook the steaks through; when you cut into one, the flesh should be a pale white colour, not translucent.

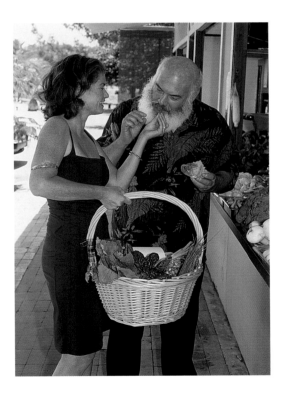

Vegetarian Shepherd's Pie

Traditional shepherd's pie is usually made with minced lamb and white potatoes. I like this one because it has sweet potatoes mixed in. The curried lentil filling is sandwiched between two layers of creamy potato filling sitting on a crouton crust baked on top of courgettes. I serve this with a simple chopped tomato salad.

SERVES 6 AS A
MAIN DISH
OR 12 AS A SIDE
DISH

PER SERVING:

CALORIES 503.1

FAT 6.8 G
  SATURATED FAT
  1.1 G
(11.8% OF CALO-
  RIES FROM FAT)

PROTEIN 22.8 G

CARBOHYDRATE
  92.2 G

CHOLESTEROL
  0 MG

FIBRE 22.3 G

2 medium or large sweet potatoes, peeled and cubed

6 medium or large white potatoes, peeled and cubed

1 tablespoon olive oil

1 tablespoon Italian seasoning herbs

1 tablespoon Cajun seasoning

CURRIED LENTIL FILLING

780 ml (3 1/4 cups) purified water

1 bay leaf

190 g (1 cup) lentils

2 teaspoons Cajun seasoning

115 g (1 cup) sliced onions

2 cloves garlic, thinly sliced

70 g (1 cup) sliced shiitake or button mushrooms

50 g (1/2 cup) broccoli florets

60 g (1/2 cup) diced yellow or red pepper

1 tablespoon olive oil

160 ml (2/3 cup) nutritional yeast

1 teaspoon salt

1 teaspoon curry powder

1 tablespoon cornflour

1 courgette, cut in rounds

45 g (1 cup) fresh breadcrumbs or baked croutons

GARNISH

50 g (1/2 cup) thinly sliced spring onions

Preheat oven to 180°C.

Bring a large pan of water to the boil. Drop the cubed sweet and white potatoes into the water and simmer for 45 minutes. They should be easily pierced with a fork. Drain the potatoes, reserving 480 ml (2 cups) of the water. Pour 240 ml (1 cup) of the water back into the pan and mash with the potatoes. Add the olive oil, Italian seasoning, and Cajun seasoning and mash again until seasonings are completely blended into the potatoes.

Meanwhile, cook the lentils: bring 3 cups of the water to the boil. Add the bay leaf, lentils, and Cajun seasoning and cook for 45 minutes. Remove from heat when completely cooked and allow to cool briefly. Drain off any liquid.

Sauté the onions, garlic, mushrooms, broccoli, and peppers in the olive oil in a large sauté pan until the onions are translucent and limp, about 4 minutes. Add the reserved 240 ml (1 cup) of potato water, the yeast, salt, and curry powder and stir until everything is blended in. Add to the cooked lentils. Mix the cornflour in the remaining water and stir it into the lentil and vegetable mixture. Continue to cook for 3 more minutes, until the sauce thickens. Remove from heat.

Line the bottom of a baking dish with the courgette rounds. Sprinkle half of the breadcrumbs or croutons on top of the courgettes. Spoon out half of the mashed potatoes and spread across the courgette rounds. Spread the curried lentils on top of the potatoes. Spoon the remainder of the mashed potatoes on the lentils, and smooth the surface. Sprinkle the rest of the breadcrumbs or croutons and the spring onions on top. Bake for 50 minutes. Leave to cool for 15 minutes before cutting and serving.

Tips from Rosie's Kitchen

Nutritional yeast is high in B vitamins, and it is often sprinkled over various foods for added flavour. You can find it in health-food shops.

ABOUT TOFU

Tofu is a traditional food of China, Japan, and Korea, now eaten in other countries of Asia and, increasingly, in the West. Sometimes called soya bean curd, it is made from soya milk in much the same way that fresh curd cheese is made from cow's milk – that is, a coagulant is added to heated milk, causing the protein to form curds that are then drained and pressed. (Soya milk is easily obtained from dried soya beans by soaking, cooking, grinding, and squeezing them.) Depending on how the curds are handled and how much liquid is pressed out of them, the finished tofu can be soft and silken or firm and 'meaty'. The former can be used as the base for puddings, pie fillings, and other Western desserts; the latter can serve as a substitute for meat or chicken.

You can now buy many varieties of tofu in supermarkets as well as health-food shops and Oriental markets, usually packed in water in plastic tubs and kept in refrigerated cases. Always check the dates on these packages and use up the tofu sooner rather than later. Tofu should have a very mild, pleasant taste and smell. It should never appear discoloured or smell sour.

Tofu is a bit scary to Westerners, who don't know all of the ways Chinese and Japanese cooks get it to absorb the flavours of sauces and take on exactly the right textures for particular dishes. You can't just dump raw tofu into a salad and expect your family and guests to like it. But you can drain firm tofu well, crumble it, and sauté it in olive oil until it becomes golden, then add it to a tomato sauce instead of beef, and most people will never know.

There are a number of advantages to learning how to cook with tofu. Not only is it extremely versatile, it is a healthful alternative to protein foods of animal origin, because it has hardly any saturated fat, and the fat it does contain is relatively good for us. In addition, tofu provides isoflavones, compounds that reduce risks of heart disease and cancer (especially breast and prostate cancer). And tofu is quite inexpensive compared with meat and poultry.

One kind of tofu I use often is the baked variety. This comes in vacuum packs and can be found in the refrigerated cases of health food shops. Baked tofu looks brown and firm. It has been pressed to a very meaty consistency and simmered in a flavoured broth. I make sandwiches with it, but I also put cubes and slices of it into stir-fries instead of meat or chicken. I think it works well to produce vegetarian versions of some of Rosie's chicken recipes. —A.W.

Slow-Baked Tofu with Stir-Fry

It is really worth the time to experiment with recipes that call for tofu. You can always marinate and bake it ahead of time to make it easier to incorporate in your favourite recipes. Once you've learned how to work with it, you can substitute it in recipes that call for chicken or meat. As we have all experienced, eating the same source of protein all the time can get boring. This dish is great because you get your help-ing of vegetables in it and they are all tossed and cooked in a delicious marinade.

This stir-fry is great over Brown Rice Pilaf (page 246) topped with Peanut Dipping Sauce (page 52) to add more protein and flavour.

720 ml (3 cups) Spanish Rice
   (page 136) or steamed rice

MARINADE

1 teaspoon toasted sesame oil
3 cloves garlic, sliced
60 ml (1/4 cup) natural soy sauce
   (such as tamari)
2 tablespoons peeled, sliced root
   ginger
1 tablespoon Dijon mustard
1 tablespoon ground cumin

450 g (1 lb) firm tofu

STIR-FRY

1/2 head broccoli
1 large onion, sliced

2 garlic cloves, sliced
2 carrots, peeled and cut into
   matchsticks (page 117)
2 tablespoons olive oil
115 g (4 oz) mange-touts, strings
   removed
35 g (1/2 cup) sliced mushrooms
2 tablespoons natural soy sauce
   (such as tamari)
60 ml (1/4 cup) purified water or
   vegetable stock (page 122)

GARNISH

360 ml (11/2 cups) Peanut
   Dipping Sauce (page 52) or
   2 tablespoons sesame seeds

SERVES 6

PER SERVING:

CALORIES 371.2

FAT 26 G
  SATURATED FAT
  4.2 G
(58.7% OF CALO-
  RIES FROM FAT)
PROTEIN 13.3 G
CARBOHYDRATE
  24 G
CHOLESTEROL
  0 MG
FIBRE 6.3 G

Prepare the Peanut Dipping Sauce, if using.

Preheat oven to 150°C.

Whisk all the marinade ingredients together in a baking dish. Drain the tofu and slice it vertically into nine 1 cm (1/2 in) seg-ments. Lay the tofu slices in the marinade and turn them gently, using a spoon, to completely coat each one. Bake on the top shelf of the oven for 30 minutes.

To cook brown rice takes about 45 minutes, so unless you are using leftover prepared rice start preparing it now.

Turn the tofu over and baste the tops with the marinade in the baking dish. Continue to bake for another 30 minutes, until the tofu slices puff up, turn light brown, and become slightly hard. Remove from the oven and leave to cool for 15 minutes. When completely cooled, cut into cubes.

Cut the florets off the head of the broccoli, slicing the large ones in half so they are all more or less the same size. Discard the stalks or save them for another stir-fry or for soups.

Sauté the onion, garlic, and carrots for 3 minutes in the olive oil in a wok or sauté pan over medium-high heat, being careful not to burn the oil. It should not smoke. Toss in the broccoli, mange-touts, and mushrooms. Stir with a wooden spoon to keep the vegetables moving, cooking for another 2 minutes.

Stir the soy sauce into the vegetables, then add the water or vegetable stock. Drop in the cubed tofu, toss a few times, and cook for 2 more minutes, then remove from the heat. Cover the pan with a lid and let the vegetables steam for about 6 minutes.

Place the prepared rice on each of 6 plates, cover with equal portions of the stir-fry, and top with some peanut sauce or 1 teaspoon sesame seeds.

Tips from Rosie's Kitchen

Although using a wok is ideal for stir-fry dishes, you can use a sauté pan and achieve excellent results.

The marinated and slowly baked tofu is another item that is very useful to have on hand in the fridge a few days in advance, to cube up and use in this or other stir-fries, or to toss in your favourite salad as a meat alternative.

BAKED PRESSED TOFU WITH GREENS

The addition of baked tofu transforms this simple recipe into a satisfying main dish with none of the saturated fat that would be present if meat or poultry were in it. Be careful not to overcook the greens. They should have a rich green colour and be just tender. You could have some balsamic vinegar and dried chilli flakes on the table in case people want to add more seasoning.

400 g (4 cups) hearty greens (kale, chard leaves, spring greens, or a mixture of these)
2 tablespoons extra virgin olive oil

1 large onion, chopped
240 ml (1 cup) baked pressed tofu, cut into cubes or slices (see *Note*)
Salt to taste

Wash the greens. Remove any coarse stalks and midribs and discard, then chop the greens coarsely.

Heat the olive oil in a large frying pan over medium-high heat and add the onions. Sauté, stirring, until the onions just begin to brown. Add the greens, tossing them until they wilt. Reduce the heat to medium and add the tofu. Stir-fry the tofu and greens for 2–3 more minutes. Season to taste with salt and serve.

Note: Baked pressed tofu that has been simmered in a flavoured broth comes in 225 g (8 oz) vacuum-sealed packs and can be found in the refrigerated cases of health food shops and supermarkets that sell tofu products. There is a choice of flavours – savoury, five-spice, and hickory-smoked, for example – all of which work in this dish, although the hickory-smoked variety is my favourite.

SERVES 4

PER SERVING:
CALORIES 93
FAT 6 G
  SATURATED FAT
  LESS THAN 1 G
  (57% OF CALO-
  RIES FROM FAT)
PROTEIN 1.8 G
CARBOHYDRATE
  7.3 G
CHOLESTEROL
  0 MG
FIBRE 1 G

Baked Spicy Tofu with Cellophane Noodles, Sweetcorn, and Mango

Tofu surprises everybody who has never had it well prepared. The real bonus of eating tofu, besides the taste, is that it's high in protein, low in both sodium and calories, and is virtually cholesterol free. See Andy's comments on the subject (page 192).

This is an uncomplicated dish, yet the flavours and textures that mingle together – sweetcorn, mango, fennel, coriander, and sweet onions – are intense. I believe that you'll develop a real taste for tofu and begin to enjoy cooking and serving this wonderful food. Tofu is really nature's gift to all of us.

SERVES 6

PER SERVING:

CALORIES 343.2

FAT 9.7 G
  SATURATED FAT
  1.4 G

(42.6% OF CALO-
  RIES FROM FAT)

PROTEIN 2.3 G

CARBOHYDRATE
  31.9 G

CHOLESTEROL
  0 MG

FIBRE 4.9 G

❋

MARINADE

60 ml (1/4 cup) toasted sesame oil
1 teaspoon ground fennel seed
1/2 teaspoon salt
1 teaspoon red chilli paste, or
  more to taste
2 tablespoons honey
60 ml (1/4 cup) freshly squeezed
  lime juice

450 g (1 lb) tofu, soft or firm

1 x 100g (3 1/2 oz) packet cellophane noodles

2 sweet onions, thinly sliced
320 g (2 cups) sweetcorn kernels
  cut off the cob
120 ml (1/2 cup) vegetable stock
  (page 122) or purified water
2 tablespoons natural soy sauce
  (such as tamari)
2 mangoes, peeled, stoned, and
  cubed
1 bunch fresh coriander, washed

GARNISH

1 bunch fresh mint

Whisk all the marinade ingredients together in a small baking dish.

Preheat the oven to 230°C.

Drain the tofu and chop it into 1 cm (1/2 in) cubes. Drop the tofu cubes into the marinade and turn them gently, using a spoon to completely coat each one. Make sure that the tofu cubes are close together and sitting in the marinade. Bake in the hot oven for 15 minutes.

Meanwhile, soak the cellophane noodles in a pan of hot water for 20 minutes, and then drain in a colander.

Simmer the onions and the sweetcorn in the vegetable stock in a large sauté pan until the onions are tender and the sweetcorn is bright yellow (about 3 minutes). Add the soy sauce, mangoes, tofu, and the juices from the marinade. Pinch the leaves off the coriander and sprinkle them in. Add the cellophane noodles and toss until everything is thoroughly coated. Cook for 2 more minutes. (Alternatively, for a handsome presentation, you can make a bed of the cellophane noodle and nestle the tofu, sweetcorn, and mango mixture on top. Then toss it all at the table.) Garnish with mint.

Tips from Rosie's Kitchen

Cellophane noodles can be found in most supermarkets, or in Chinese food shops. You will want to cut them into 15 cm (6 in) lengths with a pair of clean kitchen scissors after they have soaked in the hot water, as this will make them more manageable to work with.

The key to well-flavoured tofu is the baking dish. It must be small enough so the tofu squares are touching and sitting in the marinade. Tofu is porous, and baking the pieces this way allows all the juices to be soaked up and locked in.

Teriyaki Sampler Plate

This recipe was inspired by an evening spent with guests, some of whom were vegetarian and others who weren't. When the tofu is marinated and baked, it actually takes on an uncanny resemblance to chicken in both texture and taste.

You can marinate both the chicken and the tofu for as little as fifteen minutes or up to one full day, if you plan ahead. If you don't have that kind of time, the chicken and the tofu will still have enough teriyaki flavuor if they marinate for just 15 minutes. The teriyaki looks pretty served on a bed of buckwheat noodles (see Tips).

TERIYAKI MARINADE

80 g (1/4 cup) orange marmalade
  or apricot jam
120 ml (1/2 cup) natural soy sauce
  (such as tamari)
60 ml (1/4 cup) freshly squeezed
  orange juice
3 tablespoons grated root ginger
60 ml (1/4 cup) dry sherry

450 g (1 lb) firm tofu
2 boneless, skinless chicken
  breasts (fillets)

225 g (8 oz) asparagus, ends cut
  off, cut into 10 cm (4 in) pieces

GARNISH

1 tablespoon sesame seeds

SERVES 6

PER SERVING:
CALORIES 297.3
FAT 13 G
  SATURATED FAT
  2.7 G
(42% OF CALO-
  RIES FROM FAT)
PROTEIN 25.4 G
CARBOHYDRATE
  17.6 G
CHOLESTEROL
  39 MG
FIBRE 2 G

Preheat the oven to 200°C.

Mix the ingredients for the marinade together and pour 120 ml (1/2 cup) of it into each of 3 different baking dishes for the chicken, tofu, and asparagus.

Slice the tofu block into three 4 cm (1 1/2 in) thick pieces. Cut each of the 3 pieces at an angle from corner to corner. Lay them in a baking dish in the teriyaki marinade.

Put the chicken in a polythene bag or wrap it in cling film and gently tap it with a mallet or pounder for a few minutes,

Baked Spicy Tofu with Cellophane Noodles, Sweetcorn, and Mango

concentrating on the thicker parts of the chicken. Make 4 diagonal slices across each fillet to create 5 pieces. Lay the chicken in its own baking dish in the marinade.

Put the chopped asparagus in the last baking dish and cover with foil.

Put all 3 baking dishes in the oven and bake for 30 minutes. Sprinkle the sesame seeds on top of the chicken and tofu and serve.

Tips from Rosie's Kitchen

Tenderising the chicken not only helps it to absorb the marinade, but also helps it to cook more evenly.

I like to serve this dish with buckwheat noodles, which can be bought at some supermarkets and most health food shops. Cook the noodles in boiling water for 5 minutes, then drain and rinse them in cold water. Put them in a bowl, pour the cooking juices over them, and toss. Lay a bed of noodles on each of 6 plates and arrange the tofu, chicken, and asparagus on top.

If asparagus is out of season, broccoli is another great accompaniment. Salmon can be substituted for the chicken.

SPROUTED BEANS

In Asia, mung bean sprouts have long been used as a vegetable, usually lightly stir-fried. In the West, bean sprouts became popular only with the rise of interest in health food in the 1970s, and people mostly eat them raw. Alfalfa sprouts, especially, are a New Age staple, replacing lettuce in sandwiches, filling salad bowls, and forming great mounds of garnish on platters. Sunflower sprouts are a more recent novelty. Now I see lentil, chickpea, and radish sprouts too, and I know people who like to drink wheatgrass juice, pressed from the sprouts of our staple grain.

The idea that bean sprouts are good for health has little basis in fact. As the youngest forms of green plants, they are probably full of enzymes associated with new growth, but those compounds are destroyed in our stomachs. Actually, some sprouts might not be good for us at all. Raw bean sprouts, in particular, contain natural toxins. For example, alfalfa, a legume, makes a toxin called canavanine that is present in the sprouts and can harm the immune system. It is broken down by simple cooking, but cooking turns delicate alfalfa sprouts into an unappetising mush. So I remove raw alfalfa sprouts from any foods that I am served and recommend that you do, too. I also avoid raw clover, mung bean, lentil, chickpea, and other bean sprouts (which don't taste very good anyway). I have no problem with cooked bean sprouts and no objection to raw sprouts of non-leguminous seeds.

If you like sunflower, radish, and buckwheat sprouts, eat them. But don't try to tell me that they are any better for me than other fresh vegetables or fruits. —A.W.

Turkey Burgers

SERVES 4

PER SERVING:

CALORIES 431.9

FAT 13.3 G
  SATURATED FAT
  2.8 G

(26.8% OF CALO-
  RIES FROM FAT)

PROTEIN 33.7 G

CARBOHYDRATE
  47.8 G

CHOLESTEROL
  90 MG

FIBRE 10.8 G

Turkey meat can be a bit dry, but the addition of mushrooms in this recipe transforms the meat into a succulent and tender consistency. Grilling burgers made of well-seasoned turkey instead of traditional beef is a healthy alternative, and I think you'll really be surprised at how delicious they are.

450 g (1 lb) minced turkey
115 g (4 oz) button mushrooms,
  finely chopped
1 small onion, finely chopped
1 teaspoon barbecue sauce
1 tablespoon mild chilli powder
1 teaspoon Cajun seasoning
Cracked black pepper to taste

1 tablespoon Worcestershire sauce
Cooking oil spray
4 wholemeal burger buns

GARNISH

1 beefsteak tomato, sliced
1 red onion, sliced
1 soft-leaf lettuce

Put the minced turkey, mushrooms, and onions along with the seasonings, spices, and Worcestershire sauce in a medium bowl. With a big wooden spoon or clean hands, blend everything together, making sure that the mushrooms and onions are distributed throughout the meat. Make 4 burgers of equal size.

Preheat the grill (or cook on a sauté pan over medium-high heat). Spray burgers lightly with cooking oil spray and cook for approximately 7 minutes on each side, until completely cooked through. Warm the buns on a baking sheet on the lower level under the grill. Put the burgers on the buns and garnish each with 1 tomato slice, 1 slice red onion, and some lettuce.

Tips from Rosie's Kitchen

If you want to make your own Cajun spice blend, use 1 teaspoon paprika, 1/2 teaspoon cayenne pepper, 1 teaspoon salt, 1/2 teaspoon dried oregano, and 1/2 teaspoon dried basil.

Turkey Burger with trimmings

Hummus Pinwheels with Veggie Crudités

I love tortillas, especially when they are wrapped around something good. Here they are topped with a thick chickpea spread enlivened with the taste of orange, paprika, cayenne pepper, garlic, and lemon, then layered with fresh spinach, carrots, cucumbers, or sunflower sprouts.

These are great to take to work or for a packed lunch if you're on the run. Wrap them in greaseproof paper and seal them closed with a fancy cocktail stick.

SERVES 12

PER SERVING:

CALORIES 157.3

FAT 4.9 G
  SATURATED FAT
  0.7 G
(27.9% OF CALO-
  RIES FROM FAT)

PROTEIN 5.9 G

CARBOHYDRATE
  23 G

CHOLESTEROL
  0 MG

FIBRE 3.9 G

❋

400 g (2 cups) dried chickpeas, soaked overnight in 1.4 litres (6 cups) of water with 1 teaspoon bicarbonate of soda
1 tablespoon miso paste
2 tablespoons natural soy sauce (such as tamari)
1 teaspoon paprika
120 ml (1/2 cup) freshly squeezed orange juice
1 tablespoon grated lemon zest
60 g (1/4 cup) tahini
Pinch of cayenne pepper
2 cloves garlic
1/2 teaspoon salt
60 ml (1/4 cup) freshly squeezed lemon juice
60 ml (1/4 cup) roasted pepper purée (optional) (page 76)
1 teaspoon chopped fresh tarragon or 1/2 teaspoon dried
6 flour tortillas (wraps), flavoured or wholemeal

FILLING

225 g (8 oz) spinach, washed and tough stalks removed
165 g (11/2 cups) grated carrots
70 g (11/2 cups) sunflower sprouts or 1/2 cucumber, peeled and sliced lengthways

Do not drain the water that the beans have been soaking in overnight. Bring the water to the boil and cook the beans, covered, for 45 minutes. The beans should be easily pierced with a fork.

After the beans are cooked, drain them in a colander, reserving 60 ml (1/4 cup) of the water. Mix the water with the miso in a bowl. Put all the remaining ingredients including the red pepper purée if you are using it, but not the tarragon, in a food processor and process until smooth. Pour in the miso and process again. Fold in the tarragon.

Trim the round sides off each tortilla to make a square and spread the hummus over them. Starting 1 cm (1/2 in) up from one side of the tortillas, lay the filling ingredients on top of each other, in thin layers. Roll the tortillas up. When you get to the end of the roll, use the hummus on the inside edge to act as a sealer to keep the tortilla closed. When you are ready to serve, cut the rolled tortillas in half at an angle.

Orange Chicken Pita with Vegetables and Tahini Dressing

This recipe might inspire you to have an afternoon picnic with good friends. You'll need to plan ahead, because the chickpeas will have to soak overnight, but that takes virtually no effort (or you can use canned chickpeas to save time). If using dried chickpeas, you might also want to consider marinating the chicken overnight, because it makes a big difference in the way it tastes. The extra soaking time maximises the taste so you end up with rich, full flavour, not a weak hint of distant spices.

If you're preparing for an outdoor lunch, wrap the stuffed pitas in greaseproof paper and seal the paper with cocktail sticks that have coloured cellophane ends, or buy special sandwich bags at the supermarket. Also, when preparing stuffed pitas to go, store the dressing in a separate container with a lid until ready to use.

MAKES 6 PITAS

PER SERVING:

CALORIES 605

FAT 20.6 G
  SATURATED FAT
  5 G
(31.3% OF CALO-
  RIES FROM FAT)

PROTEIN 40.1 G

CARBOHYDRATE
  62 G

CHOLESTEROL
  82 MG

FIBRE 6.4 G

1 tablespoon Italian seasoning herbs
200 g (1 cup) dried chickpeas, soaked overnight in water to cover with 1/2 teaspoon bicarbonate of soda, or 1 x 400 g (14 oz) can chickpeas

MARINADE

240 ml (1 cup) freshly squeezed orange juice
1 tablespoon paprika
1 teaspoon turmeric
11/2 teaspoons ground cumin

4 skinless, boneless chicken breasts (fillets)

TAHINI DRESSING

60 g (1/4 cup) tahini
125 g (1/2 cup) plain low-fat yogurt
120 ml (1/2 cup) freshly squeezed orange juice
1 tablespoon natural soy sauce (such as tamari)
1 shallot, chopped
2 cloves garlic, chopped
1 tablespoon chopped fresh parsley
1 teaspoon chopped fresh chives
1 tablespoon mirin (sweet rice wine)

PITA FILLING

2 large, ripe tomatoes, cut into wedges
35 g (1/2 cup) shredded cabbage
55 g (1/2 cup) grated carrots
1 tablespoon pitted and sliced Kalamata olives
30 g (1/4 cup) thinly sliced radishes
1/2 cucumber, thinly sliced

40 g (1/2 cup) sliced red or yellow peppers
60 g (1/2 cup) thinly sliced spring onions
50 g (1/2 cup) grated low-fat Cheddar cheese

6 wholemeal pita breads

Sprinkle the Italian seasoning into the pan of water that the chickpeas have been soaking in overnight. Bring to the boil and cook for 45 minutes to 1 hour. The chickpeas should be soft and easily pierced with a fork. Drain the chickpeas well. (If using canned chickpeas, drain and rinse them well.)

Mix the orange juice, paprika, turmeric, and cumin together. Lay the chicken breasts in a baking tin and pour the marinade over them. Cover and leave to sit in the marinade for as much time as you can give it, overnight in the refrigerator if possible. Preheat the grill, then grill the chicken breasts in their marinade for 8–10 minutes on each side, basting with the marinade to keep them moist. Or you can bake the chicken in a preheated 200°C oven for about 25 minutes or until they are completely cooked, turning them over halfway through. Remove from the oven and allow to cool for 15 minutes. When completely cooled, cut into thin slices.

Mix all the dressing ingredients in a bowl and whisk together for 1 minute.

Mix the vegetable filling ingredients with the chickpeas. Cut 2.5 cm (1 in) off the top of each pita bread to make an opening. Stuff with an equal amount of chicken and vegetable filling and garnish with a dollop of dressing.

Tips from Rosie's Kitchen

If you want to store the cooked chicken in the refrigerator before assembling the pitas, or you have some leftover chicken, keep it in the cooking juices and in a covered dish so it remains moist.

Santa Fe Chicken

The marinade in this dish is what gives the chicken such a smooth flavour. Although it is ideal if the meat can soak in the marinade for at least 1 hour before cooking to absorb the intricate flavours of the marinade, if you don't have time, don't be discouraged, because the chicken will still be flavourful. If you are really planning ahead, you can soak the meat in the marinade for up to two days.

Serve with Spanish Rice (page 136) and the Jicama and Carrot Salad (page 116). The flavours together are very complementary.

SERVES 4

PER SERVING:

CALORIES 212.3

FAT 4.4 G
  SATURATED FAT
  0.8 G
(46.8% OF CALO-
  RIES FROM FAT)

PROTEIN 30.1 G

CARBOHYDRATE
  13 G

CHOLESTEROL
  72 MG

FIBRE 0.9 G

❋

MARINADE

Juice from 3 limes
60 ml (1/4 cup) low-sodium soy
  sauce
11/2 teaspoons olive oil
11/2 teaspoons mild chilli powder
11/2 teaspoons cumin seeds
11/2 teaspoons ground coriander
6 cloves garlic, finely chopped
11/2 teaspoons honey

4 boneless, skinless chicken
  breasts (fillets)

60 ml (1/4 cup) white wine
3 tablespoons chopped fresh
  coriander leaves

GARNISH

Mock Soured Cream (page 62) or
  reduced-fat crème fraîche
1 lime, sliced into 6 thin slices
6 spring onion firecrackers (see
  Tips)
60 ml (1/4 cup) fresh salsa (page
  8) or Papaya Salsa (page 185)

Mix together marinade ingredients in a bowl, stirring thoroughly. Pour into a shallow baking tin and lay the chicken breasts in it. Cover and refrigerate for 1 hour.

Preheat the grill to medium.

Pour the white wine into the baking tin. Grill the chicken for 8–10 minutes, basting it with the juices in the tin to keep it moist.

Transfer the chicken to a platter and slice it at an angle. Garnish each piece with a little of the pan juices, a dollop of Mock Soured Cream or reduced-fat crème fraîche, slices of lime, and a spring onion firecracker, as well as a dollop of salsa.

Tips from Rosie's Kitchen

The spring onion 'firecracker' is a lively garnish that gets its name from the way the leaves of the onion curl away from the body of the onion, creating a firecracker appearance. Cut 5 cm (2 in) off the green leafy side of the onion. Trim the roots at the white, bulbous end. Then, following the top illustration, cut 3 slits about 1 cm (1/2 in) down through the white, bulbous end of the onion. Fill a bowl with iced water and drop in the freshly cut spring onions.

It is never too much trouble to cook extra chicken breasts. They hold the flavour of the marinade and are wonderful for chicken sandwiches for work or school.

Rosie cutting three slits in the white, bulbous end of a spring onion

After trimming the top off the radish, she makes small cuts into the bulb all around

Soaking the radish rosettes and the spring onion firecrackers in iced water

ANDY SUGGESTS

I'd like more salsa with this, either a good commercial one or a quick salsa fresca like the one that Rosie uses (page 8).

Barbecued Fish Tacos

MAKES 12 TACOS

PER SERVING:

CALORIES 184.9

FAT 7.4 G

SATURATED FAT
3.7 G

(33.3% OF CALO-
RIES FROM FAT)

PROTEIN 14.9 G

CARBOHYDRATE
15.9 G

CHOLESTEROL
3.7 MG

FIBRE 2.1 G

Tacos (corn tortillas) filled with spicy fish cooked outdoors are just right for summertime. When buying the fish, look at it carefully to make sure it's spanking fresh. It should really glisten.

Juice from 1 lemon or 2 limes (about 60 ml/1/4 cup)
3 x 170 g (6 oz) boneless halibut steaks
1 tablespoon mild chilli powder
1 tablespoon paprika
1/2 teaspoon dried oregano
1/2 teaspoon salt
12 corn tortillas
150 g (11/2 cups) grated Cheddar cheese
210 g (3 cups) shredded cabbage
360 ml (11/2 cups) fresh guacamole (page 211)
120 ml (1/2 cup) Mock Soured Cream (page 62) or reduced-fat crème fraîche

120 ml (1/2 cup) fresh salsa (page 8), or 1 tomato, chopped, mixed with 2 teaspoons Tabasco sauce
2 limes, cut into 6 wedges

GARNISH

1 lime, cut into 6 wedges

Tips from Rosie's Kitchen

You can either barbecue or grill the fish. I like to barbecue it because I like the way the fish tastes that way, and it sets the mood for a summertime meal. If you grill the fish indoors, cook it for 4 minutes on each side, for a total of 8 minutes.

When barbecuing the fish, make sure that the fire is hot and that the fish isn't too close to the coals.

It's worth cooking extra fish so you have some left over. You can use it to make Clam Chowder (page 131) or cold fish sandwiches for the next day's lunch. Put about 55 g (2 oz) of fish between 2 slices of toasted wholemeal bread. Spread some Mock Soured Cream on the bread and top with lettuce and tomato slices.

Drizzle the lemon or lime juice over the fish and sprinkle the chilli powder, paprika, oregano, and salt on both sides. Cook on the barbecue for approximately 3–5 minutes on each side for a total cooking time of approximately 6–10 minutes. Transfer to a platter and slice the fish into 2.5 cm (1 in) thick strips.

Wrap 3 stacks of 4 tortillas in foil and place them on the barbecue for a couple of minutes to warm them up. Or, if you prefer, warm directly on the barbecue grill. Top each tortilla with equal portions of fish, cheese, and cabbage and add 2 tablespoons guacamole, 1 teaspoon soured cream, and 1 teaspoon fresh salsa. Fold the tortillas over into half moons. Garnish each plate with 1 lime wedge. Serve with more lime wedges, and the rest of the salsa and soured cream in small bowls.

Chicken Quesadillas

This is a popular dish because of everything you can taste – the marinated chicken, cheese, salsa, garlic, onions, coriander, and guacamole, all wrapped in a warm corn tortilla. It would save you some time to prepare the salsa ahead of time if you are making it fresh, but be sure to make the guacamole fresh, just before you are ready to serve.

2 skinless, boneless chicken breasts (fillets)
60 ml (1/4 cup) white wine
2 tablespoons mild chilli powder
1 red pepper
8 corn tortillas
10 Kalamata olives, pitted and sliced
5 mushrooms, sliced
200 g (2 cups) grated low-fat Cheddar cheese
120 ml (1/2 cup) fresh salsa (page 8) or 1 tomato, chopped and seasoned with Tabasco sauce to taste

GUACAMOLE

2 pinches of salt
2 small cloves garlic
1 avocado
1 sprig fresh coriander, chopped
1 tablespoon plain yogurt
11/2 teaspoons freshly squeezed lime juice (1/2 lime)
2 tablespoons finely chopped onion
1 fresh jalapeño or other green chilli, diced (optional)

SERVES 8

PER SERVING:
CALORIES 210.5
FAT 10.7 G
   SATURATED FAT
   4.2 G
(46% OF CALORIES FROM FAT)
PROTEIN 14.2 G
CARBOHYDRATE
   14.2 G
CHOLESTEROL
   38 MG
FIBRE 2.3 G

GUACAMOLE

SERVES 8

PER SERVING:

CALORIES 59.9

FAT 4 G

SATURATED FAT
0.7 G

(55.3% OF CALO-
RIES FROM FAT)

PROTEIN 1.1 G

CARBOHYDRATE
6.1 G

CHOLESTEROL
0 MG

FIBRE 1.3 G

❈

Preheat oven to 200°C.

Put the chicken breasts in a shallow glass baking dish. Pour the wine over them and sprinkle them with some of the chilli powder. Bake for 10 minutes, then turn the chicken over and sprinkle with the remaining chilli powder. Bake for 10 more minutes. The chicken breasts should be tender but not pink. Allow them to cool, then slice into strips. Pour the leftover baking juices into a covered plastic dish and refrigerate.

Grill the red pepper on a baking tray, turning it so that all sides become brown and blistered. Remove from the heat, drop it into a polythene bag and twist closed. When completely cooled, peel the skin off, scrape out the seeds, and slice the pepper into strips.

Arrange the tortillas on the baking tray and evenly distribute the chicken, pepper strips, olives, and mushrooms on top. Sprinkle 4 tablespoons of cheese on top of each tortilla and bake until the cheese melts, about 5–10 minutes. Bake longer if you want crispy tortillas.

Meanwhile, make the guacamole: sprinkle some salt into a bowl and mash the garlic against it with a fork. The grains of salt will help to mash the garlic. Add the avocado and mash with the fork. Mix in the coriander, yogurt, lime, onion, and chilli, if using. Serve the quesadillas hot with the guacamole and the salsa alongside.

TOFU FAJITAS

For a quick and exciting meal, this healthful version of a popular Mexican dish is hard to beat. The baked tofu neatly replaces beef and, along with olive oil, provides good fat. Wholemeal flour tortillas (wraps) make very good fajitas, and they give you some fibre. The freshness of the ingredients makes these fajitas both visually appealing and delicious.

2 tablespoons extra virgin olive oil
1 large onion, sliced
1 red pepper, seeded and julienned
1 green pepper, or ancho or Anaheim chilli, seeded and julienned
1 fresh jalapeño or other hot green chilli, seeded and finely chopped
70 g (1 cup) sliced chestnut mushrooms
480 ml (2 cups) sliced, baked pressed tofu (preferably hickory-smoked flavour)

Salt to taste
6 wholemeal flour tortillas (wraps), warmed

GARNISH
Reduced-fat crème fraîche, salsa, chopped fresh tomatoes, avocado, and spring onions

SERVES 6

PER SERVING:
CALORIES 303
FAT 10.5 G
  SATURATED FAT
  1 G
(31% OF CALORIES FROM FAT)
PROTEIN 23 G
CARBOHYDRATE
  32 G
CHOLESTEROL
  0 MG
FIBRE 8 G

Heat the olive oil in a large frying pan over medium-high heat, then add the onions. Sauté, stirring, until the onions are translucent. Stir in the peppers, chilli, and mushrooms and sauté until the vegetables begin to soften, about 5 minutes. Add the tofu and stir-fry for 5 minutes more. Season with salt to taste and serve in the tortillas.

Top the fajitas with reduced-fat crème fraîche, salsa, chopped fresh tomatoes, avocado, and spring onions, or a combination of these.

Baked Bean, Rice, and Cheese Burrito

An additional benefit of this dish, beside the fact that it's simple to make and really delicious, is that it's fairly nutritionally balanced. The beans provide some protein, and the rice and the tortilla provide starchy carbohydrates. I make my burritos with black beans, but you can use the traditional pinto beans if you prefer them.

FILLING

255 g (1 1/2 cups) dried black beans, soaked overnight in water to cover with 1 teaspoon bicarbonate of soda, or
2 x 400 g (14 oz) cans black beans
1 bay leaf
2 garlic cloves, peeled
1 tablespoon dried oregano
1/2 teaspoon dried chilli flakes

280 g (1 1/2 cups) brown rice

ENCHILADA SAUCE

6 large fresh tomatoes, or 225 g (8 oz) tomato passata
1 onion, diced
2 carrots, thinly sliced
Cayenne pepper to taste
1 teaspoon salt
3 tablespoons mild chilli powder
1 tablespoon olive oil
60 ml (1/4 cup) vegetable stock (page 122) or purified water
8 large flour tortillas (wraps), flavoured or wholemeal
60 g (1/2 cup) sliced spring onions
120 ml (1/2 cup) fresh salsa (page 8)
100 g (1 cup) grated Monterey jack or Cheddar cheese
3 tablespoons reduced-fat crème fraîche

GARNISH

6 black olives

Prepare the beans. Drop the bay leaf, garlic cloves, oregano, and chilli flakes into the pan of water that the beans have been soaking in overnight. Bring it to the boil and cook for 45 minutes. The beans should be soft and easily pierced with a fork. When they are ready, remove them from the heat, drain off any remaining liquid, and remove the bay leaf. If using canned beans, drain and mix with the seasonings, except the bay leaf.

Prepare the rice: bring 720 ml (3 cups) of water to the boil in a medium pan. Stir in the rice, turn down the heat, cover, and simmer for 45 minutes. The lid on the pan should be tight-fitting. Try not to remove it during the cooking, because heat and liquid will escape. When done, the rice should be firm and all the water absorbed. Remove from the heat and set aside.

Make the sauce: if using fresh tomatoes, first slice an 'X' on the base of each one and then drop them into an pan of boiling water. Leave until the skins start to loosen, about 2 minutes. Remove them with a slotted spoon and allow to cool. When cooled, peel the skin off. Squeeze each tomato over a sieve set over a bowl. Discard the seeds in the sieve. Chop the tomatoes and set aside in the bowl with the squeezed-out juice.

Preheat oven to 180°C.

Sauté the onion and carrots with the cayenne, salt, and chilli powder in the olive oil for about 2 minutes. Add the chopped tomatoes with their juice, or the passata, and the stock, and cook over medium heat until the carrots begin to soften (about 10 minutes). Remove from the heat and leave to cool. When cool, pour into a food processor and process until smooth and with a sauce-like consistency.

Lay the tortillas flat on a clean work space. Divide the beans and rice among them, placing it in the middle. Sprinkle each tortilla with 1 tablespoon sliced spring onions, 1 tablespoon salsa, 3 tablespoons grated cheese, and 1/2 tablespoon crème fraîche. Fold the sides in, then roll up the tortillas. Lay them in a baking dish, seam side down, and pour the enchilada sauce on top. Sprinkle the tops with the remaining cheese and cover the pan with foil. Bake for 30 minutes. Garnish each burrito with 1 black olive and serve.

GALLO PINTO (COSTA RICAN RICE AND BEANS)

This is a typical Costa Rican dish, often eaten with scrambled eggs for breakfast. The universal Costa Rican condiment, Salsa Lizano, is used to flavour it. A combination of Worcestershire and Tabasco sauces makes a good approximation. The fresh coriander is an essential ingredient, adding colour and an authentic Latin American flavour. Beans and rice are used together in dishes all round the world. This is a particularly good one.

SERVES 6

PER SERVING:

CALORIES 199

FAT 3 G
  SATURATED FAT
  0.5 G

(14% OF CALO-
  RIES FROM FAT)

PROTEIN 6.5 G

CARBOHYDRATE
  37.5 G

CHOLESTEROL
  0 MG

FIBRE 3 G

❈

175 g (1 cup) white rice
400 ml (1¾ cups) cold purified water
1 tablespoon extra virgin olive oil
1 medium onion, diced
½ red pepper, seeded and diced
1 green chilli, seeded and finely chopped
2 cloves garlic, finely chopped

1 handful fresh coriander leaves, chopped
1 x 400 g (14 oz) can black beans, drained
Salt to taste
1 teaspoon Tabasco sauce mixed with 2 tablespoons Worcester-shire sauce, or to taste (see *Note*)

Wash the rice in cold water, drain, and put it in a pan with the water and a pinch of salt. Bring to the boil, stir, cover, and lower the heat to a simmer. Cook the rice until the water is absorbed, about 20 minutes. Let the rice stand for 10 minutes, then fluff it with a fork.

Heat the olive oil in a frying pan over medium-high heat. Add the onion, pepper, and chilli and sauté, stirring, for 5 minutes. Stir in the garlic and sauté for another 2 minutes. Add the coriander and sauté for 1 minute more.

Spoon the rice and beans into the pan, mix well, and heat everything through. Season to taste with salt and the mixed sauces.

Note: You may be able to find Salsa Lizano in shops that sell Latin American foods. Pickapeppa Sauce from Jamaica also works well in this dish.

Tostadas with Salsa and Guacamole

Plan this dish for a festive evening with friends. You can prepare the beans and salsa one day in advance. Take a casual approach and create a 'tostada buffet' by putting all the toppings out in separate bowls. This way, everybody participates in creating their own meal, piling on whatever they want. Kids love it.

BEANS

285 g(1 1/2 cups) dried pinto beans, soaked overnight in 1.4 litres (6 cups) of water with 1 teaspoon bicarbonate of soda
2 garlic cloves, peeled
1 onion, chopped
1 bay leaf
2 teaspoons dried basil
90 g(1/2 cup) chopped ripe tomatoes
1 tablespoon ground cumin
1 tablespoon mild chilli powder
1 teaspoon paprika
Pinch of dried chilli flakes

SALSA

1 bunch fresh coriander
180 g(1 cup) chopped ripe tomatoes
30 g(1/4 cup) diced red pepper
40 g(1/4 cup) diced red onion
1 fresh jalapeño or other green chilli, seeded and finely chopped
2 tablespoons freshly squeezed lime juice

8 corn tortillas or small flour tortillas (wraps)

TOPPINGS

100 g(1 cup) grated Monterey jack or Cheddar cheese
1 cos lettuce, shredded
1 carrot, grated
1/2 red cabbage, shredded
10 g(1/4 cup) fresh coriander leaves
Fresh guacamole (page 211)

MAKES 8

PER SERVING:
CALORIES 282
FAT 6.1 G
 SATURATED FAT
 2.9 G
(18.5% OF CALO-
RIES FROM FAT)
PROTEIN 15.3 G
CARBOHYDRATE
 44.7 G
CHOLESTEROL
 12 MG
FIBRE 13.8 G

Prepare the beans: add the garlic, onion, bay leaf, and dried basil to the pan of beans that has been soaking overnight. Bring to the boil and cook for 45 minutes to 1 hour. The beans should be soft and easy to mash with the back of a spoon. When they are ready, drain off any remaining water and remove the bay leaf. Add the tomatoes, and mash the beans and tomatoes with a potato masher. Add the cumin, chilli powder, paprika, and the chilli flakes and mash again. (Reheat before serving if prepared ahead of time.)

Make the salsa: hold the bunch of coriander under running water, making sure that all the dirt is washed off. Pinch the leaves off the stalks and put them in a small bowl with the remaining salsa ingredients, mixing with a spoon until everything is thoroughly blended. Serve immediately or cover and refrigerate until you are ready to use.

Lay the tortillas on a baking tray. Spread an equal amount of beans on each one and sprinkle 1 tablespoon of cheese on top. Heat under a medium grill for about 2 minutes. Layer on the toppings or let everyone do this for their own tostada.

SALSA

SERVES 8

PER SERVING:

CALORIES 21

FAT 0.3 G
  SATURATED FAT
  0 G

(9.6% OF CALO-
  RIES FROM FAT)

PROTEIN 1.1 G

CARBOHYDRATE
  4.7 G

CHOLESTEROL
  0 MG

FIBRE 1.1 G

Tips from Rosie's Kitchen

You've probably heard that dried beans can soak for just a few hours and be ready to cook, but I always soak my beans overnight. It is a fail-safe method. You can be sure they will be evenly cooked. Fill a large pan with enough water to thoroughly cover the beans, add a little bicarbonate of soda, and leave to soak. Salt your beans after they are cooked, not before, to flavour them. If you put salt in the water while soaking or cooking, it may prevent them from softening.

To prepare lettuce, pull the leaves off at the end of the head and rinse them well under cold running water. Pat them dry gently with a clean tea towel, then lay them out and cut into thin slices at an angle, using a sharp knife.

To shred the cabbage, cut the half head in half, then cut the core from each of these quarters. Lay one quarter flat side down on a cutting board and cut into paper-thin slices, at an angle.

You could also include the Santa Fe Chicken (page 208) in your tostada buffet. It makes a great topping.

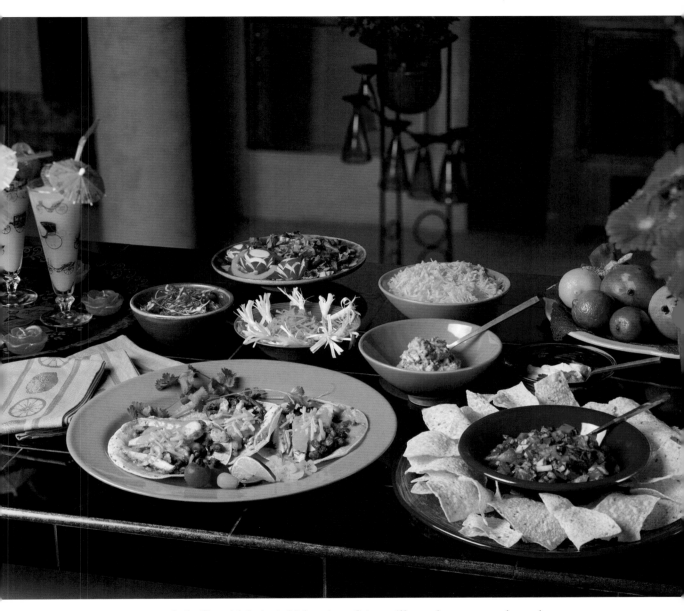

A tostada buffet with baked chicken (or tofu), tortillas, salsa, guacamole, and various toppings

USING LEFTOVERS

No one likes to waste food. It should be painful to throw out unused leftovers. I find it useful to have a plan for leftovers so that I don't wind up ignoring them until they clearly have to be discarded. Rosie agrees with me on this. In her Tips she gives numerous suggestions for using leftovers.

Orthodox Hindus refuse to eat leftovers. They try to eat only freshly prepared food for its healthful energetic qualities, which they think dissipate when food is left standing or is reheated. In my experience, some foods are just fine on reheating – bean dishes, including lentil and split pea soups, and some casseroles. Other foods definitely suffer, like pasta, most vegetables, and fish, but with some forethought they can be prepared in very satisfying ways. In some cases, recipes must be made with leftovers. It is not possible to make good Chinese fried rice with freshly cooked rice; you have to use cold, leftover rice in order to have the grains separate and absorb oil and flavour. —**A.W.**

STEAMED BROCCOLI WITH GLUTEN

I keep cans of braised gluten in my storecupboard and open one when I want a super-quick, satisfying meal that provides protein (derived from wheat). I like to combine it with a fresh vegetable. The name 'gluten' is unfortunate; maybe 'wheat protein medallions' would sound more appetising. What's called for here is a Chinese product that is surprisingly good: the ready-to-eat medallions have a rich taste and satisfying texture that make them a delicious replacement for animal protein in stir-fries.

1 large head broccoli
120 ml (1/2 cup) purified water
1 tablespoon grapeseed oil
Salt to taste
4 cloves garlic, chopped

280 g (10 oz) canned braised gluten
 (see *Note*)

Slice off the bottom ends of the broccoli stalks and cut the thick stalks away from the tops. Separate the tops into florets. Peel the fibrous stalks down to the tender inner flesh and cut them into bite-sized chunks. Place the broccoli in a saucepan with the water, oil, a bit of salt, and the garlic.

Bring the broccoli to the boil, then cover tightly, and cook, stirring once, until the broccoli is bright green and very crunchy-tender, no more than 5 minutes. Do not overcook. Remove from heat, drain off all the liquid, and add the contents of the can of gluten. Stir thoroughly to break up the pieces of gluten. Heat through and serve.

Note: Braised gluten is available at shops that stock Chinese canned goods. The Chinese name is *Cha'i Pow Yü,* and the best brand is Companion, from Taiwan.

SERVES 6

PER SERVING:

CALORIES 132.2

FAT 10.8 G
 SATURATED FAT
 1.7 G

(72.4% OF CALO-
RIES FROM FAT)

PROTEIN 7.1 G

CARBOHYDRATE
 1.8 G

CHOLESTEROL
 0 MG

FIBRE 1 G

CAULIFLOWER WITH CURRIED GLUTEN

Curry-flavoured braised gluten is another versatile prepared-wheat protein food, so well seasoned that it can simply be combined with a fresh vegetable for a quick and easy main dish.

1 large cauliflower
120 ml (1/2 cup) purified water
Salt to taste
1 tablespoon grapeseed oil
1 medium onion, chopped

280 g (10 oz) canned curry-flavoured braised gluten (see *Note*)
30 g (1/2 cup) chopped fresh coriander leaves (optional)

Separate the cauliflower into florets and cut into bite-sized chunks. Put the cauliflower in a saucepan with the water and a bit of salt. Bring to the boil, then cover tightly, and cook until the cauliflower is crunchy-tender, no more than 5 minutes. Remove from the heat and drain well.

Heat the oil in a frying pan, add the onions, and sauté over medium-high heat until the onions just begin to brown. Add the contents of the can of curry-flavoured braised gluten and the steamed cauliflower, stirring well to break up the pieces of gluten, and heat thoroughly. Add the coriander, if used, cook for another minute, and serve.

Note: The Chinese name for curry-flavoured braised gluten is *Curry Cha' i Pow Yü,* and, again, the best brand is Companion.

Accompaniments

(Side Dishes, Breads, and Sauces)

Pickled Vegetables

Lemon Dill Baby Carrots

Seasonal Vegetable Medley

Mashed Potatoes and Parsnips

Shiitake Mushrooms and Mange-touts

Portobello Burger

Warm Tomatoes Stuffed with Quinoa and
Courgette

Wilted Spinach with Mushrooms

Brussels Sprouts for People Who Think
They Hate Brussels Sprouts

Beetroot in Mustard Sauce

Steamed and Roasted Baby Red Potatoes

Greens with Tangy Miso Dressing

Toasted Grain Pilaf

Fresh Apple Sauce

Potato Griddle Cakes

Pear Relish

Serrano Chilli and Coriander Cornbread
Muffins

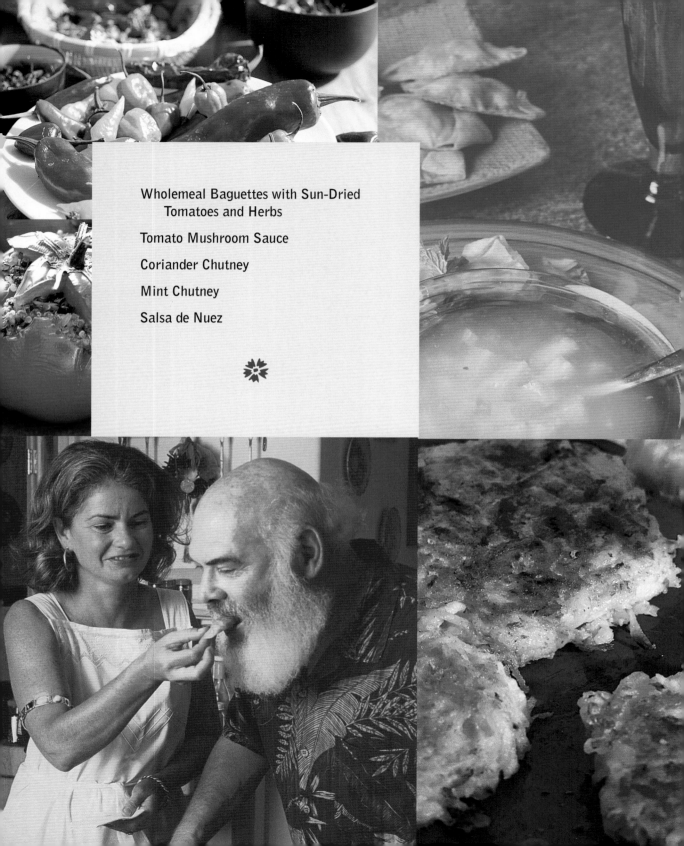

Wholemeal Baguettes with Sun-Dried
    Tomatoes and Herbs

Tomato Mushroom Sauce

Coriander Chutney

Mint Chutney

Salsa de Nuez

COOKING TECHNIQUES

I like to cook in ways that are efficient and clean, give good results, and do not decrease the nutritional values of foods. One technique I employ frequently is steaming. It uses little energy, results in little mess, and does the least damage to nutrients. I steam many vegetables and fish. Chinese cooks will also steam dumplings, buns, and pancake wrappers encasing other foods. Another technique I like is 'steam frying': that is, sautéing food briefly in a little oil, then adding water, stock, or wine, covering the pan, and allowing the food to cook until it is done. You can uncover the pan and quickly boil off excess liquid near the end of the preparation if you want to.

I often boil less delicate vegetables, like corn on the cob, potatoes, and beetroot. (But if you have never tasted baked whole beetroot, you will be surprised at how much more delicious they are.) If you boil tender vegetables, be aware that you will lose some of their nutrients to the cooking water.

Grilling, baking, and roasting use a lot of energy and often require more cleaning up, but they produce very good results. Try not to add excessive fat to foods you cook in the oven. Also try to avoid browning them excessively, especially flesh foods, which become carcinogenic when they are cooked brown or black. Be careful not to inhale the smoke from high-temperature cooking of foods containing fat and animal protein; it is also carcinogenic. Of course, these same precautions also apply to barbecuing. (See page 51 for more on outdoor cooking.)

I urge you not to fry foods, especially not to deep-fry them. Frying puts excessive fat into dishes and also exposes you to the health risks of chemically altered fats. Stir-frying is perfectly acceptable if you use reasonable amounts of good oils and keep them below the smoking point.

I use my microwave oven for rapid heating and defrosting of food, especially of small portions, never for serious cooking. As a cooking method microwaving just does not produce as good results as conventional baking or grilling, and it may alter the chemical composition of food in ways that could be harmful. You should also know that if you microwave food in plastic containers or cling film, the microwaves can drive plastic molecules into the food. Never put food into a microwave oven in anything other than a glass or ceramic dish, and never cover it with cling film.

A word on cookware: I use enamel-coated cast-iron pans that are easy to clean and conduct heat fairly well. I also like stainless steel cookware with copper or aluminium bottoms to improve conductivity. (Stainless steel by itself is not a great conductor.) High-quality non-stick pans are also very useful, because they make it possible to sauté with little or no fat, and the non-stick coating does not interact with food. Avoid uncoated aluminium cookware; the metal can get into food you cook in it, and aluminium is probably toxic. —A.W.

Pickled Vegetables

Pickled carrots, jicama, cauliflower, and green beans make a healthy snack to have on hand. The carrots offer a great deal of beta-carotene and iron. The jicama and cauliflower provide vitamin C and potassium, and the green beans have a good deal of antioxidants and also add some colour to the combination. The vinegar here is well seasoned with the essence of mustard, dill, and garlic, all offset with a hint of sweet and balancing brown sugar. The pickling liquid makes an excellent dressing for any salad.

SERVES 20
(30 G/1 OZ SERV-
INGS)

PER SERVING:

CALORIES 23.1

FAT 0.2 G
  SATURATED FAT
  0 G

(5.4% OF CALORIES
  FROM FAT)

PROTEIN 0.6 G

CARBOHYDRATE
  5.7 G

CHOLESTEROL 0 MG

FIBRE 1.2 G

225 g (8 oz) carrots, peeled and
    cut in rounds on the diagonal
225 g (8 oz) green beans
1 small cauliflower, broken into
    florets
1/2 jicama, peeled, cut in half and
    then into sticks

DRESSING

480 ml (2 cups) purified water
600 ml (2 1/2 cups) cider vinegar
60 ml (1/4 cup) olive oil

3 tablespoons soft light brown
    sugar
1 teaspoon salt
1 tablespoon dried dill
6 cloves garlic
pickling spices: 5 bay leaves,
    1 tablespoon mustard seed,
    1 tablespoon dill seed, and
    1 1/2 teaspoons dried chilli
    flakes

Fill a large pan with water and bring to the boil. First drop in the carrots and parboil for 2 minutes, then quickly scoop them out with a strainer or large slotted spoon and transfer to a basin filled with cold water and ice to stop the cooking. Drop the green beans into the boiling water and cook just until they turn bright green (about 3 minutes), then quickly transfer them to the ice dwater. The cauliflower will only need to parboil for 1 minute. Let all the vegetables sit in the iced water for a few minutes to cool. Drain well, then transfer the cooled vegetables to a big bowl and add the jicama.

Put all the dressing ingredients, including the pickling spices, in a stainless steel pan set over medium heat. Bring to the boil and cook for 2 minutes. Pour the hot dressing over the vegetables and allow them to cool at room temperature. Once cooled, put the vegetables into a large glass jar or lidded plastic container and fill it with as much dressing as the jar will hold. Cover and refrigerate for 2 days before eating.

Tips from Rosie's Kitchen

Blanching your vegetables makes them porous enough to absorb flavour from the dressing. Cooling them rapidly shocks the vegetables and stops any further cooking; ensuring that your pickles are crisp and crunchy rather than limp and rubbery. The jicama is porous enough raw, so it doesn't need to be blanched. Each vegetable is blanched separately because some vegetables need more time than others, and we want them all to be crisp and flavourful.

Lemon Dill Baby Carrots

It really helps to know how to make a side dish that doesn't call for a lot of time or fuss. These carrots are the answer. They are healthy, take almost no time to prepare, and are great with lunch or dinner, or even by themselves.

SERVES 6

PER SERVING:

CALORIES 45.5

FAT 0.6 G
  SATURATED FAT
  0.1 G
(10.6% OF CALO-
  RIES FROM FAT)

PROTEIN 0.9 G

CARBOHYDRATE
  9.9 G

CHOLESTEROL 0 MG

FIBRE 2.9 G

675 g (1 1/2 lb) baby carrots
1 tablespoon freshly squeezed
  lemon juice
1 teaspoon cornflour
80 ml (1/3 cup) purified water
2 teaspoons chopped fresh dill

1/8 teaspoon salt (optional)
Freshly ground black pepper to
  taste

GARNISH

Fresh dill sprigs

Put the carrots in a steamer basket in a large pan filled with enough boiling water to reach the bottom of the basket. Steam for 6–8 minutes. The carrots should be tender yet firm.

Combine the lemon juice and the cornflour in a large saucepan, stirring until well mixed. Gradually add the water and cook over medium heat until the liquid becomes thick and bubbly, stirring constantly. Remove from the heat. Stir in the dill and salt.

Drain the carrots when they are finished steaming and arrange them on a platter. Pour the lemon dill sauce over the top. Sprinkle with black pepper and garnish with dill sprigs.

Tips from Rosie's Kitchen

Make sure that you prepare the barbecue well ahead of time so that the coals are hot and the heat is consistent. This always ensures even cooking. You can cook indoors, using the grill or a ridged grill pan instead. A grill pan sears the food, much like cooking over hot coals.

Seasonal Vegetable Medley

Cooking outdoors is a summertime tradition for me. Once you barbecue vegetables, you will find yourself preparing them this way quite a bit. It imparts a smoky flavour that people love, especially kids. In fact, serving barbecued vegetables to kids is a good way to get them to actually enjoy eating them!

Use any leftover barbecued vegetables to toss into a cold pasta salad.

During the winter months, my kitchen is full of the aroma of the seasoned roasted winter vegetables baking in the oven. These are great alone or paired with simple fish or chicken dishes such as the chicken in the Simple Marinated Chicken Salad recipe (page 94), or the Seared Salmon with Orange Glaze (page 178).

BARBECUED SUMMER VEGETABLES

3 large courgettes, preferably
   1 green and 2 yellow, cut
   lengthways into 1 cm (1/2 in)
   thick slices
1 medium aubergine, sliced
   lengthways into 1 cm (1/2 in)
   thick slices
1 onion, cut into 5 mm (1/4 in)
   thick slices
1 red pepper, cut lengthways into
   1 cm (1/2 in) strips

OLIVE OIL SEASONING

60 ml (1/4 cup) olive oil
1/4 teaspoon dried oregano
1/4 teaspoon dried thyme
1 tablespoon dried basil
1/8 teaspoon cayenne pepper
   (optional)
1/2 teaspoon crushed fennel seeds
1/4 teaspoon salt
1/8 teaspoon coarsely cracked
   black pepper
60 ml (1/4 cup) freshly squeezed
   lemon juice

SERVES 8

PER SERVING:
CALORIES 185.1
FAT 9.8 G
  SATURATED FAT
  1.4 G
(42.4% OF CALORIES FROM FAT)
PROTEIN 4.3 G
CARBOHYDRATE
  24.4 G
CHOLESTEROL
  0 MG
FIBRE 9.5 G

Put all the sliced vegetables in a large bowl. Mix all the seasoning ingredients together in a separate bowl, then pour it over the vegetables. Toss thoroughly with a big spoon until all the vegetables are completely coated.

Spread the vegetables on the barbecue grill, over medium-low coals, and cook for 21/2 minutes. Turn them over and cook for a further 11/2 minutes.

ROASTED WINTER VEGETABLES

150 g (1 cup) potatoes, scrubbed and cut into 2.5 cm (1 in) cubes

150 g (1 cup) turnips or sweet potatoes, scrubbed and cut into 5 cm (2 in) cubes

170 g (1 cup) carrots, sliced into 1 cm (1/2 in) rounds

160 g (1 cup) parsnips, cut into 2.5 cm (1 in) rounds

2 small onions, quartered

1/2 teaspoon caraway seeds

Preheat oven to 190°C.

Put all the vegetables in a large bowl. Mix all the olive oil seasoning ingredients together in a separate bowl and pour them over the vegetables. Toss thoroughly with a big spoon until all the vegetables are completely coated. Using kitchen paper, oil a baking tray with olive oil. Spread the vegetables on the tray and roast for 20 minutes. Carefully turn the vegetables over, using a palette knife, and roast for a further 15 minutes, until the vegetables are tender and golden brown.

SERVES 8

PER SERVING:

CALORIES 107.5

FAT 6.9 G
  SATURATED FAT 0.9 G
  (55.5% OF CALORIES FROM FAT)

PROTEIN 1.4 G

CARBOHYDRATE 11.1 G

CHOLESTEROL 0 MG

FIBRE 1.8 G

❄

ANDY SUGGESTS

Pumpkin or butternut squash would be good in the winter vegetable mixture too.

Mashed Potatoes and Parsnips

Mashed potatoes make a hearty, honest dish. It has sometimes been referred to as comfort food because it evokes memories of both big, special-occasion dinners and the simple, family dinner intended for no other reason than to share a good meal. This version of mashed potatoes tastes good because it's dense with the mildly sweet flavour of parsnips and just enough butter to please, but without the extra calories you usually find in mashed potatoes.

8 medium new potatoes (see Tips), scrubbed and cubed
4 parsnips, cubed
240 ml (1 cup) milk
45 g (1¹/2 oz) butter

1 tablespoon chopped parsley
Pinch of cayenne pepper
Several grindings of black pepper
1 teaspoon salt

SERVES 6

PER SERVING:
CALORIES 260.8
FAT 7.5 G
 SATURATED FAT
 4.5 G
(25% OF CALO-
 RIES FROM FAT)
PROTEIN 5.6 G
CARBOHYDRATE
 45 G
CHOLESTEROL
 21 MG
FIBRE 6.9 G

Put the potatoes and parsnips in a large pan with water to cover them. Bring to the boil, then lower the heat to medium, cover and simmer for 20–30 minutes, stirring occasionally with a spoon. Test the tenderness of the potatoes with a fork; they should pierce easily and be tender, yet firm. Drain well, then mash the vegetables with a potato masher until there are no visible lumps. Add the milk and butter and continue to mash until the vegetables are smooth and creamy. Stir in the parsley, cayenne pepper, black pepper, and salt, and beat thoroughly with a wooden spoon until all the seasonings are completely mixed in. Serve warm.

Tips from Rosie's Kitchen

New potatoes have softer, thinner skins and can be mashed with the skins to preserve all the nutrients they offer. However, if you prefer to use floury potatoes, you will probably want to peel them as they have thicker, tougher skins.

This is a great recipe because the liquid that remains from cooking the potatoes is instant stock! Save it and use it to make Cold Cucumber Soup (page 134).

SHIITAKE MUSHROOMS AND MANGE-TOUTS

Fresh and dried shiitakes are practically different mushrooms; they are so unalike in texture and flavour. But both are delightful when combined with mange-touts, which provide a vivid contrast of green, sweetness, and crunchiness (if you do not overcook them). This dish makes a good accompaniment to fish and to grain dishes.

SERVES 4

PER SERVING:

CALORIES 279 G

FAT 4 G
   SATURATED FAT
   0.5 G

(13% OF CALORIES
   FROM FAT)

PROTEIN 8.5 G

CARBOHYDRATE
   55 G

CHOLESTEROL
   0 MG

FIBRE 9.5 G

❄

450 g (1 lb) mange-touts or sugar snap peas
225 g (8 oz) fresh shiitake mushrooms, or 60 g (1 cup) dried shiitake
2 teaspoons grapeseed oil
1 teaspoon toasted sesame oil
2 teaspoons soft light brown or demerara sugar
60 ml (1/4 cup) sake or dry sherry
2 tablespoons shoyu or other natural soy sauce

Trim the ends and any strings from the mange-touts.

If using fresh mushrooms, trim the stalk ends and discard (or save for soup). Cut the mushrooms into 1 cm (1/2 in) wide slices. If using dried mushrooms, put them in a bowl with enough cold water to cover. Place bowl in microwave, uncovered, and microwave on high for 1 minute. Let the mushrooms sit in warm water until completely softened, about 30 minutes, then drain, squeeze out the liquid (save for soup), and cut off and discard the tough stalks. Cut the caps into 1 cm (1/2 in) wide slices.

Heat the oils in a frying pan and add the mushrooms. Sauté over medium-high heat, stirring, until the mushrooms just begin to brown. Sprinkle the sugar over the mushrooms and add the wine and shoyu. Cook and stir for 1 minute, then add the mange-touts. Cover, reduce the heat to medium, and steam until the mange-touts are just tender-crunchy and bright green, about 2 minutes.

Uncover and continue to cook until most of the liquid has evaporated. Serve immediately.

Shiitake Mushrooms and Mange-touts

COOKING MUSHROOMS

Nutritionists often teach that mushrooms have little value as food, that they are useful mainly as interesting garnishes or sources of unusual flavours and textures. This view is a product of a general fear of mushrooms common in the English-speaking world. It goes along with another wrong idea, that mushrooms have no medicinal value. I am a longtime mushroom hunter, eater, and enthusiast, and I have long extolled both their nutritional and health benefits.

Mushrooms are respectable protein sources, intermediate between foods of animal origin and vegetables. (Actually, we share more DNA sequences with mushrooms than with plants and so are more closely related to them.) Their protein is of good quality and, when combined with grains, provides all essential amino acids. On a dry-weight basis, the protein content of many species approaches that of meat. The carbohydrates in mushrooms are mostly indigestible, and there is little fat – a great plus. They provide useful amounts of some B vitamins and trace minerals.

I always stress the importance of cooking mushrooms thoroughly. Cell walls of mushrooms are tough, making it difficult for the digestive system to get at the nutrients inside them. Mushrooms often contain chemical compounds that either interfere with digestive enzymes or block absorption of nutrients. In addition, even many edible species contain natural toxins. These problems all have a common solution: heat. Sufficient cooking breaks down the tough cell walls, inactivates the anti-digestive elements, and destroys many toxins. It also makes mushrooms taste better, bringing out their best flavours and textures. I strongly advise against eating any mushrooms raw, whether wild or cultivated.

Many fanciers of mushrooms sauté them in lots of butter, often adding whole milk or cream on top of that. These dishes are not healthy for hearts and arteries, however good the mushrooms are to begin with. When I try a new species for the first time, I will usually sauté it in a little olive or grapeseed oil in order to determine whether it has a good enough flavour and texture to recommend it for further experimentation. If it does, I will then look for ways to prepare it to enhance its qualities without flouting principles of healthy eating.

For example, many thick-fleshed mushrooms can be cooked over charcoal and basted with a low-fat or non-fat sauce. Fresh shiitakes, barbecued with a little teriyaki sauce, are universally popular at mushroom cook-and-tastes. (Mix one part dry sherry or sake, one part reduced-sodium Japanese shoyu [soy sauce], and one tablespoon of sugar for each 240 ml/1 cup of liquid to make an easy teriyaki sauce.)

In general, Asian cooking methods work very well for mushrooms, use little fat, and result in dishes that are much more healthful than most of those described in books on mushroom cookery or dishes that are served at restaurants. In addition to barbecuing, other methods include simmering in broth and stir-frying with vegetables.

The only innovation in mushroom cultivation in the West has been the introduction of the portobello, a large variety of the common button mushroom that is allowed to grow to maturity. When the caps expand, their flavour intensifies as spores ripen. Grilled or barbecued portobello caps are thick and meaty, lending themselves to the creation of tasty vegetarian burgers.

A number of cultivated Oriental varieties are now available in our markets. Fresh shiitakes are easy to find. They are more flavourful than button mushrooms and also have anti-cancer and cholesterol-lowering properties. Several kinds of oyster mushrooms are in cultivation. They also offer protection from cancer, and are cheaper than shiitakes, but less flavourful. Look for maitake, a newer arrival from Japan. It is meaty, tasty (especially grilled with teriyaki sauce), and one of the best-studied species for immune-enhancing effects. In the spring, wild morels are often for sale, usually for exorbitant prices; and in the fall, yellow chanterelles are available, sometimes more reasonably. You can also find several kinds of dried mushrooms in Oriental and Italian food shops. Soak them in water until they soften, save the soaking liquid (after straining) for soups or sauces, and add the reconstituted mushrooms to your recipes. Dried shiitakes, maitakes, and porcinis (ceps) are especially good to have on hand. —**A.W.**

SERVES 1
(1 BURGER
WITH GARNISHES)

PER SERVING:

CALORIES 471.3

FAT 33.5 G
  SATURATED FAT
  3.8 G

(63.7% OF CALORIES
  FROM FAT)

PROTEIN 0 G

CARBOHYDRATE
  0 G

CHOLESTEROL
  0 MG

FIBRE 0 G

Portobello Burger

For a simple vegetarian alternative to a meat or turkey burger, try barbecuing or grilling a whole portobello mushroom cap and serving it on a toasted bun with your favourite garnishes (lettuce, tomato, onion, pickle, ketchup, mustard). Choose large, firm, fresh-looking portobellos and remove the stalks. Brush the caps with olive oil and place them gill side up on a heated barbecue grill or on a sheet of foil under a hot grill. Cook until the caps are soft and begin to brown. Sprinkle with salt and pepper, turn them over, and cook until caps brown on that side, too. Sprinkle with additional salt and pepper and slide the cooked mushrooms onto waiting buns.

Warm Tomatoes Stuffed with Quinoa and Courgette

Quinoa, like other grains, is bursting with B vitamins and iron; however, it varies from other grains because it contains more protein without a lot of carbohydrates. Quinoa actually contains all 8 essential amino acids, which makes it a unique complete food. The ancient Incas honoured this protein-dense food, making it a staple in their everyday diet. It is now gaining more recognition and becoming a valuable vegetarian source of protein.

100 g (1/2 cup) quinoa
2 tablespoons olive oil
360 ml (11/2 cups) purified water
  or vegetable stock (page 122)
1/4 teaspoon salt
1/4 teaspoon freshly ground black
  pepper
1 teaspoon Italian seasoning herbs
1/2 medium onion, chopped
130 g (1 cup) grated courgettes
2 tablespoons currants or raisins

1 tablespoon chopped fresh
  parsley or basil
1/2 teaspoon curry powder or
  ground cumin
1/4 teaspoon paprika
2 tablespoons freshly squeezed
  lemon juice
6 medium tomatoes
2 teaspoons fresh breadcrumbs
2 tablespoons freshly grated
  Parmesan cheese

Tips from Rosie's Kitchen

If you don't have quinoa on hand, you can make this recipe using millet or amaranth. Amaranth tends to have a slightly sweet flavour, while millet and quinoa tend to taste like natural rice, with a delicate, nut-like flavour.

Stuffed Winter Squash*: You can use the stuffing from this recipe to stuff baked squash. Buy 3 acorn squashes or 6 baby pumpkins. Puncture the surface of the squash 4 times with a knife, making sure that each stab is spaced apart. Cut the squashes lengthways in half and scoop out the seeds with a big spoon; discard them. Lay the squash halves cavity side down in a baking tin. Add a little water and bake for 30–45 minutes. When completely cooked, the squash can be easily pierced with a fork. Remove from the oven and cool in the tin. Keeping all the liquid from the squashes in the tin; turn the squash halves over so the cavity side is up, and spoon in the stuffing to fill the cavity. Cover with foil and bake for 15 minutes in the same oven. Garnish a platter or each of 6 plates with a few sprigs of fresh parsley, lay the squash halves on top, and serve.*

SERVES 6

PER SERVING:

CALORIES 164.1

FAT 3.4 G
  SATURATED FAT
  0.7 G
(17.3% OF CALO-
  RIES FROM FAT)

PROTEIN 5.9

CARBOHYDRATE
  30.6 G

CHOLESTEROL
  1 MG

FIBRE 4.2 G

Preheat oven to 180°C.

In a small saucepan, toss the quinoa in 1 tablespoon olive oil, then pour in the water, and add the salt, black pepper, and Italian seasoning. Bring to the boil. Cover and simmer over low heat for 20 minutes. Remove from the heat.

Pour 1 tablespoon olive oil into a non-stick pan and sauté the chopped onions, courgettes, and currants with the parsley or basil, curry powder, paprika, and lemon juice over medium heat for about 2 minutes. Scoop the quinoa into the sauté pan and mix thoroughly until it is blended with the vegetables to make an aromatic stuffing. Remove from heat.

Create a lid for each tomato by cutting a star shape around the stalk about 5 mm (1/4 in) deep. Remove the top and set it

aside. Scoop out the seeds of each tomato and some of the loose pulp, being careful to leave a strong wall of tomato all around. Spoon equal amounts of the stuffing into the cavities of each tomato, filling them up generously. Put the tomatoes in a small ceramic or glass baking dish and garnish with a sprinkle of breadcrumbs and 1 teaspoon Parmesan cheese per tomato. Cover the baking dish with a glass lid or foil and bake for 25 minutes. Tomatoes should be firm and easy to transfer from the baking dish to the serving plates. Garnish by putting the star-shaped tomato lids back on top of each tomato.

Wilted Spinach with Mushrooms

This is a side dish that you can call upon a lot because it complements so many things. In presenting the Seared Salmon with Orange Glaze (page 178), I use the Wilted Spinach with Mushrooms as a fancy bed beneath the fish, which appeals to the eye as well as the taste buds. You can also toss it with your favourite pasta to add colour, flavour, and nutritional value. And you can venture out into the world of greens and use some Swiss chard or kale along with the spinach in this recipe. Just replace one of the bunches of spinach with the vegetable of your choice. All of them offer ample amounts of vitamins A, B, and C, and minerals. I have to warn you, though, that once you start incorporating more greens in your meals, you'll be addicted – they make you feel great!

3 cloves garlic, sliced
2 tablespoons olive oil
70 g (1 cup) sliced mushrooms
3 tablespoons vegetable stock
   (page 122) or water
900 g (2 lb) spinach, washed well
   and tough stalks removed
Salt to taste
Freshly ground pepper to taste

GARNISH

6 tablespoons goat's cheese, or
   3 tablespoons sesame seeds
   (optional)

SERVES 3

PER SERVING:

CALORIES 84.4

FAT 7.2 G
  SATURATED FAT
  2.4 G
  (73.4% OF CALO-
  RIES FROM FAT)

PROTEIN 3.5 G

CARBOHYDRATE
  2.3 G

CHOLESTEROL
  7 MG

FIBRE 1.2 G

Warm Tomatoes Stuffed with Quinoa and Courgette

Sauté the garlic in the olive oil in a sauté pan over medium heat until it becomes soft. Add the mushrooms and cook for 1 minute, stirring once or twice. Pour in the vegetable stock or water and pile in the spinach. Rotate the spinach with tongs so that the leaves are coated in the cooking juices. When the spinach turns bright green and is thoroughly wilted, remove from the heat. Sprinkle individual servings with goat's cheese or sesame seeds, if you wish, then season to taste with salt and black pepper. Serve immediately.

Tips from Rosie's Kitchen

If you're using Swiss chard and/or kale, remove the leaves from the stalks and wash them well. Wash the stalks and chop them up coarsely. Cook the chard leaves and the stalks the same way as in this recipe. If you haven't used kale, which offers an amazing amount of calcium, you'll find that it tastes similar to cabbage. However, kale takes a little longer to cook, so put it in with the mushrooms to give it more time to soften.

BRUSSELS SPROUTS FOR PEOPLE WHO THINK THEY HATE BRUSSELS SPROUTS

I understand why Brussels sprouts top the list of detested vegetables for many people. When they are large, old, or overcooked, they tend to have an obnoxious, barn-yardy flavour that some people are sensitive to whereas others are not. You can minimise this by choosing smaller, fresh-looking sprouts and cooking them just until they are crunchy-tender and bright coloured. (Do not use frozen sprouts.) The secret of this dish is balancing ingredients to mellow the strong flavour of these miniature cabbages. Olive oil, garlic, chilli, Parmesan, and, especially, nutmeg do the trick admirably.

450 g (1 lb) Brussels sprouts
1 teaspoon salt
2 tablespoons extra virgin olive oil
1 teaspoon dried chilli flakes, or to
   taste

5 cloves garlic, finely chopped
1/4–1/2 teaspoon nutmeg, or to taste,
   preferably freshly grated
50 g (1/2 cup) freshly grated
   Parmesan cheese

SERVES 4

PER SERVING:
CALORIES 162
FAT 10 G
   SATURATED FAT
   3 G
(56% OF CALORIES
   FROM FAT)
PROTEIN 8.3 G
CARBOHYDRATE
   12 G
CHOLESTEROL
   8 MG
FIBRE 4.5 G

Trim the ends off the Brussels sprouts, and remove and discard any discoloured outer leaves. If sprouts are large (more than 2.5 cm/1 in in diameter), cut them in quarters lengthways through the stalk end. If smaller, cut them in half.

Bring a pan of water to the boil, and add the salt and sprouts. Cook the sprouts uncovered until they are just crunchy-tender, about 5 minutes. Do not overcook them. Drain the sprouts well.

Wipe and dry the pot and heat the olive oil in it. Add the chilli flakes and garlic and sauté for 1 minute. Add the sprouts and nutmeg and sauté for another minute. Mix in the Parmesan cheese and toss the sprouts until the cheese melts.

BEETROOT IN MUSTARD SAUCE

SERVES 4

PER SERVING:

CALORIES 176

FAT 14 G

SATURATED FAT
2 G

(72% OF CALORIES
FROM FAT)

PROTEIN 2 G

CARBOHYDRATE
12 G

CHOLESTEROL
0 MG

FIBRE 3 G

❋

The sharp taste of beetroot is masked in this recipe by the simple mustardy vinaigrette. Be sure to allow the beetroot to marinate for a full day in order for the flavours to marry.

450 g (1 lb) beetroot
3 tablespoons prepared mustard, preferably whole grain or Dijon
3 tablespoons red wine vinegar

60 ml (¼ cup) extra virgin olive oil
1 medium onion, chopped
Salt to taste

Cut the tops off the beetroot, leaving 2.5 cm (1 in) of stalk attached. Place the beetroot in a pan of cold water to cover and bring to the boil, then reduce heat, and cook until the beetroot can easily be pierced through with a sharp knife, 45–60 minutes depending on their size.

Meanwhile, put the mustard in a bowl and whisk in the vinegar. Then whisk in the olive oil in a steady stream until the sauce is smooth and creamy. Add the onions.

When the beetroot are done, drain them, and submerge them in several changes of cold water until they are just cool enough to handle. Cut off the roots and tops, slip the skins off, and slice the warm beetroot into the mustard sauce. Mix well, cover, and leave to marinate in the refrigerator for at least 24 hours. Before serving, mix well and add salt if desired.

Steamed and Roasted Baby Red Potatoes

Potatoes are packed with energy-enhancing vitamins C and B₆ that give your body and mind some pep. Baby red potatoes or new white potatoes are particularly good because the peel is tender, pretty, and full of minerals like iron and potassium. The basic seasonings we add truly transform the taste of a simple potato. The garlic really enhances the flavour of the olive oil, and the rosemary, pepper, salt, and paprika give the potatoes a robust, seasoned taste.

These potatoes, steamed or roasted, make a perfect complement to many dishes. They go very well with the Roasted Pepper Turkey with Orange Liqueur (page 168), or alongside Eggs Florentine with Orange and Dill Sauce (page 4) for a fancy breakfast.

18 baby red potatoes, scrubbed
　　and halved

SEASONING FOR ROASTING

2 tablespoons olive oil
5 small cloves garlic, peeled

1 tablespoon fresh rosemary
　　or 1 teaspoon dried
1 teaspoon salt
1/4 teaspoon freshly ground black
　　pepper
1/4 teaspoon paprika

Preheat the oven to 230°C.

Steam the potatoes: pour about 5 cm (2 in) of water into a large pan and bring to the boil. Place a steaming basket in the pan raised just above the boiling liquid, put the halved potatoes into the basket, cover the pan, and allow to steam until the potatoes are easily pierced with a fork (about 8 minutes). Remove from the heat and lift the steaming basket from the pan.

Roast the potatoes: pour the olive oil and seasonings into a large baking dish or casserole, add the steamed potatoes, and gently toss them until they are completely coated with the mixture. Roast for 12 minutes until the outsides of the potatoes are crusty, occasionally moving them around to ensure even browning.

Tips from Rosie's Kitchen

Steaming involves cooking something at a low temperature in a covered container with a small amount of boiling liquid. If you do not have a steaming basket, pour about 1 cm (1/2 in) of water into the bottom of a pan, put the potatoes into the water, cover the pan, and cook on low heat.

STEAMED
SERVES 6

PER SERVING:

CALORIES 270.3

FAT 0.4 G
　SATURATED FAT
　0.1 G

(1.3% OF CALORIES
　FROM FAT)

PROTEIN 7.2 G

CARBOHYDRATE
　61.5 G

CHOLESTEROL
　0 MG

FIBRE 5.5 G

❁

STEAMED AND
ROASTED
SERVES 6

PER SERVING:

CALORIES 310.1

FAT 4.9 G
　SATURATED FAT
　0.7 G

(13.8% OF CALORIES FROM FAT)

PROTEIN 7.2 G

CARBOHYDRATE
　61.5 G

CHOLESTEROL
　0 MG

FIBRE 5.5 G

SERVES 4

PER SERVING:

CALORIES 108

FAT 4 G
   SATURATED FAT
   0.6 G
(34% OF CALO-
RIES FROM FAT)

PROTEIN 4 G

CARBOHYDRATE
   16 G

CHOLESTEROL
   0 MG

FIBRE 3 G

GREENS WITH TANGY MISO DRESSING

The tangy miso dressing for cooked greens provides an unlikely and surprising combination of ingredients and flavours – salty, sour, and sweet, plus the distinctive earthy tang of turmeric. It manages to be a perfect accompaniment to sautéed greens that are quickly pre-pared and is attractive to the eye.

115 g (1 cup) onions, cut into thin
   half-moons
1 tablespoon toasted sesame oil
100 g (1 cup) seeded and julienned
   red pepper
400 g (4 cups) julienned kale leaves
160 ml (2/3 cup) purified water

400 g (4 cups) julienned Chinese
   leaves or pak choy
1 tablespoon shoyu or other natural
   soy sauce
8 tablespoons Tangy Miso Dressing
   (see below)

MISO DRESSING

MAKES ABOUT
240 ML (1 CUP)
SERVES 6

PER SERVING:

CALORIES 68

FAT 3 G
   SATURATED FAT
   0.5 G
(40% OF CALO-
RIES FROM FAT)

PROTEIN 2.5 G

CARBOHYDRATE
   8.5 G

CHOLESTEROL
   0 MG

FIBRE 1 G

In a large frying pan over medium-high heat, sauté the onions in the sesame oil for 5 minutes. Add the red pepper, toss, and sauté for 3 minutes. Add the kale and 80 ml (1/3 cup) water. Cook until the liquid has evaporated. Add the Chinese leaves, soy sauce, and the remain-ing water. Cook until the greens are tender, about 5 minutes.

Divide into 4 portions and spoon 2 tablespoons Tangy Miso Dressing over each serving.

Tangy Miso Dressing

60 ml (1/4 cup) white miso
2 tablespoons tahini
60 ml (1/4 cup) freshly squeezed
   lemon juice
60 ml (1/4 cup) purified water

1 tablespoon honey or brown rice
   syrup
2 teaspoons chopped fresh dill or
   1 teaspoon dried
1/2 teaspoon turmeric

Stir the miso and tahini together in a bowl. Add the lemon juice and water and mix well. Stir in the remaining ingredients.

Andy with a wok full of his Greens with Tangy Miso Dressing

Toasted Grain Pilaf

SERVES 6

PER SERVING:

CALORIES 153.9

FAT 6.2 G
  SATURATED FAT
  1.0 G

(34.1% OF CALORIES
  FROM FAT)

PROTEIN 4.2 G

CARBOHYDRATE
  22.7 G

CHOLESTEROL
  1 MG

FIBRE 3.0 G

400 g (2 cups) millet, quinoa, or amaranth, or a combination
1/8 teaspoon curry powder (optional)
1 litre (4 cups) chicken stock (page 124) or vegetable stock (page 122), or more as needed
30 g (1/4 cup) dry-pack sun-dried tomatoes
120 ml (1/2 cup) boiling purified water
130 g (1 cup) grated courgettes, preferably a mixture of green and yellow
30 g (1/4 cup) diced red pepper
30 g (1/4 cup) chopped spring onions
Salt to taste

Toast the millet (or other grains) in a large saucepan set over low heat, stirring it constantly until it turns a light brown colour, less than 1 minute. Stir in the curry powder until it is blended in. Remove from heat and cool for 5 minutes. Add the chicken or vegetable stock and bring to the boil. Reduce heat, cover, and simmer. Check after 20 minutes. If the stock has boiled away, add a little more. Cook until the millet has absorbed all the liquid, about 25 minutes in all.

Meanwhile, soak the dried tomatoes in the boiling water for 15 minutes. Drain them in a colander set over a bowl to reserve the liquid, then chop them. Mix the tomatoes, reserved liquid, courgettes, red pepper, and spring onions together in a small frying pan set over low heat and cook until most of the liquid is absorbed. Pour into the cooked grain and toss until everything is completely mixed together. Taste and add salt if you think it is needed. Fluff with a fork and serve.

Tips from Rosie's Kitchen

Traditionally, a Middle Eastern pilaf is made with white rice, but here we use a healthful grain, toasting it first to bring out its flavour, and mixing in aromatic vegetables to create a delicious, more nutritious dish. For more about grains, see Andy's comments opposite. You can also make this recipe with brown rice, but the cooking time would be about 45 minutes.

ABOUT GRAINS

Cereal crops are cultivated relatives of grass that have sustained human life throughout the world and often define the diets of whole populations. We rely on wheat as our staple grain, Asians on rice, Native Americans on maize (corn), eastern Europeans on rye, and so forth. Grains are very nourishing, providing a mix of carbohydrate, protein, and fat, but how we prepare and process them can influence our health in ways both good and bad.

When people first discovered grains and domesticated the plants that produced them, they made the seeds edible by simply parching them – that is, heating them in a dry pan over a fire. Parched maize is still a common snack in Peru. Some grains, if they have sufficient water content and soft enough hulls, also lend themselves to popping. Popcorn is an ancient food that remains popular today. Another simple solution is to boil whole or cracked grains into porridges and gruels.

People also quickly developed other uses for grains, mixing them with water, grinding them, and letting them ferment into alcoholic beverages such as beer or into dough that would rise and could be baked into bread. Until the early 1800s bread was rough, dense, and chewy – peasant bread – often with visible pieces of cracked grains. Since then it has mostly been made with white flour, a product of modern food technology. White flour is pure wheat starch in the form of superfine particles that are digested very differently from whole or cracked grains; it is devoid of the fibre and fat of whole wheat. The same technology has been applied to maize and rice, and supermarkets are filled with products made from these refined starches: breads, pastries, sweet and savoury biscuits, crisps, pretzels.

As I explained in the section on nutrition, increasing consumption of these refined carbohydrate foods is a major cause of the epidemic of obesity we are seeing in America and wherever American-type fast and processed foods are popular. In my opinion, it also contributes to the prevalence of cardiovascular disease and adult-onset diabetes. This does not mean that grains and carbohydrates are bad for health. It does suggest that modern ways of processing grains have dramatically lowered their nutritional qualities.

Rosie and I both like to cook grains, but we favour unrefined, less processed ones, and we enjoy experimenting with less familiar varieties. Try boiling whole wheat grains (wheat berries) until they are tender, then mixing them with sautéed vegetables or turning them into a cold salad with walnuts, dried cranberries, and a light vinaigrette. Try some of the exotic varieties of rice now on the market, including black rice and red rice, both beautiful and delicious. Use wild rice more; it is now cultivated extensively in California and is no longer an expensive luxury. Get to know buckwheat groats (kasha) and quinoa, grain-like seeds from Eastern Europe and South America, respectively, with distinctive flavours and textures.

Even if you are watching your weight and feel you are sensitive to carbohydrates, you can enjoy these nutritious foods. Well-prepared whole and cracked grains are filling and satisfying, enjoyable both as main dishes and as accompaniments to protein foods. They are also quick and easy to cook and lend themselves to endlessly varied dishes. —**A.W.**

Fresh Apple Sauce

When you make this apple sauce, your guests and family will never forget it and you will probably never buy it in a jar again.

You can use any type of apple you'd like, and because apples are pretty much available year round, you can serve it as a warm side dish in the winter, or a cold side dish, or dessert, any time of year.

6 apples, peeled, cored, and sliced (about 675 g/6 cups)
120 ml (1/2 cup) apple juice

1 teaspoon ground cinnamon (see Tips)

Put the apple slices and the apple juice in a saucepan with a lid. Cook, covered, over low heat, until the apples are tender and most of the liquid is absorbed, about 10–20 minutes, depending on the type of apple you are using. Break up the apples using a fork or pour the mixture into a blender and blend until smooth. Sprinkle in the cinnamon and stir until it is thoroughly integrated into the apples. Leave the apple sauce to cool for a few minutes or longer, depending on whether you want to serve it warm or cold.

SERVES 6

PER SERVING:

CALORIES 94.1

FAT 0.6 G
  SATURATED FAT
  0.1 G
(4.9% OF CALORIES
  FROM FAT)

PROTEIN 0.3 G

CARBOHYDRATE
  24.4 G

CHOLESTEROL
  0 MG

FIBRE 4.4 G

Tips from Rosie's Kitchen

Always let your taste buds be your guide! Cinnamon, an aromatic spice, can do wonders to enhance any type of apple, as well as pastries, curries, soups, and stews. However, if you are starting out with apples that taste great raw, you might not want to disguise their wonderful flavour with too much cinnamon. So add only as much cinnamon as you'd like to taste.

Potato Griddle Cakes

I have made these at the house of a friend who gives a party featuring potato griddle cakes every year. He loves making them and gets really creative, tossing in Tabasco sauce or different herbs. You can be as creative as you like with yours. Mine are a simple version, and I like to serve them with Fresh Apple Sauce.

MAKES 8 GRIDDLE-
CAKES

PER SERVING:
CALORIES 246
FAT 7.8 G
  SATURATED FAT
  1.3 G
(28.3% OF CALO-
  RIES FROM FAT)
PROTEIN 5.4 G
CARBOHYDRATE
  39.1 G
CHOLESTEROL
  27 MG
FIBRE 3 G

❈

900 g (2 lb) floury potatoes
1 large sweet onion
100 g (1 cup) matzo meal
1 egg
1 teaspoon salt, or more to taste
60 ml (1/4 cup) olive oil

GARNISH

Reduced-fat crème fraîche
Fresh Apple Sauce (page 249)

Peel and grate the potatoes and onion by hand or in a food processor and put them in a large bowl. (If you grate the potatoes ahead of time, make sure to keep them in water to prevent them from turning brown, then drain and squeeze when ready to use.) Add the matzo meal and the egg. Sprinkle in the salt and blend everything together until the onions and potatoes are coated with the egg and matzo meal. Let stand for 5 minutes.

With clean hands, roll a ball of dough just big enough to fit into the palm of your hand, and flatten it out with your palms to make a round cake. Repeat the process until you have used up all the dough. Set a medium sauté pan over medium-high heat with 1 tablespoon of olive oil. Lay 4 cakes in the hot oil and cook for 1 minute on each side, until they turn golden brown. Transfer the cakes to kitchen paper to soak up any excess oil. Repeat, adding more olive oil to the pan, until all cakes are cooked. Serve with crème fraîche and Fresh Apple Sauce.

Tips from Rosie's Kitchen

I sometimes add 15 g (1/4 cup) chopped fresh sorrel leaves or chives to the batter. Sorrel, a herb that belongs to the buckwheat family, is in season during the spring. Its leaves are similar in shape to spinach, although smaller and more narrow. Don't buy it if the leaves look wilted.

Rosie turning her Potato Griddle Cakes

Pear Relish

This tastes wonderful on meat or poultry. It is similar to fruit chutney and it will change the way your meal tastes. I serve it with the Roasted Pepper Turkey with Orange Liqueur (page 168).

1 pear
60 g (1/4 cup) finely chopped
  onion
2 tablespoons finely chopped
  yellow pepper

2 tablespoons finely chopped red
  pepper
480 ml (2 cups) cranberry or
  apple juice
2 sprigs fresh mint, chopped

MAKES ABOUT
480 ML (2 CUPS)

PER SERVING:

CALORIES 68.1

FAT 6.2 G
  SATURATED FAT
  0 G
(2.5% OF CALORIES
  FROM FAT)

PROTEIN 0.2 G

CARBOHYDRATE
  17.2 G

CHOLESTEROL 0 MG

FIBRE 0.8 G

Halve the pear and scoop out the core. Peel, then chop into bite-size pieces.

Put the pear, onion, peppers, and cranberry or apple juice into a small saucepan and set over medium heat. Cook until the onions and peppers become limp and the pear becomes soft.

Remove from the heat, add the mint, and drizzle over your favourite poultry dish.

Tips from Rosie's Kitchen

You'll encounter a variety of pears that range in textures at your greengrocer throughout the year. Some pears, like Anjou, are soft when raw, while others, like Bosc, are very hard. All pears taste good in this recipe, but the naturally hard types will take a bit longer to cook. Softer pears will take about 7 minutes to soften, and harder pears will need about 15 minutes.

Serrano Chilli and Coriander Cornbread Muffins

These muffins are moist and chewy, spicy and sweet. When you make them, they won't last long! They are excellent eaten warm, with some butter, or as a side dish to a main dish such as Santa Fe Chicken (page 208) or Mexican Chicken Soup (page 136).

2 small fresh serrano chillies, or
   55 g (2 oz) canned green
   roasted chillies
190 g (1¹/2 cups) unbleached
   plain flour
65 g (¹/2 cup) cornmeal or polenta
1 tablespoon baking powder
1 teaspoon salt
Pinch of cayenne pepper
160 ml (²/3 cup) semi-skimmed
   milk or soya milk
2 medium eggs
120 ml (¹/2 cup) grapeseed oil or
   115 g (4 oz) softened butter
3 tablespoons pure maple syrup or
   sugar

15 g (¹/4 cup) chopped fresh
   coriander

HONEY BUTTER TOPPING
(Optional)
3 tablespoons honey
3 tablespoons soft butter

MAKES 10 CORN-BREAD PIECES OR 12 MUFFINS

PER SERVING:
CALORIES 178
FAT 8.1 G
  SATURATED FAT
  0.8 G
(40.4% OF CALO-RIES FROM FAT)
PROTEIN 4.7 G
CARBOHYDRATE
  22.1 G
CHOLESTEROL
  36 MG
FIBRE 1.8 G

Preheat the oven to 180°C.

Put the fresh chillies on a baking tray and grill until they blister and turn black, turning so they cook evenly. Remove them from the grill and drop them into a polythene bag to cool. The skin will become loose and flaky as they cool.

Mix together all the dry ingredients in a large bowl. Whisk together the milk, eggs, oil or butter, maple syrup or sugar, and the coriander in a separate bowl. Stir the wet ingredients into the dry ingredients with a wooden spoon until thoroughly mixed.

Take the chillies out of the bag and slice them in half, directly down the middle. Open them up and remove the seeds. Peel the skin off. Cut the chillies into small pieces and stir them into the batter until they are completely mixed in.

Smear a little butter or oil on the bottoms and sides of a 23 cm (9 in) square baking tin or 12 American-style muffin tins and pour in the batter. Bake for 20 minutes if using muffin tins or 25 minutes if you're using a baking tin. Remove from the oven and leave to cool.

Make the Honey Butter: simply blend the softened honey and butter together in a bowl with a fork, whipping lightly to create a creamy spread. Scoop the spread into a ramekin and serve with the cornbread.

To cut the cornbread, make 1 slice directly down the middle of the tin and 4 slices across to yield 10 rectangular pieces.

Tips from Rosie's Kitchen

The traditional way to peel chillies is to roast them over an open fire. If you're feeling really motivated and have the time to do it, you, too, can do this, over a barbecue or using a burner on a gas cooker. Hold the chillies 10 cm (4 in) away from the flame and rotate until all sides of the chilli turn black. When peeling and seeding the chillies, do not touch your eyes, because the oil from the chillies will sting. If you'd prefer an alternative to chillies, just sauté 80 g (1/2 cup) chopped onions in a tablespoon of olive oil and use them instead.

Wholemeal Baguettes with Sun-Dried Tomatoes and Herbs

The sun-dried tomatoes and herbs really cling to the dough of this baguette, which is similar in consistency to pizza dough. It is wonderful toasted and smeared with the spread in the Goat's Cheese Toasties with Sun-Dried Tomato and Basil recipe (page 83).

1 tablespoon dried yeast
360 ml (1¹/2 cups) warm water
1 teaspoon salt
155 g (1¹/4 cups) wholemeal flour
375 g (3 cups) unbleached bread
   flour, or more as needed
2 tablespoons olive oil
2 garlic cloves, finely chopped
60 g (¹/2 cup) dry-pack sun-dried
   tomatoes

1 teaspoon finely chopped dried
   rosemary leaves
2 tablespoons chopped fresh basil
   (optional)

MAKES 2 LOAVES

PER SERVING:
CALORIES 278.9
FAT 4.4 G
  SATURATED FAT
  0.6 G
  (14% OF CALO-
  RIES FROM FAT)
PROTEIN 8.6 G
CARBOHYDRATE
  52.2 G
CHOLESTEROL
  0 MG
FIBRE 4.6 G

Dissolve the yeast in the warm water in a large bowl. Stir in the salt, all the wholemeal flour, and about 315 g (2¹/2 cups) of the white flour. Turn the dough out onto a floured work surface and knead, adding more flour as necessary when the dough gets sticky, until smooth and elastic, about 8–10 minutes. Return the dough to the cleaned bowl, cover with a tea towel, and leave to rise until tripled in volume, about 2 hours.

Heat the olive oil in a small pan and sauté the garlic gently for 1–2 minutes

Rosie putting the baguettes into her patio bread oven

Tips from Rosie's Kitchen

If you don't have a paddle and a pizza stone, simply bake the loaves on the baking sheet (without the baking parchment).

until it just begins to colour. Soak the dried tomatoes in 240 ml (1 cup) boiling water until rehydrated and plump. Drain the tomatoes and chop finely.

Knock back the dough in the bowl, and scatter the garlic with its cooking oil, the herbs, and the tomatoes on top. Knead these ingredients into the dough until evenly distributed. Turn the dough out onto a floured surface, cut in half, and form it into 2 baguettes by rolling the dough with the floured palms of your hands into rolls about 25 cm (10 in) long. Place on a sheet of baking parchment on a paddle or a rimless baking sheet. Make 3 diagonal slashes with a sharp knife down the length of each loaf, cover with a tea towel, and leave to rise until doubled in volume, about 45 minutes.

Preheat oven to 200°C, with a pizza stone, if you have one, on the middle shelf. Slide the risen baguettes onto the pizza stone and bake for 40 minutes. Remove to a rack to cool. Makes 2 loaves, 12 slices per loaf.

Tomato Mushroom Sauce

It's nice to make your own tomato sauce. Of course, time doesn't always permit it, but when it does, try it. This is a favourite of mine that I use quite a bit in pasta and vegetable dishes.

12 medium, ripe tomatoes or
   1 x 400 g (14 oz) can peeled
   organic tomatoes
2 medium onions, chopped
1 green pepper, diced
1 tablespoon olive oil
450 g (1 lb) mushrooms, diced or
   chopped

120 ml (1/2 cup) white wine
2 teaspoons dried oregano
11/2 teaspoons dried basil
1/2 teaspoon salt (optional)
1 bay leaf
1 tablespoon tomato purée
1 teaspoon honey

If using fresh tomatoes, slice an 'X' on the bottom of each one and drop them into and pan of boiling water. Blanch until the skins start to loosen, about 2 minutes. Drain and cool completely. When cool, squeeze each tomato over a sieve set over a bowl; discard the seeds. Purée the tomato flesh and juice in a food processor until smooth. If you are using canned tomatoes, simply scrape out the excess seeds, then mash the tomatoes with their juice by hand or with a fork.

Sauté the onions with the green peppers in the olive oil in a large sauté pan for 5 minutes over low heat. Add the mushrooms, wine, herbs, salt, puréed tomatoes, and bay leaf. Simmer for 30 minutes. Remove the bay leaf. Mix in the tomato purée and the honey and cook for 10 more minutes.

MAKES ABOUT 1 LITRE (4 CUPS)
SERVES 6

PER SERVING:
CALORIES 146
FAT 3.2 G
    SATURATED FAT 0.4 G
(18.9% OF CALORIES FROM FAT)
PROTEIN 4.6 G
CARBOHYDRATE 26.2 G
CHOLESTEROL 0 MG
FIBRE 4.9 G

❃

Tips from Rosie's Kitchen

If you don't have a food processor, you can purée the tomatoes using your hands. Wash your hands very well and then squeeze each tomato over a sieve, trapping the seeds which should be discarded, but keeping the juice and the pulp.

If ripe, juicy tomatoes are out of season, use organic canned tomatoes that you can find in your supermarket. They come peeled whole, chopped, and with or without herbs. Be sure to include their liquid.

CORIANDER CHUTNEY

This recipe and the variation that follows are from south India, from the region around Mysore, where 'chutney' denotes more of a savoury spread than the sweet-hot relishes we associate with the term. Indians make these rich condiments with freshly grated coconut, but that is full of saturated fat. Raw cashews taste just as good and provide monounsaturated fat, which is much better for the cardiovascular system and general health. South Indians spread these on dosas, the fabulous (and sometimes gigantic) pancakes of the region, made from rice and lentils.

MAKES ABOUT 480 ML
(2 CUPS)
SERVES 16

PER SERVING:

CALORIES 56

FAT 4.8 G

SATURATED FAT
LESS THAN 1 G

(77% OF CALO-
RIES FROM FAT)

PROTEIN 1.6 G

CARBOHYDRATE
2.8 G

CHOLESTEROL
0 MG

FIBRE LESS THAN
1 G

140 g (1 cup) raw cashew nuts
180 g (4 cups, loosely packed) fresh coriander leaves
1 jalapeño or serrano chilli, or other green chilli, stalk removed

Purified water
Salt to taste
1 tablespoon grapeseed oil
1 teaspoon black mustard seeds

Grind the cashews in a food processor to a fine powder. Add the coriander leaves and chilli and process for 30 seconds. Scrape the mixture together and continue to process, pouring in just enough water to make a mayonnaise like cream. Salt to taste.

Heat the oil in a small pan over medium-high heat. Add the mustard seeds and cook, stirring, until they start to pop. Stir the seeds and oil into the chutney.

Use as a spread for chapatis, wholemeal tortillas (wraps), or pita bread, or as a sauce for fish or vegetables. Chutney will keep in the refrigerator for several days.

Mint Chutney

Follow the above recipe, substituting fresh spearmint leaves for the coriander.

SALSA DE NUEZ

I discovered this sauce in Oaxaca, the southern Mexican state, where South American Indian culture and indigenous foods abound. It is rich and highly flavoured, and absolutely delicious. Use it sparingly on almost anything.

220 g (2 cups) pecan halves
1 tablespoon extra virgin olive oil
5 cloves garlic, crushed
1–2 tablespoons ground red chilli or
    cayenne pepper, or more to taste
Purified water
Salt to taste

Fry the pecans in the olive oil over medium-high heat, stirring constantly, until the nuts just begin to brown. Put them in a food processor or blender with the garlic and 1 tablespoon of the chilli powder or cayenne, and blend until the nuts form a paste. Taste and add more chilli powder or cayenne, if you wish. Add just enough water to bring the consistency to a medium-thick sauce. Season to taste with salt.

Store the salsa in the refrigerator in a tightly covered container. Use it as a sauce for steamed or grilled fish and steamed vegetables, and as a spread for tortillas (wraps), savoury biscuits, or bread.

MAKES ABOUT
480 ML (2 CUPS)
SERVES 16

PER SERVING:

CALORIES 99

FAT 10 G
  SATURATED FAT
  0.8 G
(91% OF CALO-
  RIES FROM FAT)

PROTEIN 1 G

CARBOHYDRATE
  2.8 G

CHOLESTEROL
  0 MG

FIBRE 1 G

Desserts

Almond Fruit Tart

Apple Tart with Jam Glaze

Apple Strudel with Almond Sprinkles

Honey Nut Baklava

Angel Cake with Fresh Berries

Banana Cupcakes with Orange Cream
   Cheese Glaze

Peach and Blueberry Cobbler

Blueberry Pie with Lattice Top

Apple Cake Squares

Berries with Sorbet

Pistachio Dream

Lemon Sponge Cake

Lemon Yogurt Sorbet

Ginger Biscuits

Orange Oat and Sultana Cookies

Poached Pears

Figs in Wine

Raspberry Sorbet Tarts with Chocolate
    Whipped Cream

Rice Pudding

Apple Cranberry Crisp

Apricot Mousse

Dark Chocolate with Fruit

SUGAR AND OTHER SWEETENERS

Human beings are born with an innate craving for sweetness, because sugar represents almost instant energy. Long ago, our ancestors were only likely to encounter sugar in the form of ripe fruit or an occasional honeycomb; today it is everywhere – not only on every table but hidden in the ingredients of many prepared foods, from soups to ketchup. Some nutritionists say that sugar is a dietary evil, the cause of mood swings, hyperactivity in children, and systemic yeast infections in adults. Others tell us that refined white sugar is the problem and urge us to use honey and other more 'natural' sweeteners in its place. And today, a large number of people are using artificial and non-nutritive sweeteners in place of sugar, a significant change in eating habits.

You will find sugar, honey, and maple syrup in some of the recipes in this book. Neither Rosie nor I think that sugar is evil, but we worry that most people eat much too much of it and feel that it should be consumed consciously and in moderation. Sugary foods and drinks certainly contribute to obesity in our society and to dental decay. They may raise the glycaemic index of meals, putting a burden on the pancreas and raising the risk of insulin resistance and its attendant problems (see page xx).

I do not think there is much difference between sugar and other natural sweeteners. Honey, maple syrup, molasses, and sorghum contain trace minerals and have novel flavours, but to the body they are all sugar to be converted to glucose for metabolic fuel. Until recently, all so-called raw or natural sugars were actually white sugar coloured and flavoured with the addition of some molasses (the residue of concentrated sugar cane juice after removal of most of its content of sucrose). In other words, they were the same as light and dark brown sugars. Today, real raw sugar is on the market, which is straw-coloured with a rich flavour that I prefer in many dishes to that of white sugar. Of the other natural sweeteners, my personal favourite is maple syrup. I love it. As for honey, I much prefer the flavour and texture of raw varieties to those of cooked ones.

Some non-nutritive sweeteners are natural: sorbitol and xylitol, for example, which are made from wood pulp and are used in sugarless chewing gum, sweets, and toothpaste. But be aware that they can cause flatulence and can aggravate irritable bowel syndrome. Stevia is also in this category. It is the leaf of a South American shrub, from which a very sweet compound, stevioside, can be isolated. This is so sweet that it is best dissolved in water and dispensed from a dropper bottle. It has a liquorice flavour that I do not find agreeable, but it might be worth trying if you are diabetic or intolerant to sugar.

Artificial sweeteners are of more concern to me as a physician. In the first place, there is no evidence that they help anyone lose weight, although that is why people use them. (I love watching people put artificial sweeteners in their coffee after they have downed rich desserts.) Second, most of them taste funny. And, most important, the highly popular ones may be harmful. Saccharin, which has been around the longest, may increase risks of bladder cancer and other forms of the disease. Aspartame (NutraSweet) may damage brain cells; many people note symptoms that appear to correlate with their use of it: headaches, for example, or intensification of menstrual problems. If you must use an artificial sweetener, I recommend the newest one on the market, sucralose. It tastes better than aspartame and appears safer.

Because sugar can add to the pleasure of food and eating, it should be part of the optimum diet. The dessert recipes in this book offer some examples of using it wisely. —A.W.

BUTTER AND BUTTER SUBSTITUTES

I do not cook with butter and do not keep it in my house, because it provides too much saturated fat for me. I like good cheese and get enough butterfat from it. On the very rare occasions that I make muffins, pastry, or topping for a fruit crisp or crumble I prefer to substitute healthier fats for butter. In many cases neutral-tasting oil will do, such as grapeseed oil or expeller-pressed canola oil. (Expeller-pressed oil is pressed mechanically at relatively low pressure and temperature rather than extracted with high-pressure, high-temperature methods or with solvents. The oil suffers less damage as a result.) I make a great crumb crust with digestive biscuits, sesame tahini, and maple syrup. And occasionally I use Spectrum Spread as a butter substitute. Unlike margarine, this product contains no hydrogenated or trans fats. It uses a mechanical process to emulsify oil and water to make a spread that has the flavour of butter and good baking qualities. I introduced Rosie to it and she has included it as an option in recipes calling for significant quantities of butter. You will find Spectrum Spread in the refrigerated sections of some shops that sell natural foods. —A.W.

Almond Fruit Tart

This is a less rich rendition of the popular French tart. It makes a lovely complement to a shared pot of freshly brewed tea.

SERVES 12

PER SERVING:

CALORIES 249.9

FAT 10.9 G
  SATURATED FAT
  4.8 G
(42.3% OF CALO-
  RIES FROM FAT)

PROTEIN 4.1 G

CARBOHYDRATE
  329 G

CHOLESTEROL
  36 MG

FIBRE 2.7 G

PASTRY

110 g (1 cup) oat flour
125 g (1 cup) unbleached plain
  flour
25 g (1/4 cup) ground almonds
1 tablespoon freshly squeezed
  orange juice
55 g (2 oz) diced cold butter or
  Spectrum Spread
4–5 tablespoons cold purified
  water

FILLING

35 g (1/4 cup) pine nuts
45 g (11/2 oz) butter
2 tablespoons soft light brown
  sugar
30 g (1/4 cup) unbleached plain
  flour
60 ml (1/4 cup) frozen orange
  juice concentrate

1 egg yolk
2 egg whites
2 tablespoons Amaretto

JAM GLAZE AND FRUIT TOPPING

155 g (1/2 cup all-fruit strawberry
  or apricot jam
3 tablespoons purified water
2 kiwi fruits, peeled and sliced
360 g (3 cups) raspberries (or
  Poached Pears, page 294)

Make the pastry: put all the ingredients with 3 tablespoons water in a food processor and pulse briefly about 6 times, just until smooth, about 30 seconds. If the dough seems very dry, add 1 or 2 more tablespoons water and pulse briefly again. Cut a piece of baking parchment or greaseproof paper that measures 25 cm (10 in) square. Roll the dough into a ball, wrap it in the paper, and chill it in the refrigerator for 10 minutes. The paper square may seem large for the dough ball, but you will be using it later in the recipe.

After the dough has chilled, unwrap it and roll it out, on the baking parchment using a rolling pin, to make a circle that is about 30 cm (12 in) in diameter. Flip the pastry, on the paper, over onto a 23 cm (9 in) pie tin and peel off the paper. Press the pastry down with your fingers, moulding it to the bottom and sides of the tin. Trim off excess pastry with a knife so that it is flush with the edge of the tin. Cover and chill for 15 minutes.

Preheat the oven to 180°C.

Remove the tin from the refrigerator and bake the pastry case for 15 minutes or until it is dry in the centre. You can test by inserting a wooden cocktail stick; if the stick comes out dry, the pastry is done. Set aside to cool for 15–20 minutes. Leave the oven on.

Meanwhile, make the filling: combine all the filling ingredients in a food processor and process until smooth. Pour into the pastry case. Bake for 20 minutes, until the top puffs up and is golden brown. Leave to cool.

Make the glaze: heat the jam and water together in a saucepan on low heat until syrupy. Strain the glaze through a wire sieve over a bowl. Brush the glaze over the tart.

Arrange the kiwi slices around the perimeter of the tart and the fresh raspberries (or Poached Pears) in the middle. Brush another layer of jam glaze over the raspberries and kiwi to make the fruit shine and to hold them together. To serve, quarter the pie, then cut each quarter into 3 pieces.

SERVES 8

PER SERVING:

CALORIES 276.5

FAT 8.9 G
  SATURATED FAT
  5.4 G

(28.5% OF CALORIES
  FROM FAT)

PROTEIN 3.6 G

CARBOHYDRATE
  46.8 G

CHOLESTEROL
  23 MG

FIBRE 38 G

✳

Apple Tart with Jam Glaze

Tarts are a dessert that can be served for any occasion. I like to make them during the Christmas holidays because they have such a dressy presentation.

PASTRY

85 g (3 oz) cold butter or
  Spectrum Spread
250 g (2 cups) unbleached plain
  flour, plus 2 tablespoons for
  dusting
1/2 tablespoon sugar
1/4 teaspoon salt
4–5 tablespoons cold purified
  water

3 Granny Smith apples, peeled
  and thinly sliced vertically
2 tablespoons caster sugar
1 teaspoon ground cinnamon

GLAZE

155 g (1/2 cup) apricot jam
3 tablespoons purified water

Preheat oven to 180°C.

Cut the butter into small pieces. Put the butter, flour, sugar, and salt in a food processor and pulse on and off about 10 times, until crumbs start to form. Slowly add the cold water and pulse again. If you don't have a food processor, rub the butter into the dry ingredients, then bind with the water. Shape the dough into a ball, wrap in a 25 cm (10 in) square of baking parchment or greaseproof paper and chill in the refrigerator for 15 minutes or in the freezer for 10 minutes.

Unwrap the dough. Sprinkle a little bit of flour on the baking parchment and, using a floured rolling pin, roll out the dough on the paper to a 30 cm (12 in) circle. Flip it over onto a 23 cm (9 in) pie tin. Peel off the paper. Trim off excess pastry so that it is level with the rim of the tin.

Tips from Rosie's Kitchen

The pastry case can be made ahead of time and kept, covered with cling film, in the freezer until ready to use.

Arrange the apple slices in rows in the pastry case, slightly overlapping them. Combine the sugar and cinnamon and sprinkle over the apples. Bake for 30 minutes, then cover the tart with foil and bake for a further 35 minutes. The apples should be soft and juicy. Remove from the oven.

Heat the jam with the water in a small saucepan until it becomes syrupy. Using a pastry brush, brush the jam glaze over the tart. Allow to cool for 15 minutes or so, but serve warm (reheat if necessary).

Apple Strudel with Almond Sprinkles

Strudel is usually made with apples, but cherries also make a terrific filling when they're in season (see Tips). Granny Smith apples are my favourites but use whatever good, flavourful apples are in season when you make this strudel.

Like the Honey Nut Baklava recipe that follows, this strudel calls for clarified butter. Clarified butter can be made a couple of days in advance (see Tips) or the night before. It is one of those ingredients that is great to have on hand in the refrigerator because it is a good substitute for oil when sautéing and can be used in making dishes with filo pastry.

SERVES 9

PER SERVING:

CALORIES 306.9

FAT 17.1 G
SATURATED FAT
8 G

(48.7% OF CALO-
RIES FROM FAT)

PROTEIN 2.8 G

CARBOHYDRATE
37.7 G

CHOLESTEROL
31 MG

FIBRE 2.8 G

FILLING

2 tablespoons clarified butter

330 g (3 cups) peeled, cored, and thinly sliced apples

80 ml (1/3 cup) maple syrup

1 tablespoon ground cinnamon

1 teaspoon freshly squeezed lemon juice

3 tablespoons cornflour

60 ml (1/4 cup) water

2 tablespoons honey

40 g (1/4 cup) currants

Few drops of almond essence

1 tablespoon pure vanilla extract

1 teaspoon grated lemon zest

PASTRY

120 ml (1/2 cup) clarified butter or walnut oil

6 filo pastry sheets, defrosted if frozen

50 g (1/2 cup) finely chopped or ground almonds

50 g (1/4 cup) caster sugar

Preheat the oven to 200°C.

Make the filling: put the clarified butter and apples in a sauté pan and add the maple syrup, 2 teaspoons of the cinnamon, and the lemon juice. Sauté over medium heat for 2–3 minutes until the apples are tender. Mix the cornflour with the water in a small bowl. Stir into the apples, and simmer, stirring, on low heat until the mixture becomes thick. Stir in the honey, currants, almond essence, vanilla extract, and lemon zest. Remove from the heat and leave to cool.

While the apple mixture cools, begin preparing the pastry. Warm the clarified butter (walnut oil does not need to be warmed). Working quickly, lay 1 filo sheet on a piece of baking parchment and lightly brush with a generous tablespoon of the clarified butter. Combine the almonds with the sugar. Sprinkle about 1 1/2 tablespoons of the almond and sugar mixture evenly over the filo and lay a second sheet on top.

Brush clarified butter evenly over the surface and sprinkle on another

Brushing the filo pastry with clarified butter

Tips from Rosie's Kitchen

Clarified Butter: Melt 170 g (3/4 cup) unsalted butter (clarifying reduces the butter by about one-third) in a small, heavy saucepan over low heat for 20 minutes. The butterfat will separate and sink to the bottom of the pan and foam will start to accumulate on the surface. Skim the foam off the top and throw it away. Allow the liquid that remains in the pan to cool for about 5 minutes, then strain the milky residue through a fine sieve. Pour the completely cooled golden liquid that remains into a small bowl, jar, or plastic container. Cover and keep in the refrigerator.

If you don't have the time to prepare clarified butter, you can use walnut oil, which will different in flavour but just as delicious.

You will need a pastry brush and baking parchment, which you can find at any kitchen shop and many supermarkets.

Chop the almonds in a food processor, or see instructions on grinding almonds in a blender (page 34). You need to create a finely ground meal. Or buy ready ground almonds to save time and effort.

Spooning the filling down one side of the layered pastry. (In this instance, Rosie is using her cherry filling. See Tips, page 272.)

1 1/2 tablespoons of almond sugar. Repeat the process until all 6 sheets have been lightly brushed with the clarified butter, sprinkled with the almond sugar mixture, and stacked on top of each other.

Spoon the apple filling along the length of the top layer, about 5 cm (2 in) from the edge. Gently roll up the filo from this long side to enclose the filling.

Brush the top of the strudel with the remaining clarified butter and sprinkle evenly with the remaining 1 teaspoon cinnamon and the rest of the almond sugar mixture. Put a piece of baking parchment or grease-proof paper on a baking tray and lay the strudel, seam side down, on top. Bake for 20 minutes until the top is golden brown. Remove from the oven and leave to cool a bit. Slice acros into 9 pieces while still warm and serve.

Rolling up the strudel

Brushing the top of the strudel with clarified butter before baking

Tips from Rosie's Kitchen

Cherry Strudel: *If you'd like to try this recipe with cherries instead of apples, you'll need to make the following substitutions: 400 g (3 cups) fresh (or frozen) stoned cherries instead of apples, and 115 g (1/2 cup) softened cream cheese instead of the currants. Begin by blending the cream cheese with the honey, vanilla extract, and lemon zest in a small bowl until smooth. Then just follow the rest of the recipe instructions.*

Honey Nut Baklava

Layers of flaky filo pastry sheets lightly brushed with butter and capped by a thick honey and nut spread are what make this classic Greek dish so popular around the world.

Plan to start the baklava one day in advance if the filo pastry needs to be defrosted (do this in the refrigerator overnight). The clarified butter can also be prepared the night before and refrigerated until you are ready to use it.

60 g (1/2 cup) walnut pieces
70 g (1/2 cup) blanched almond
680 g (2 cups) honey
1 tablespoon pure vanilla extract
120 ml (1/2 cup) clarified butter
  (see Tips, page 271)

9 sheets filo pastry, defrosted if frozen
90 g (1/2 cup) dark chocolate chips or small chunks

MAKES 36 PIECES

PER SERVING:

CALORIES 145.3

FAT 7.3 G
  SATURATED FAT
  3.3 G

(42.5% OF CALORIES FROM FAT)

PROTEIN 1.4 G

CARBOHYDRATE
  20.7 G

CHOLESTEROL
  11 MG

FIBRE 0.6 G

Preheat oven to 200°C.

Process the nuts briefly in a food processor to chop them. Pour the honey and vanilla extract into a medium bowl and stir with a wooden spoon until the vanilla is completely incorporated into the honey. Add the nuts and stir until they are all coated with the honey. Grease a rectangular baking tin and line with parchment or greaseproof paper cut to fit.

Warm the clarified butter in a small pan.

Open the packet of filo and unroll the sheets flat on the work surface. Cover with a large piece of foil to prevent the pastry from drying out. You are going to create 2 separate stacks of filo sheets. The first stack will consist of 6 sheets cut in half, and the second of 3 sheets folded in half.

Prepare the first stack: place 1 filo sheet on the work surface and quickly brush with clarified butter using a pastry brush. Lay another sheet on top and brush with butter. Continue layering the 6 sheets. Using kitchen scissors, cut the stack in half and lay one half in the tin. Spread half of the honey and nut mixture evenly on the pastry, then lay the other half of the stack on top. Spread the remaining honey and nut mixture over this. Next, layer the remaining 3 sheets of filo pastry, brushing each one with clarified

Spooning the filling over the layered filo pastry

butter, then fold the stack over in half. Lay it on top of the filling in the tin.

Place the tin in the oven and bake until the top is golden and the honey is bubbling, about 20 minutes. Remove the baking tin from the oven and leave to cool slightly.

Cut the baklava lengthways into 6 even slices, then cut 6 even slices at a 45° angle from top to bottom to create 36 triangular pieces.

Melt the chocolate chips in a stainless-steel double boiler or in a small heatproof bowl set over a pan of hot water. Stir until the chocolate is smooth. Remove from the heat. Working quickly, dip a fork into the chocolate and drizzle it horizontally across the cooling baklava.

Cherry Strudel and Honey Nut Baklava for tea

Angel Cake with Fresh Berries

Angel cake can be eaten so many ways. Here, it is served with fresh fruit, but it can be served topped with vanilla ice cream, Chocolate Whipped Cream (page 296), or any fruit combination of your choice. Because it isn't overly sweet, but just sweet enough, sometimes I just cut a small piece and eat it plain.

125 g (1 cup) unbleached plain flour
300 g (1 1/2 cups) caster sugar
12 egg whites, at room temperature
1/2 teaspoon cream of tartar
1/4 teaspoon salt
1 teaspoon pure vanilla extract

1/4 teaspoon almond essence

FRESH FRUIT TOPPING

500 g (2 cups) sliced strawberries
60 ml (1/4 cup) freshly squeezed orange juice
1 tablespoon honey
300 g (1 pint) blueberries

MAKES 1 CAKE
SERVES 12

PER SERVING:
CALORIES 257
FAT 0.3 G
  SATURATED FAT
  0.1 G
(0.9% OF CALO-
  RIES FROM FAT)
PROTEIN 4.7 G
CARBOHYDRATE
  61.6 G
CHOLESTEROL
  0 MG
FIBRE 1.3 G

Preheat oven to 170°C.

Mix the flour and sugar together in a bowl. Whisk the egg whites with the cream of tartar using an electric mixer until they become firm and peaks begin to form. Sift one-third of the flour and sugar mixture into the bowl and gently fold into the whites. Repeat by sifting and folding in the remaining sugar and flour mixture in 2 batches. Finally, fold in the salt, vanilla extract, and almond essence until everything is evenly combined.

Spoon the mixture into an ungreased angel cake tin, scraping the bowl with a spatula to get all of it. Bake for 1 hour or until the top is light brown. Remove from the oven and leave to cool for 1 hour on a wire rack.

When completely cooled, slide a knife around the edge of the tin to loosen the cake. Turn out onto a platter. Mix together the strawberries, orange juice, honey, and blueberries and spoon this fresh fruit mixture on top.

Tips from Rosie's Kitchen

I make angel cakes for birthday cakes. I give them a little flair by using the Apricot Mousse recipe (page 300) as a filling, and replace the strawberries with apricots. When the cake is completely cooled, I cut it in half horizontally and spread the apricot mousse in the centre. It adds some flavour without a lot of calories, and it looks very pretty.

It is very important that the bowl in which the egg whites are whisked is clean and complete grease-free or the whites will not stiffen. A tiny bit of egg yolk will also prevent them from forming peaks, so take care when you are separating the whites from the yolks.

You can also bake the mixture in American-style muffin tins, to make individual angel cakes. Baking time will be about 30 minutes and this amount of mixture will make 12 small cakes.

Banana Cupcakes with Orange Cream Cheese Glaze

Using very ripe bananas is the key to giving these little cakes such abundant flavour. Alternatives to the cupcake tins are mini loaf tins or a big standard-size loaf tin. The latter produces a teabread with a dressier presentation. Whatever you choose, the combination of bananas and ginger, along with carrots or courgettes, makes a healthy cake with a distinctive flavour.

ORANGE CREAM CHEESE GLAZE

230 g (1 cup) softened reduced-fat
  cream cheese
60 ml (1/4 cup) freshly squeezed
  orange juice
85 g (1/4 cup) honey
1/2 teaspoon pure vanilla extract
1/2 teaspoon grated orange zest

GARNISH

12 walnut halves

CAKE MIXTURE

250 g (2 cups) wholemeal flour
20 g (1/2 cup) oat or wheat bran
1 tablespoon bicarbonate of soda
1/4 teaspoon salt
1/8 teaspoon ground cloves or
    mixed spice
1/8 teaspoon ground ginger
4 ripe bananas
1/2 large carrot or 1/2 courgette,
    grated
85 g (3 oz) softened butter
200 g (1 cup) soft light brown
    sugar
2 eggs
1/4 teaspoon pure vanilla extract
30 g (1/4 cup) chopped walnuts

MAKES 12 CUPCAKES,
4 MINI LOAVES,
OR 1 STANDARD
LOAF
SERVES 12

PER SERVING:

CALORIES 354

FAT 14.6 G
    SATURATED FAT
    6.3 G
(37.1% OF CALO-
    RIES FROM FAT)

PROTEIN 7.9 G

CARBOHYDRATE
    53.4 G

CHOLESTEROL
    60.6 MG

FIBRE 4.4 G

Let the cream cheese for the glaze soften at room temperature while you prepare the cake mixture.

Preheat oven to 190°C.

Mix the flour, bran, bicarbonate of soda, salt, and spices together in a bowl. Mash the bananas in a separate bowl with a fork until all fruit chunks are completely squashed. Drop in the grated carrots or courgette, and stir thoroughly with a spoon until they are completely covered in bananas. In a medium bowl, cream together the softened butter, brown sugar, eggs, and vanilla extract, using an electric mixer or a whisk, until smooth, with no sign of lumpy sugar granules. Add the walnuts and stir with a spoon until they are completely coated. Slowly mix in the dry ingredients for 1 minute, using a wooden spoon or electric mixer set on low, until all ingredients are thoroughly blended. Pour in the mix of mashed banana and grated carrot or courgette and stir everything with a big wooden spoon until the bananas and vegetables are completely blended in.

Spray the tins you are using with non-stick cooking spray, then pour in the cake mixture, scraping the bowl with a spatula to get all of it.

Bake the cupcakes and the mini loaves for 20 minutes; the large loaf will take 45 minutes. Remove from the tins and leave to cool on a wire rack before glazing.

To make the glaze: whisk together the softened cream cheese, orange juice, honey, vanilla extract, and orange zest in a bowl until smooth and thick. For cupcakes, use 1 tablespoon of glaze per cake. For mini loaves, use 60 ml (1/4 cup) for each one. For a standard loaf, use half of the glaze. Garnish with the walnuts before the glaze sets.

Peach and Blueberry Cobbler

This is an old-fashioned dessert that most people thoroughly enjoy eating. The baked fruit filling is crowned with a thin scone topping. It can be eaten warm or cold, plain or with vanilla ice cream.

FILLING

5 peaches, peeled and sliced
145 g (1 cup) fresh blueberries
60 ml (1/4 cup) freshly squeezed
   orange juice
100 g (1/2 cup) caster sugar
Pinch of grated nutmeg
2 teaspoons cornflour

SCONE TOPPING

70 g (2 1/2 oz) softened butter or
   Spectrum Spread

250 g (2 cups) unbleached plain
   flour plus 30 g (1/4 cup) for
   rolling out
1 tablespoon caster sugar
1 tablespoon baking powder
1/2 teaspoon salt
180 ml (3/4 cup) milk

GLAZE

2 tablespoons granulated sugar

SERVES 10

PER SERVING:
CALORIES 241.8
FAT 6.9 G
   SATURATED FAT
   4.1 G
(25% OF CALO-
   RIES FROM FAT)
PROTEIN 3.9 G
CARBOHYDRATE
   42.3 G
CHOLESTEROL
   19 MG
FIBRE 2 G

Preheat oven to 200°C.

Bring all the filling ingredients to the boil in a large saucepan, then turn down heat and simmer until the filling becomes thick, stirring occasionally. Spoon the thickened fruit filling into a medium baking dish (at least 25 x 20 cm/10 x 8 in), and spread it out evenly .

Make the topping: rub the butter into the flour until the mixture is crumbly. Mix in the caster sugar, baking powder, and salt and slowly stir in the milk to make a soft dough. Sprinkle the work surface with the 30 g (1/4 cup) flour. Knead the dough lightly a few turns on the floured surface, then roll out to the size of your baking dish. With a round biscuit cutter cut out 10 scones and lay them, slightly overlapping, on top of the fruit filling. Use the scraps of leftover dough to fill in any uncovered spots.

Sprinkle the top with the granulated sugar for the glaze. Bake in the preheated oven for 20 minutes until the scone top-

Peach and Blueberry Cobbler

ping turns golden brown. Allow to cool for 10 minutes. To serve, scoop out a scone and a spoonful of the fruit filling and transfer to each dessert bowl or plate.

Tips from Rosie's Kitchen

*The topping on our cobbler tastes delicious baked on its own as scrumptious scones. To make **Fresh Herb Scones**, just replace the sugar with fresh herbs (I use 1 teaspoon chopped parsley, 1 teaspoon chopped oregano, 1 teaspoon chopped thyme, and a pinch of cayenne pepper). Prepare the dough as for the cobbler, cut out 6 scones, lay them on a greased baking sheet, and bake in the preheated oven for 12 minutes.*

Blueberry Pie with Lattice Top

As a child, I picked blueberries during walks through our back woods to make pie, but collecting enough blueberries for a pie was impossible because they usually made their way to my mouth instead of the basket! Frozen blueberries can be substituted for fresh as long as they're well drained.

PASTRY

170 g (6 oz) cold butter
315 g (2 1/2 cups) unbleached
  plain flour, plus 30 g (1/4 cup)
  for dusting
1 tablespoon caster sugar
1/2 teaspoon salt
8–10 tablespoons cold purified
  water

FILLING

435 g (3 cups) fresh blueberries
120 ml (1/2 cup) maple syrup
2 tablespoons plain flour
1 tablespoon cornflour
1 teaspoon grated lemon zest
2 tablespoons freshly squeezed
  lemon juice

TO FINISH

2 tablespoons granulated sugar

Preheat oven to 180°C.

Cut the butter into small pieces. Put the butter, flour, sugar, and salt in a food processor and pulse on and off about 10 times, until crumbs start to form. Add the cold water and pulse again. If you don't have a food processor, rub the butter into the flour, sugar and salt, then bind with the water. Turn the dough out and shape into 2 equal balls. Wrap in greaseproof paper and chill in the refrigerator for 15 minutes or in the freezer for 10 minutes.

Sprinkle a little bit of flour from the 30 g (1/4 cup) on a piece of baking parchment or greaseproof paper. Roll out one of the balls of dough in the floured paper, using a floured rolling pin, to a circle about 30 cm (12 in) in diameter. Flip over the pastry on the paper onto a 23 cm (9 in) pie tin. Peel off the paper, then gently press the pastry into the tin to line it. Trim off any excess pastry. Toss the blueberries with the maple syrup, flour, corn-flour, lemon zest, and lemon juice in a bowl, then pour into the pastry case.

Roll out the other ball of dough, on the flour-dusted paper, to a circle a little larger than the top of the pie. Cut out 1 cm (1/2 in) wide strips on the diagonal. Lay half of them across the filling, spaced a little bit apart, using the longer ones for the centre of the pie. Lay the remaining strips in the opposite direction, creating a 'lattice' effect. Press the strips onto the edge of the pastry case, using a fork, so that they are secured in place.

Bake for 1 hour. When the pie is done, remove from the oven and sprinkle the top with the granulated sugar.

SERVES 8

PER SERVING:

CALORIES 386.8

FAT 17.7 G
 SATURATED FAT
 10.9 G

(40.6% OF CALO-
 RIES FROM FAT)

PROTEIN 4.8 G

CARBOHYDRATE
 53.5 G

CHOLESTEROL
 46 MG

FIBRE 2.9 G

❄

Apple Cake Squares

The bonus of this cake is that it's fast to make. It's a moist cake with a mellow cinnamon and apple taste. You can serve it for dessert or you can wrap slices up to take to school or to the office.

125 g (1 cup) wholemeal flour
1/4 teaspoon salt
3/4 teaspoon grated nutmeg
1 teaspoon bicarbonate of soda
1 teaspoon ground cinnamon
3 tablespoons caster sugar
45 g (11/2 oz) softened butter or
    Spectrum Spread
2 eggs
225 g (2 cups) peeled, cored, and
    grated apples

40 g (1/4 cup) finely chopped
    dates
30 g (1/4 cup) icing sugar

GARNISH (optional)

30 g (1/4 cup) finely chopped
    walnuts
60 ml (1/4 cup) maple syrup

SERVES 9

PER SERVING:

CALORIES 201.2

FAT 7.5 G
  SATURATED FAT
  2.9 G
(39.9% OF CALO-
  RIES FROM FAT)

PROTEIN 3.6 G

CARBOHYDRATE
  31.6 G

CHOLESTEROL
  58 MG

FIBRE 1.4 G

Preheat oven to 180°C.

Mix the flour, salt, nutmeg, bicarbonate of soda, and cinnamon together in a medium bowl and stir thoroughly. Cream the sugar and butter together in a large bowl. Beat in the eggs and beat until smooth. Stir in the grated apples and dates until they are evenly distributed throughout. Slowly stir in the dry ingredients, mixing thoroughly.

Spray the bottom and sides of a 23 cm (9 in) square baking tin with non-stick cooking spray, or grease it with 1/4 teaspoon of butter, and pour in the mixture. Bake in the preheated oven for about 45 minutes.

Put the icing sugar in a small sieve and sift it over the surface of the cake. Cut the Apple Cake into 9 squares. If you want to garnish, mix the walnuts with the maple syrup and drizzle over individual servings.

Blueberry Pie with Lattice Top

BERRIES WITH SORBET

For this simple yet very light and satisfying dessert, use raspberries, blackberries, blueberries, organic strawberries, or a mixture of these. Look for high-quality fruit sorbets with a minimum of ingredients. This is perfect after a heavy meal and provides a good measure of protective phytochemicals in the red and purple pigments of the fruit.

SERVES 6

PER SERVING:

CALORIES 63.1

FAT 0.4 G
  SATURATED FAT
  0 G

(4.8% OF CALORIES
  FROM FAT)

PROTEIN 0.6 G

CARBOHYDRATE
  16 G

CHOLESTEROL
  0 MG

FIBRE 2.3 G

300–450 g (2 pints) fresh berries
1 litre (2 pints) fruit sorbet (one or
    more flavours)

Wash the berries, drain them, and distribute them in 6 serving bowls. Let guests add their own sorbet. Serve with biscuits, if you wish.

PISTACHIO DREAM

The combination of pistachios, sugar, almond essence, and rosewater is an exotic and irresistible flavour signature of the Near East. This is a non-dairy frozen dessert, essentially a frozen, flavoured nut milk, made practical by the welcome availability of natural, shelled pistachios, now grown in abundance in California and Arizona. You need only serve small portions of this dessert, perhaps accompanied by plain biscuits.

360 ml (1½ cups) cold purified
   water
65 g (⅓ cup) caster sugar
135 g (1 cup) raw, unsalted, shelled
   pistachio nuts

Pinch of salt
½ teaspoon almond essence
1 teaspoon rosewater (see *Note*)

Mix the water and sugar in a saucepan. Cover and heat to boiling. Reduce the heat and boil for 1 minute. Remove the saucepan from heat and uncover.

Place the pistachios in a blender and grind to a fine powder, stopping the motor occasionally to stir in any large pieces.

Add half of the hot sugar syrup in a stream and blend at high speed for 1 minute, stopping occasionally to stir in any unblended nuts. Add the remaining sugar syrup and blend at high speed for 1 minute more. Pour the mixture through a fine sieve, pressing the residue with the back of a spoon to extract as much liquid as possible. Discard the residue. Stir in the pinch of salt, almond essence, and rosewater, and chill in the freezer until cold.

Pour the mixture into the chilled container of an ice cream maker and freeze according to the manufacturer's directions.

Serve the frozen dessert in small chilled cups with fresh fruit or biscuits.

Note: Rosewater is available in food shops that stock Middle Eastern or Indian foods.

SERVES 4

PER SERVING:

CALORIES 250

FAT 15.5 G
  SATURATED FAT
  2 G

(56% OF CALORIES
  FROM FAT)

PROTEIN 6.5 G

CARBOHYDRATE
  24.5 G

CHOLESTEROL
  0 MG

FIBRE 3.5 G

❋

Lemon Sponge Cake

Finally, a recipe that uses the whole egg! We use the egg whites in the Sponge Cake to make it a fluffy complement to our creamy, lemony custard, where we use the egg yolks. These counterparts may taste familiar, as they are used in classic desserts like lemon meringue pie.

I serve this cake with Spiced Tea (page 42) when I'm having some friends over for a casual afternoon tea.

Makes 1 cake
Serves 8

Per serving:

Calories 251.5

Fat 5 g
  Saturated fat
  1.9 g
(17.7% of calories from fat)

Protein 8.8 g

Carbohydrate
  43.5 g

Cholesterol
  17.7 mg

Fibre 0.6 g

SPONGE CAKE

4 egg whites, at room temperature
1/4 teaspoon salt
1 tablespoon pure vanilla extract
100 g (1/2 cup) caster sugar
65 g (1/2 cup) unbleached plain
  flour
50 g (1/2 cup) ground almonds

LEMON CUSTARD

100 g (1/2 cup) caster sugar
2 tablespoons cornflour
240 ml (1 cup) milk (or water for
  lighter recipe)
Pinch of salt

2 egg yolks
60 ml (1/4 cup) freshly squeezed
  lemon juice
1/2 teaspoon grated lemon zest
3 tablespoons icing sugar

GARNISH

150 g (1 cup) blueberries,
  raspberries, blackberries, or a
  combination

Preheat oven to 170°C.

Make the cake: whisk the egg whites with the salt until they become stiff. Fold in the vanilla extract. In a separate bowl combine the sugar, flour, and almonds. Mix thoroughly, then fold gently into the whisked egg whites.

Line the bottom of a 20 x 30 cm (8 x12 in) Swiss roll tin or baking tray with a sheet of baking parchment. Scrape the cake mixture into the tin and spread it out evenly into a rectangle about 15 x 25 cm (6 x 10 in). Bake for 15 minutes.

Meanwhile, put the caster sugar and the cornflour into a medium saucepan set over low heat. Gradually stir in the milk (or water) and keep stirring until smooth. Turn up the heat to medium and, using a whisk, mix in the salt and the egg yolks.

Bring to the boil. Whisk in the lemon juice and lemon zest and continue to boil for 1 minute more. Allow to cool for 10 minutes.

Remove the cake from the oven and cool for 10 minutes. Lay a clean piece of baking parchment on the work surface and sprinkle with the sifted icing sugar. Invert the cake on top of the sugar-sprinkled parchment. Trim off the crusty edges. Spread a thin layer (about 300 ml/1 1/4 cups) of the cooled lemon custard over the surface. Starting at the long end near you, roll the cake up and wrap it securely in the parchment, twisting the ends of the paper to keep it closed (some custard might ooze out of the sides of the cake). Chill for 3 hours.

Cut across into 5 cm (2 in) thick slices, and place each slice on a plate with a dollop of the remaining custard. Sprinkle over the berries and serve.

Tips from Rosie's Kitchen

You can buy almonds already ground, but they won't have as fresh a flavour as those you grind yourself. Use a food processor or, for the finest ground nuts, a special electric nut mill or clean coffee grinder.

You will find that you use only about half the custard for the filling. But it is lovely to have extra on hand to serve with fruit salads and berries. If you prefer, you can make only half the amount.

Lemon Yogurt Sorbet

A simple combination of mellow fruit and tangy citrus, this lively dessert can complete a meal or serve as a palate cleanser between courses. An appealing way to serve this sorbet is to scoop it into a hollowed-out lemon cup.

SERVES 12

PER SERVING:

CALORIES 49.7

FAT 0.7
  SATURATED FAT
  0.4 G
(11.1% OF CALO-
RIES FROM FAT)

PROTEIN 0.8 G

CARBOHYDRATE
  11.3 G

CHOLESTEROL
  2 MG

FIBRE 0.4 G

❊

500 g (2 cups) plain yogurt
120 ml (1/2 cup) freshly squeezed
  lemon juice
80 g (1/2 cup) chopped crystallized
  ginger
1 teaspoon grated lemon zest

170 g (1/2 cup) honey
60 g (1/2 cup) raspberries
60 g (1/2 cup) green grapes

GARNISH

Sprigs fresh mint

Blend all the ingredients together, except the berries and the grapes, in a blender or with a whisk. Pour the mixture into a big bowl, cover with cling film, and put it in the freezer until thoroughly chilled, about 30 minutes. Then pour into an ice cream machine and freeze according to manufacturer's instructions. To serve, centre a scoop of sorbet on top of each portion of raspberries and grapes, and garnish with mint.

Alternative Method

If you don't have an ice cream maker or sorbet machine, simply freeze the mixture in a covered, stainless steel bowl until set and crystallized, about 3 hours. Place the crystallized mixture in a food processor and pulse for about 30 seconds. Return to the bowl, cover with cling film, and freeze until solid.

Tips from Rosie's Kitchen

Make your own yogurt: *use 1 litre (4 cups) of fresh whole milk (or semi-skimmed milk, if you prefer) and 1 tablespoon plain yogurt. Bring the milk to boiling point, stirring constantly. Pour into a bowl and cool until you can stick a finger in and hold it there comfortably. Whisk in the yogurt, mixing well. Cover the bowl and leave at room temperature overnight. If your kitchen is cold, just set the bowl in a turned-off oven, or on the top of the cooker over the pilot light. When the yogurt has thickened, put it into the refrigerator to chill for 6 hours. It will keep for up to 1 week.*

Lemon Yogurt Sorbet with heart-shaped Ginger Biscuits

Ginger Biscuits

Ginger biscuits are fun to make and kids will love to be involved in the cutting and decorating. I like heart-shaped biscuits, but you can use any shape cutter including those that make gingerbread people. Whatever cutter you use, you're sure to enjoy these soft, scrumptious biscuits.

MAKES ABOUT
32 BISCUITS
(7.5 CM/3 IN EACH)

PER SERVING
  (ONE BISCUIT):

CALORIES 96.9

FAT 1.8 G
  SATURATED FAT
  0.1 G
  (1.6% OF CALO-
  RIES FROM FAT)

PROTEIN 1.6 G

CARBOHYDRATE
  19 G

CHOLESTEROL
  0 MG

FIBRE 0.5 G

220 g (2/3 cup) molasses
75 g (1/3 cup) softened butter or
  Spectrum Spread
60 ml (1/4 cup) apple juice
  concentrate
1 teaspoon pure vanilla extract
2 egg whites
500 g (4 cups) unbleached plain
  flour
100 g (1/2 cup) caster sugar
2 teaspoons ground ginger
1 teaspoon ground cinnamon
1/4 teaspoon ground cloves
1/4 teaspoon ground allspice

1/2 teaspoon salt
1 teaspoon bicarbonate of soda
1/2 teaspoon baking powder
1/8 teaspoon grated orange zest

GLAZE

60 ml (1/4 cup) apple juice
  concentrate

Mix the molasses, butter, apple juice concentrate, and vanilla extract together in a large bowl. Whisk the egg whites in a separate bowl using an electric mixer for 3 minutes, then whisk them into the wet ingredients.

Mix all the dry ingredients together, including the orange zest, in a separate, large bowl. Slowly add the dry ingredients to the wet ingredients, using a wooden spoon to mix everything together until the dough becomes stiff. Knead the dough with clean hands for a couple of minutes, and then divide it in half. Flatten each half into a disc, wrap in cling film, and chill in the freezer for at least 2 hours, or overnight in the fridge.

Preheat the oven to 180°C.

Roll out the dough on a floured surface to about 3 mm (1/8 in) thick. Cut out shapes with a biscuit cutter. Using a pastry brush, lightly brush the shapes with the apple juice concentrate.

Smear a baking sheet with 1/4 teaspoon of butter and

arrange the biscuits on it. Bake for 10–12 minutes until they turn a light golden brown. Remove the biscuits from the oven and allow them to cool for a few minutes on the baking sheet before transferring to a wire rack to cool completely.

Tips from Rosie's Kitchen

Ginger biscuits don't have to be plain. You can liven them up by adding dried cranberries or cherries, extra grated citrus zest, sunflower seeds, flaked almonds, or raisins. Allow the biscuits to cool after baking until they are warm, then gently press the dried fruit, seeds, or nuts into the soft biscuit.

In order to glaze the biscuits before baking, you will need a pastry brush that you can buy at any kitchen shop.

Molasses has a strong flavour and is less sweet than sugar or honey. You can substitute golden syrup, which is sweeter but not as nutritious as molasses.

If you want to involve kids in baking, these biscuits are a great place to start. During the holiday season, you can use gingerbread cutters and let the kids make their own gingerbread people. Children love biscuits no matter what shape they are cut into, especially if they have a hand in adorning them with delicious, edible, bite-size decorations.

Orange Oat and Sultana Cookies

These cookies are excellent because of the orange flavour, the banana mixed into the batter, and the clumps of sultanas or chocolate chips. They taste less like just a sugary mass of oats and more like a real cookie: dense with genuine flavour and satisfying. I like to freeze these cookies in a polythene bag because they are refreshing and delicious when cold!

Makes 16 large cookies

Per serving:

Calories 205.3

Fat 14.2 g

  Saturated fat 6 g

(53.9% of calories from fat)

Protein 3.1 g

Carbohydrate 24.1 g

Cholesterol 29 mg

Fibre 2.9 g

✳

115 g (1/2 cup) butter, at room temperature, or Spectrum Spread

1 egg

40 g (1/4 cup) mashed ripe banana (about 1/2 banana)

1 teaspoon pure vanilla extract

100 g (1/2 cup) light soft brown sugar

11/2 teaspoons grated orange zest

125 g (1 cup) wholemeal flour

1/4 teaspoon salt

1 teaspoon baking powder

120 g (11/2 cups) rolled oats

20 g (1/4 cup) desiccated coconut

60 g (1/2 cup) chopped walnuts

75 g (1/2 cup) sultanas, or 90 g (1/2 cup) dark chocolate chips

Preheat oven to 180°C.

Cream the butter and egg together until well blended and smooth. Gradually beat in the banana, vanilla extract, and brown sugar. Add the orange zest. Mix well with a wooden spoon until all the ingredients are thoroughly blended.

In a large bowl mix the flour, salt, baking powder, oats, coconut, walnuts, and sultanas or chocolate chips. Use a wooden spoon to combine the dry ingredients until they are evenly mixed. Stir the dry ingredients into the wet ingredients and mix thoroughly until there is no sign of dryness.

Smear 1/4 teaspoon of butter on a baking sheet. Drop heaping tablespoonsful of the dough onto the greased baking sheet , leaving 5 cm (2 in) space around each one, and press down lightly to flatten. Bake for 20 minutes until lightly browned. Cool on a wire rack.

Tips from Rosie's Kitchen

If you want to turn these cookies into a treat that provides more fibre, replace one-third of the rolled oats with a whole-grain cereal that includes rolled oats, cracked wheat, cracked rye, and cracked barley. The oats will ensure that you get the benefits of vitamins E, B$_1$, and B$_2$, and the other grains will offer their own nutritional goodies.

Poached Pears

There are many poached pear recipes using various liquids. I like to poach pears in fruit juices because the juice from the pears when combined with apple or cranberry juice has a delicately sweet flavour. Choose pears that are ripe and firm. Poaching pears that are too ripe will just make them mushy.

If you have leftover pears you can use them ito make Pear Relish (page 252), to drizzle over warm turkey or any other type of poultry dish.

SERVES 6

PER SERVING:

CALORIES 143.7

FAT 1.3 G
  SATURATED FAT
  0.2 G
(7.1% OF CALO-
  RIES FROM FAT)

PROTEIN 0.7 G

CARBOHYDRATE
  36.4 G

CHOLESTEROL
  0 MG

FIBRE 5.6 G

3 pears, cut in half lengthways
480 ml (2 cups) cranberry or
   cranapple juice
2 cinnamon sticks
3 whole cloves

GARNISH

6 fresh mint leaves

Scoop the cores out of the pear halves using a melon scooper or a teaspoon. Peel the skin off with a small knife.

Put the pears and the fruit juice in a saucepan with the cinnamon sticks and cloves. Make sure the pears are entirely covered by the juice. Cook them over medium heat until they are soft. If the pears are already ripe, this will take about 7 minutes; for harder pears, cook them for about 15 minutes. They should be easily pierced with a fork. Remove the pears using a slotted spoon, and set aside to cool on a clean cloth. Lower the heat and cook the poaching liquid for 45 minutes until it is reduced to a third of the original amount, and it is thick and syrupy. Remove it from the heat.

Lay each pear half, flat side down, on a plate. Cut into 6 thin slices lengthways without cutting through the stalk end. Fan the slices out and drizzle the poaching syrup on top. Serve warm or chilled. Garnish each with a mint leaf before serving.

FIGS IN WINE

This is an unusual and healthful dessert, full of flavour and devoid of fat. You want the figs to swell up and become very tender as they absorb the wine. To do so they must be moist and pliable to begin with. Very hard, dry figs will not do the job.

500 ml (2 cups) dried white figs
   (Turkish or Calimyrna), the softer
   the better
500 ml (2 cups) red wine, such as
   Merlot or Pinot Noir
Grated zest of 1 large, organic
   orange (optional)

Put the figs in a glass or ceramic bowl and pour the red wine over them to cover. Cover the bowl with cling film and chill for 24 hours until the figs are very soft.

   Drain the figs and toss them with the optional orange zest.

SERVES 6

PER SERVING:
CALORIES 236
FAT 0.8 G
  SATURATED FAT
  LESS THAN 1 G
(3.5% OF CALORIES FROM FAT)
PROTEIN 2 G
CARBOHYDRATE
  47 G
CHOLESTEROL
  0 MG
FIBRE 6.5 G

Raspberry Sorbet Tarts with Chocolate Whipped Cream

Chock full of berries embraced by a thin, crunchy chocolate crust, these miniature frozen pies are loaded with heavy flavour without being a heavy dessert. They make the perfect light and gratifying way to end a special meal.

SERVES 8

PER SERVING:

CALORIES 323.8

FAT 15.1 G
   SATURATED FAT
   6.5 G
(49% OF CALO-
   RIES FROM FAT)

PROTEIN 3.4 G

CARBOHYDRATE
   40.3 G

CHOLESTEROL
   32 MG

FIBRE 2.3 G

TART CASES

3 tablespoons grapeseed oil
150 g (1 1/2 cups) plain chocolate digestive biscuits, crushed into fine crumbs
1 egg white

SORBET FILLING

280 g (10 oz) unsweetened frozen raspberries with juice, slightly thawed
280 g (10 oz) unsweetened frozen strawberries, slightly thawed (or 150 g/1 cup fresh strawberries)
145 g (1 cup) fresh blackberries
100 g (1/2 cup) caster sugar
120 ml (1/2 cup) apple juice

CHOCOLATE WHIPPED CREAM

120 ml (1/2 cup) whipping cream
2 tablespoons icing sugar
1 tablespoon cocoa powder
1/2 teaspoon pure vanilla extract

GARNISH

Fresh strawberries
8 sprigs fresh mint

Preheat oven 180°C.

Make the tart cases: lightly grease the bottom and sides of 8 tartlet tins or ramekins with 1 tablespoon of the oil. Mix the remaining oil with the digestive biscuit crumbs and egg white in a bowl. Distribute equal amounts of the chocolate crumb mixture among the 8 tins. Press into the tins with your fingers to line the bottom and sides evenly. Bake for 10 minutes, then remove from the oven and chill while you prepare the filling.

Process all the filling ingredients in a blender or food processor until smooth. Strain the seeds out of the filling, using a spoon to push the purée against the sieve; discard seeds. Scoop the purée into the cooled tart cases. Freeze for 2 hours.

Make the Chocolate Whipped Cream: whip the cream in a clean, stainless steel bowl, using an electric mixer or whisk. Whip until the cream becomes thick, about 3 minutes. Add the sifted icing sugar, cocoa powder, and vanilla extract and whip for 1 more minute until fluffy and light. Cover and set aside.

Take the Raspbery Sorbet Tarts out of the freezer and garnish each with a dollop of Chocolate Whipped Cream, fresh strawberries, and a mint sprig.

Tips from Rosie's Kitchen

If you want to make this an entirely dairy-free dessert, use Andy's almond milk (page 34) as a garnish instead of the Chocolate Whipped Cream. Turn out the tarts and set in the centre of dessert plates. Pour a thin pool of almond milk around the tarts, then garnish with strawberries and mint sprigs.

Rice Pudding

This eggless rice pudding is not as sweet and heavy as traditional rice pudding. I like to use jasmine rice because I think it tastes sweeter. Basmati rice has a nuttier flavour and a finer grain. They both make a fine rice pudding; it just depends on what flavour of rice appeals to you. I serve this light dessert after a main dish salad .

MAKES 6

PER SERVING:

CALORIES 349

FAT 4.2 G
   SATURATED FAT
   3.3 G
(13.4% OF CALORIES
   FROM FAT)

PROTEIN 8 G

CARBOHYDRATE
   72.6 G

CHOLESTEROL
   6 MG

FIBRE 1.2 G

❉

FRUIT SAUCE

2 peaches, peeled and sliced
240 ml (1 cup) freshly squeezed
   orange juice
2 tablespoons honey

RICE PUDDING

720 ml (3 cups) semi-skimmed
   milk
180 g(1 cup) jasmine rice or
   brown basmati rice

1 teaspoon grated lemon zest
1 teaspoon pure vanilla extract
1/8 teaspoon grated nutmeg or
   ground mace
170 g (1/2 cup) honey
120 ml (1/2 cup) evaporated
   skimmed milk
45 g (1/2 cup) desiccated coconut

Make the fruit sauce: put the peaches, orange juice, and honey in a bowl and toss to coat the peaches with the honey and juice. Cover and chill until ready to use.

Preheat oven to 170°C.

Bring the milk and rice to the boil in a large saucepan. Reduce the heat and simmer, covered, for 15 minutes, until all the liquid is absorbed. Remove from the heat. Stir in the lemon zest, vanilla extract, nutmeg or mace, honey, and evaporated milk. Add the coconut. Use a fork to mix everything together and break up the rice grains. Spoon into 6 ramekins and cover each with foil. Arrange them in a baking tin containing warm water that comes about two-thirds of the way up the sides of the ramekins. Bake for 30 minutes, then carefully remove

Tips from Rosie's Kitchen

If you want to make this a completely dairy-free dessert, substitute either rice milk or vanilla soya milk for the cow's milk called for here. Use the same amount and cook it the same way.

the foil. Bake for another 15 minutes until the tops of the puddings puff up. Remove from the oven and leave to cool.

When completely cooled, slide a knife around each pudding to loosen it from the sides of the ramekin. Turn over onto a plate and lift off the ramekin. Spoon equal portions of chilled fruit sauce on top of each pudding and serve.

APPLE CRANBERRY CRISP

Cranberries give this crisp a delightful colour and tartness. A moderate amount of oil replaces the large amount of butter usually called for in toppings for this kind of dessert. It is best served warm.

12 large tart apples, peeled, cored, and sliced
225 g (8 oz) fresh or frozen cranberries
Juice of 1 lemon
80 ml (1/3 cup) brandy
65 g (1/3 cup) soft light brown sugar
1 teaspoon ground cinnamon
2 tablespoons wholemeal flour

TOPPING
120 g (1 1/2 cups) rolled oats
50 g (1/2 cup) toasted wheat germ
3/4 teaspoon salt
1 1/2 teaspoons ground cinnamon
100 g (1/2 cup) soft light brown sugar
80 ml (1/3 cup) grapeseed oil
80 ml (1/3 cup) maple syrup

SERVES 12

PER SERVING:
CALORIES 279.5
FAT 7.7 G
  SATURATED FAT 0.8 G
(24.8% OF CALORIES FROM FAT)
PROTEIN 4.1 G
CARBOHYDRATE 48.7 G
CHOLESTEROL 0 MG
FIBRE 5.8 G

Preheat oven to 190°C.

Toss the sliced apples in a large bowl with the cranberries, lemon juice, brandy, light brown sugar, cinnamon, and flour. Pile the apple mixture into a 20 x 25 cm (8 x 10 in) baking dish.

Mix together the ingredients for the topping and spread over the apples. Cover the baking dish with foil and bake for 20 minutes. Uncover and bake for 40 minutes more until the apples are soft and the topping is crisp. Serve hot.

Apricot Mousse

You will have a hard time refusing seconds with this dessert. You can taste every bit of fruit in it, from the apricots to the raspberries. Every foamy, sweet bite just melts in your mouth.

SERVES 6

PER SERVING:

CALORIES 103.3

FAT 0.3 G
   SATURATED FAT
   0 G
(2.2% OF CALO-
   RIES FROM FAT)

PROTEIN 2.5 G

CARBOHYDRATE
   25.7 G

CHOLESTEROL
   0 MG

FIBRE 1.7 G

3 tablespoons agar-agar (vegetarian gelatine)
360 ml (1 1/2 cups) cold purified water
115 g (1 cup) dried apricots (preferably unsulphured)
1 tablespoon honey
480 ml (2 cups) apple juice
260 g (2 cups) frozen vanilla yogurt

GARNISH

About 6 tablespoons plain low-fat yogurt
250 g (1 pint) fresh raspberries
1 lime, thinly sliced

Dissolve the agar-agar in 240 ml (1 cup) of the water in a small bowl.

Drop the apricots into a second bowl. Bring the remaining water to the boil in a small pan, then add the honey and stir. Pour the liquid over the apricots and set aside to rehydrate.

Bring the apple juice to the boil, then stir in the dissolved agar-agar and continue to cook, while stirring, for 5 minutes. Drain the apricots in a colander, then add them to the boiling juice mixture. Stir again a few times and remove from the heat. Allow to cool for 1 minute, then pour into a glass bowl. Chill, covered, for at least 2 hours or overnight, until the apricots in jelly are set.

Put the apricot jelly and frozen yogurt into a blender or food processor and blend until well mixed and foamy. Scoop it into glasses. Garnish each with a dollop of yogurt, a sprinkling of fresh raspberries, and a slice of lime.

Tip's from Rosie's Kitchen

Agar-agar is a natural gelatine made from dried seaweed. It is a strong setting ingredient and you can find it at any health food shop.

Though you can chill the jelly for just 2 hours to set it, I always chill it overnight. Whatever you choose, you'll need to plan accordingly.

This recipe is actually two in one because you have the option of serving it simply as a fruit jelly, or you can blend it with the frozen yogurt to make the mousse. Instead of yogurt, you can garnish the jelly option with a dollop of real whipped cream.

This dessert is exceptionally easy to make, requiring minimal ingredients, and the bonus to your friends and family is that it's preservative-free.

CHOCOLATE

Most people love chocolate; many are passionate about it. Some say dessert is either chocolate or something other than chocolate. But this food of the gods, enjoyed as a sacred drink by natives of ancient Mexico and Meso-America, has developed a bad reputation in our times. Considered a 'guilty pleasure', it has been demonised because of its fat content and is said to have no place in a good diet. Some health-food producers have even come up with a wretched imitation of it – carob – that they use to make 'nutritious' fake chocolates, cakes, and biscuits. In fact, chocolate not only beats carob hands down in both the taste and health categories, it has many attributes that recommend it for inclusion in an optimum diet.

Cocoa butter, the fat in chocolate, turns out not to be so bad. Although it is a saturated fat, the body turns it into monounsaturated fat, processing it like olive oil. Chocolate appears to be neutral, at worst, in regard to cardiovascular health and may actually lower serum cholesterol. In addition, chocolate has strong antioxidant activity, equivalent to that of red wine and green tea. It is a stimulant because it contains theobromine, a relative of caffeine, but, for unknown reasons, it is also, for many people, a rapid-acting antidepressant.

The best form of chocolate from a health standpoint is high-quality, plain, dark chocolate. I say 'high-quality' because cheaper brands contain less actual chocolate, often replacing expensive cocoa butter with unhealthful hydrogenated vegetable oils. The first ingredient on a bar of high-quality chocolate should be chocolate – usually indicated as 'chocolate liquor', 'cacao', or 'cocoa solids'. It should not be sugar. The brands I like best contain 70 per cent cocoa. (Bitter baking chocolate is 100 per cent cocoa; more than 80 per cent is too bitter for most people to enjoy.)

I say 'plain' because chocolates often contain butter and cream, sources of highly saturated animal fats, as well as other ingredients much less good for us than the natural constituents of cocoa beans. And I say 'dark' because milk chocolate contains much less cocoa and more butterfat and sugar.

When I want a sweet, I usually go for a piece (or chunk) of high-quality dark chocolate, which I regard as a pleasure, but not one I need to feel guilty about. I often serve dark chocolate with fruit as a dessert (the recipe follows) and keep dark chocolate sorbet in the freezer. In moderation, these treats are not fattening, provide important nutrients, are perfectly fine for people following low-carbohydrate diets – and they certainly add to the pleasure of eating. —A.W.

DARK CHOCOLATE WITH FRUIT

SERVES 6

✳

This couldn't be simpler, and your guests will love it. Serve an assortment of fresh fruit that is perfectly ripe and flavourful. Also serve some high-quality dark chocolate broken into pieces, and let people help themselves.

45 g (1¹/₂ oz) dark chocolate
1 pear or apple

Rosie's Tips on Planning Menus

The menus Andy and I have designed here should give you an idea of how to mix and match our dishes to create a healthy diet throughout the week. As well, we offer two exciting menus for celebratory meals.

But often, menu planning is and should be prompted by the season – what the weather is like and what fresh produce is in the market. Also, keep in mind what you may have left over from a meal so that you can use it in a creative way the next day or so. I even plan for leftovers, deliberately making more so I have something to work with – which saves me time. As a general rule, I serve my meals with something fresh, like a slice of melon or a spring salad mix. I also like to use edible flowers, such as nasturtiums, geraniums, pansies, and lavender as a garnish. It's good to have these items available because they taste good and dress up the plate.

A spring meal after a visit to the farmers' market (or, if you're so fortunate, your own garden), where you find baby salad greens and small spinach leaves, might feature Mixed Greens with Potato Crouton Salad (page 101). The Vegetable 'Quiche' (page 11), served hot or cold, would be perfect with the salad to complete a lovely light spring lunch.

In summer, you can enjoy the breeze while barbecuing outside. Sip on a glass of iced Berry Herbal Tea (page 41), while you prepare Thai Prawn Brochettes (page 67), having set up a Tostada Buffet (page 217) for a casual supper for friends. The Spanish Seafood Cocktail, Gazpacho-Style (page 64) would make a pleasant chilled starter that goes well with the Spanish Tostada. Both dishes use salsa and other common summer ingredients, which you can prepare ahead of time. I usually like to end a meal with a cup of herbal tea and/or fresh fruit. At the weekends, when you have more time, you may want to make a special treat, like a Blueberry Pie with Lattice Top (page 280), to make the most of the delicious seasonal berries.

On a chilly autumn evening when it's nice to have the oven warming up the kitchen, you could prepare ahead some Apple Cake Squares (page 283), which would make a fine ending for a dinner starting with Baked Curried Sea Bass (page 188) accompanied by Stuffed Winter Squash (page 236) instead of Barbecued Summer Vegetables (page 156).

In the winter months, again it's nice to warm up the kitchen on a leisurely Sunday afternoon by baking an Apple Cranberry Crisp (page 299) and roasting at the same time the Savoury Roasted Poussins (page 150). The whole roasted heads of garlic that are part of that recipe are delicious over Mashed Potatoes and Parsnips (page 231), another winter treat. In the middle of that pleasant day of cooking, you might stir up some simple Miso Soup (page 125) for a wholesome lunch or snack.

So I have added some additional seasonal menus that make the most of the year's changing bounty.

NOTE: The nutritional analyses for these menus are not written in stone – there will inevitably be slight variables in the kind of fruit or cheese or bread or nuts you might choose. But they serve as guidelines for planning a healthy diet through the week and allow for some additional rounding out of the meals, as you see fit, since the calorie counts come in well under the recommended guidelines. The holiday and special dinners are more indulgent, but we all need to celebrate on occasion and you can simply cut back on the rest of the day's intake or adjust your meals accordingly on the ensuing days.

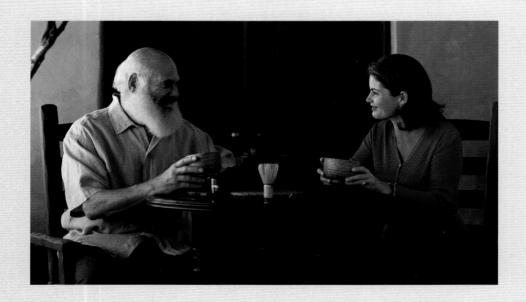

Daily Menus

Monday

B R E A K F A S T
    Scrambled Eggs with Fresh Salsa
    Sunrise Orange Grapefruit Juice
    Toast

S N A C K
    Pineapple Almond Shake

L U N C H
    Lebanese Salad
    Wholemeal Baguette
    Fresh Fruit

D I N N E R
    Grilled Fish with Tropical Relish
    Lemon Dill Baby Carrots
    Brown Rice
    Figs in Wine
    Berry Herbal Tea

CALORIES 1534.8
FAT 37 G
  SATURATED FAT 9.6 G
(26.3% OF CALORIES FROM FAT)
PROTEIN 71.3 G
CARBOHYDRATE 104.9 G
CHOLESTEROL 204 MG
FIBRE 12.3 G

❄

Tuesday

B R E A K F A S T
    Frosted Orange and Ginger Fruit Salad
    Frittata

S N A C K
    Orange Oatmeal and Sultana Cookie

CALORIES 1474
FAT 49 G
  SATURATED FAT 14.7 G
(31.9% OF CALORIES FROM FAT)
PROTEIN 31.9 G
CARBOHYDRATE 196.1 G
CHOLESTEROL 224 MG
FIBRE 43.1 G

LUNCH

    Mixed Bean Minestrone Stew

    Cheese and Biscuits

DINNER

    Baked Spicy Tofu with Cellophane Noodles,
        Sweetcorn, and Mango

    Shiitake Mushrooms and Mange-touts

    Berries with Sorbet

Wednesday

BREAKFAST

    Muesli or Granola

SNACK

    Frozen Fruit Smoothie

LUNCH

    Tabbouleh Salad

    White Bean Spread

    Pita Bread

DINNER

    Escarole Soup

    Grilled Salmon with Mustard Sauce

    1 Slice Baguette

    Wilted Spinach with Mushrooms

    Grapes and Cheese

CALORIES 1394.3

FAT 54 G
  SATURATED FAT
  12.9 G
(34.4% OF CALO-
  RIES FROM FAT)

PROTEIN 106.3 G

CARBOHYDRATE
  125.7 G

CHOLESTEROL
  246 MG

FIBRE 18.9 G

Thursday

BREAKFAST

    Two-Coloured Fruit Gazpacho

    Apple Sauce Muffins

SNACK

    Honey Ginger Lemonade

    A Handful of Nuts

LUNCH

    Vegetable Nori Rolls

    Broccoli Salad with Avocado

DINNER

    Tomato, Sweetcorn, and Basil Soup

    Turkey Burgers or Portobello Burgers

    Lemon Yogurt Sorbet and

        (optional) Ginger Biscuits

WITH TURKEY BURGERS

CALORIES 1512.8

FAT 50.1 G

  SATURATED FAT 8.4 G

(27.9% OF CALORIES FROM FAT)

PROTEIN 55.5 G

CARBOHYDRATE 235.2 G

CHOLESTEROL 110 MG

FIBRE 36.9 G

WITH PORTOBELLO BURGERS

CALORIES 1552.3

FAT 70.3 G

  SATURATED FAT 9.5 G

(38.5% OF CALORIES FROM FAT)

PROTEIN 29.9 G

CARBOHYDRATE 222.4 G

CHOLESTEROL 20 MG

FIBRE 30.9 G

CALORIES 2008.2

FAT 70.4 G
  SATURATED FAT
  13.7 G
(18.2% OF CALO-
  RIES FROM FAT)

PROTEIN 56.6 G

CARBOHYDRATE
  305.1 G

CHOLESTEROL
  54 MG

FIBRE 37.3 G

Friday

BREAKFAST

Scrambled Tofu with Fresh Salsa
Slice of Melon
Wholemeal Toast

SNACK

Spiced Tea

LUNCH

Cold Vegetable Pasta Primavera
Fresh Fruit

DINNER

Barbecued Fish Tacos
Spanish Rice
Dark Chocolate with Fruit

CALORIES 2088.1

FAT 52.2 G
  SATURATED FAT
  11.3 G
(21.3% OF CALO-
  RIES FROM FAT)

PROTEIN 51.3 G

CARBOHYDRATE
  383 G

CHOLESTEROL
  30 MG

FIBRE 54.3 G

Saturday

BREAKFAST

Pancakes or Waffles with Fruit Compote

SNACK

Citrus Mango Freeze

LUNCH

Roasted Butternut Squash and Apple Soup
Hummus Pinwheels with Veggie Crudités

DINNER
Vegetable Lasagne
Green Bean Salad
Poached Pears

Sunday

BREAKFAST
Eggs Florentine with Orange and
Dill Sauce
Fresh Fruit

SNACK
Low-Fat Vanilla Shake

LUNCH
Cold Cucumber Soup
Thai Prawn and Papaya Salad

DINNER
Tofu Fajitas
Greek Salad with Mild Chilli Dressing
Blueberry Pie with Lattice Top

CALORIES 1659.1

FAT 73.5 G
SATURATED FAT
23.6 G
(38% OF CALO-
RIES FROM FAT)

PROTEIN 64.6 G

CARBOHYDRATE
205 G

CHOLESTEROL
366 MG

FIBRE 31.6 G

Menus for Special Occasions

CALORIES 1099.9

FAT 49.6 G

SATURATED FAT
10.7 G

(24.9% OF CALO-
RIES FROM FAT)

PROTEIN 211.3 G

CARBOHYDRATE
125.9 G

CHOLESTEROL
87 MG

FIBRE 20.2 G

CHRISTMAS LUNCH
WITH FISH,
1 SERVING

CALORIES 1417.2

FAT 49.5 G

SATURATED FAT
9.7 G

(30.1% OF CALO-
RIES FROM FAT)

PROTEIN 51.4 G

CARBOHYDRATE
207 G

CHOLESTEROL
29 MG

FIBRE 40.6 G

Christmas Lunch

Miso Pâté

Spinach Toasts

Roasted Pepper Turkey with Orange Liqueur
    or Fish with Spinach *En Papillote*

Vegetarian Shepherd's Pie with Sweet Potato
    and Lentil Filling

Andy's Brussels Sprouts

Jicama and Carrot Salad

Pistachio Dream and Biscuits

Apple Strudel

Cranberry Barley Tonic

Dinner Party for Friends

Smoked Fish with Horseradish Sauce
Goat's Cheese Toasties with Sun-Dried Tomatoes
   and Basil
Mediterranean Stuffed Vine Leaves
(A) Celery, Artichoke, Hearts of Palm, and Prawn Salad
   or (B) Mixed Greens with Potato Croutons and
   Tarragon Dressing
(A) Savoury Mushroom Lobster Crêpes,
   or (B) Aubergine Rollatini with Spinach and
   Cheese Filling
(A) Apple Tart,
   or (B) Raspberry Sorbet Pie

DINNER FOR FRIENDS
WITH MAIN COURSE
AND DESSERT
SELECTION (A)
1 SERVING

CALORIES 1511.8

FAT 72.2 G
   SATURATED FAT
   17.8 G

(41.7% OF CALO-
   RIES FROM FAT)

PROTEIN 78.8 G

CARBOHYDRATE
   148 G

CHOLESTEROL
   102 MG

FIBRE 24.8 G

DINNER FOR FRIENDS
WITH MAIN COURSE
AND DESSERT
SELECTION (B)
1 SERVING

CALORIES 1692.7

FAT 69 G
   SATURATED FAT
   23 G

(36.8% OF CALO-
   RIES FROM FAT)

PROTEIN 116.4 G

CARBOHYDRATE
   150.3 G

CHOLESTEROL
   527 MG

FIBRE 15.6 G

Seasonal Menus

Spring Brunch

Vegetable Quiche with Radish Rosettes
Fresh Herb Scones (made from leftover cobbler dough)
Angel Cake with Fresh Berries

Summer Garden Party

Chicken Satay with Peanut Dipping Sauce
Warm Tomatoes Stuffed with Quinoa and Courgette
Greens with Tangy Miso Sauce
Apricot Mousse

Summer Dinner

Barbecued Summer Vegetables
Lemon Baked Halibut with Papaya Salsa
Spanish Rice
Two-Coloured Fruit Gazpacho

Autumn Dinner

Warm Mediterranean Stuffed Vine Leaves
Baked Curried Sea Bass with Lentils
Greek Salad with Mild Chilli Dressing
or Green Salad
Lemon Sponge Cake

Winter Dinner

Roasted Butternut Squash and Apple Soup
Poussins with Roasted Garlic
Apple Cranberry Crisp

Anytime Vegetarian Menu

Miso Soup
Teriyaki Sampler Plate
    with Spring Onion Firecrackers
Rice Pudding

A Note About the Authors

Rosie Daley was born in New Jersey to a large family. She trained as a chef at Cal-a-Vie spa just north of San Diego, California, then relocated to Chicago to work as the personal chef for Oprah Winfrey for five years. She is the author of *In the Kitchen with Rosie*, published in 1994. Since then she has been busy teaching cookery classes to small and large groups, promoting healthy eating. She now lives in California with her son Marley.

Andrew Weil, M.D., a graduate of Harvard College and Harvard Medical School, is Clinical Professor of Medicine at the University of Arizona and director of the Program in Integrative Medicine at that institution. Dr. Weil produces a monthly newsletter, *Self-Healing,* maintains a popular website, DrWeil.com, and writes a monthly column in *Prevention* magazine. He is a frequent guest on radio and television and lectures widely on nutrition and natural medicine. This is his ninth book.

A Note on the Types

Rosie's text was set in a typeface called Méridien, a classic roman designed by Adrian Frutiger for the French type foundry Deberny et Peignot in 1957. Adrian Frutiger was born in Interlaken, Switzerland, in 1928 and studied type design there and at the Kunstgewerbeschule in Zurich. In 1953 he moved to Paris, where he joined Deberny et Peignot as a member of the design staff. Méridien, as well as his other typeface of world renown, Univers, was originally created for the Lumitype photoset machine.

Andy's text was set in Meta Plus. Heralded as the Helvetica of the nineties, the definitive sans serif face Meta was originally commissioned for the German Post Office (Bundespost) in 1984. Although the project was eventually cancelled in favour of staying with Helvetica, Erik Spiekermann completed the design as a digital font in 1989, and it was published in 1991 by FontShop International. Since that time, the family has been expanded to its current comprehensive state of twenty weights and has been warmly embraced by the international design market.

Designed by Virginia Tan